CHARTED Courses

Treasured Recipes from the Auxiliaries of
Child and Family Agency of Southeastern Connecticut, Inc.

Carol Connor, our cover artist, was born and raised in the small coastal Connecticut village of Noank. She is now back there painting seascapes and still-lifes. Her artistic talents were nurtured through her childhood by her mother-teacher. Carol has studied at the Lyman Allyn Art Museum and the Mystic Art Gallery and her works have been shown in New England galleries.

◆ ◆ ◆ ◆

Nautical charts donated by The Bookstore at Mystic Seaport Museum

Additional copies of *Charted Courses* may be obtained from:
Child and Family Agency of Southeastern Connecticut, Inc.
255 Hempstead Street
New London, Connecticut 06320
(203) 443-2172
For your convenience, order blanks are included in the back of this book.

Published by: Child and Family Agency of Southeastern Connecticut, Inc.

Library of Congress Catalog Number: 95-60895
ISBN: 0-87197-431-2

Edited, Designed and Manufactured by
Favorite Recipes® Press
P.O. Box 305142
Nashville, Tennessee 37230
1-800-358-0560

Manufactured in the United States of America
First Printing: 1995   10,000

CONTENTS

♦ ♦ ♦ ♦ ♦ ♦ ♦ ♦ ♦ ♦ ♦ ♦ ♦

COOKBOOK COMMITTEE

♦ ♦ ♦ ♦ ♦ ♦ ♦ ♦ ♦ ♦ ♦ ♦ ♦

Charted Courses is the result of dedication of the following committee members and their families.

Co-Chairmen

Suzie Canning
Sue Curtiss

Cookbook Committee Members

Hetsy Bisbee ♦
Joyce Brennan
Carol Connor
Jamie Doubleday
Deb Fuller ♦
Phyllis Gada ♦
Dorothy Gorra ♦
Barbara Hallwood
Ann-Marie Howell
Alby Johnson
Ellie Krusewski

Jeanne Lena
♦ Elaine Livingston
Judy Lovelace
Kathi Lynch
Gail Mayhew
Lil Paul
♦ Jane Potter
Denise Russo
♦ Toni Slifer
♦ Betty Steadman

♦ Test Kitchen Co-ordinators

Marketing Co-Chairmen

Lois Geary
Michele Welch

Distribution Chairman

Peggy Callahan

Treasurer

Joyce Brennan

CHARTING A COURSE SINCE 1809...

◆ ◆ ◆ ◆ ◆ ◆ ◆ ◆ ◆ ◆ ◆ ◆ ◆ ◆

The history of Child and Family Agency of Southeastern Connecticut, Inc., begins in 1809 with the formation of its forerunner, the Female Benevolent Society of Hartford. Initially, the group focused on adoption and temporary foster care for children of tubercular parents. Through the years and several name changes, the Child and Family Agency has grown, adapted, and anticipated the evolving needs of the community. The heart of Child and Family's mission continues to be *children in the context of their family.* Agency programs deal with children's health care, child abuse, family violence, teen pregnancy, parent education, and child guidance. It has become the largest nonprofit children's service provider in southeastern Connecticut. For 186 years Child and Family Agency has meant hope and opportunity for children.

In 1944, a group of 12 women organized to aid the Agency and its work. Today, Child and Family Agency has more than 800 members in seven auxiliaries located in Essex, Old Lyme/Lyme, East Lyme, New London, Groton, Mystic/ Noank, and Stonington. The members are a diverse group of volunteers who give generously of their time and talent—caring for children, fund raising and supporting educational services to further the mission of the Agency. All proceeds from this cookbook, an all-auxiliary effort, will ensure that the many programs of this private, nonprofit charitable organization continues into the future.

INTRODUCTION

♦ ♦ ♦ ♦ ♦ ♦ ♦ ♦ ♦ ♦ ♦ ♦ ♦ ♦ ♦

Living on the shoreline, we are mindful of the unique nature of our area. Bounded by the Connecticut River on the west and the Pawcatuck River on the east, the Sound and its estuaries enrich our lives, providing leisure activities, panoramic views, livelihoods and the bountiful seafood enjoyed by all.

However, *Charted Courses* is not only about seafood. Generations of Connecticut families have farmed this land. Farmers' markets still dot the landscape offering locally grown produce—berries for spring fruit desserts, sweet corn and tomatoes for summer feasts and apples and pumpkins to make fall cooking special.

No longer during the winter months must we rely on what has been preserved or "put up" in the root cellar. No longer are exotic fruits and vegetables just memories from a sea captain's voyage. Our markets abound with foods from around the world. The cook's horizon is unlimited.

We hope you will explore our collection of menus and recipes. It is an eclectic blend from the traditional to the contemporary. If we can lead you in new directions, be assured the passage will be delightful. These are not uncharted waters. Whether preparing a "carry-along" picnic or planning an elegant dinner, we wish you fair sailing as you chart your courses.

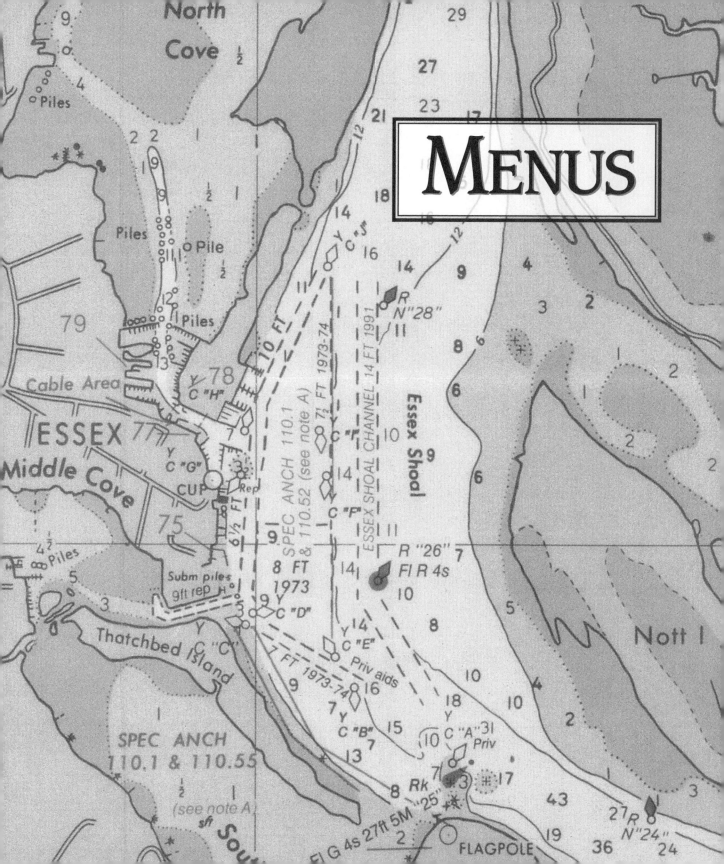

MENUS

MENUS

♦ ♦ ♦ ♦ ♦ ♦ ♦ ♦ ♦ ♦ ♦ ♦ ♦

BED AND BREAKFAST

♦ ♦ ♦ ♦ ♦ ♦ ♦ ♦ ♦ ♦ ♦ ♦ ♦

Cranberry and Orange Juice
Fruit Kabobs with Lemon-Mint Sauce

All-Seasons Muffins   Yankee Applesauce Muffins
English Muffin Bread
An assortment of preserves and butter

Freshly brewed coffee and tea

♦ ♦ ♦ ♦ ♦ ♦

Orange Juice
Grapefruit Halves

Skier's French Toast
Spicy Turkey Sausage Patties

Freshly brewed coffee, tea and Mocha Coffee

East Lyme has eleven miles of coastline and some of the most beautiful beaches in Connecticut. The development of each of her two villages—Flanders, originally a farming community, and Niantic, a seaside town—was spurred by better transportation. Flanders grew as farmers cultivated fields near the Boston Post Road, the main thoroughfare from New York to Boston. Niantic evolved in the 1850s from a shipbuilding and shipping center to a summer retreat when the steam railroad made travel for passengers on holiday from New York quick, comfortable and convenient. Boarding houses and hotels prospered, and eventually a colony of private summer homes was built by vacationers enchanted by the area's scenic charm.

Guests are the wonderful inevitability of living on the shore. Some visitors still arrive from the city by train ready to sail, fish, swim and relax at the beach. In fall, others prefer to drive the many byways (perhaps part of the old Post Road) and enjoy the foliage, apple picking, museums or antiquing. Whatever their penchant, they arise early in anticipation of both a day out-of-doors and a special breakfast to get them on their way.

Impressive Spring Luncheon

♦ ♦ ♦ ♦ ♦ ♦ ♦ ♦ ♦ ♦ ♦ ♦ ♦

Sage-Pecan Cheese Wafers

White Sangria

Citrus Tea Punch

Tarragon Chicken Salad

Asparagus Bundles with Lemon Mayonnaise

The Rectory's Sally Lunn Bread

Frozen Lemon Mousse with Strawberries

Ginger Spice Cookies

Old Lyme's tidal salt marshes filled with ospreys, herons and ducks and its farms of unassailable pastoral beauty have inspired many an artist. At the turn of the twentieth century, Old Lyme was touted for its similarities to the environs of Paris and young artists sought its stimulation. Florence Griswold, daughter of a sea captain and friend of the arts, opened her family's home to boarders and it became the summer salon of the new American impressionists. The community embraced its young artists and has fostered creative expression. The Florence Griswold House is now a museum.

Wake up from winter. Create a spring luncheon from a whole palate of flavors... savory, spicy, tart and sweet. When the meal is light, colorful and fresh, it will always be impressive!

SHORELINE SEAFOOD BAKE

♦ ♦ ♦ ♦ ♦ ♦ ♦ ♦ ♦ ♦ ♦ ♦ ♦

Crudités with Zesty Vegetable Dip

Clam Digger's Chowder

Trash Can Clambake
Lobsters, clams, chicken, corn-on-the-cob, potatoes

Watermelon, sliced to order

New England Hermits

Soda and Beer

Noank fishing "smacks" were often lovely schooners with spiked bowsprits, some as elegant as any yacht. Built for short-haul "market" fishing, they often had "live" wells to keep the catch fresh. Launched in Mystic, *Whistler*, a lobster smack, operated out of Noank in the 1880s. She supplied lobster to a burgeoning New York market.

The quintessential shoreline feast of lobsters and clams, the Trash Can Clambake, is so much the better because everyone helps. Family and guests will whistle a happy and expectant tune while collecting driftwood and seaweed, or bagging clams. Their whistles will soon be replaced by the sounds of a crackling fire, popping seaweed, smacking lips and kudos for the chefs, one and all!

FALL TAILGATE PICNIC

♦ ♦ ♦ ♦ ♦ ♦ ♦ ♦ ♦ ♦ ♦ ♦ ♦ ♦

Harvest Popcorn

Farmhouse Cheese Soup

Beef Barbecue

Carolina Coleslaw

Crunchy Oatmeal Cookies

Apples and Pears

Cider

Mystic became a preeminent shipbuilding center of necessity and by providence. Farming the rocky land was difficult. However, the hillsides were covered with the timber necessary for tall ships; the river was navigable. From the end of the seventeenth century until the apex of shipbuilding in the mid-nineteenth century, many Mystic men were warm-weather farmers and cold-weather shipwrights. At the Mystic Seaport Museum, a re-creation of a nineteenth-century seafaring village, this heritage is preserved.

Organizing an autumn tailgating picnic can be difficult. Out of necessity it must be convenient to keep and serve; with a little luck and a great menu, a picnic becomes a fabulous feast.

SUMMER DINNER ON THE DECK

♦ ♦ ♦ ♦ ♦ ♦ ♦ ♦ ♦ ♦ ♦ ♦ ♦

Frozen Margaritas

Hot Artichoke Dip with crackers

Chilled Spinach and Pea Soup

Caesar Salad

Grilled Tuna with Salsa

Fiesta Salad

Perfect No-Peek Rice

Blueberry Tart

Mystic shipyards launched a number of clipper ships. These packets were designed for speed and seaworthiness. The gold rush in California inspired many additional blueprints for rapid passage from the East Coast to San Francisco. The *Andrew Jackson*, built in Mystic in 1860, was one of the fastest clippers of her time. She sailed around the Horn in eighty-nine days and four hours, handily beating the internationally-acclaimed *Flying Cloud*.

An easy but elegant summer dinner after a day of beaching or sailing is worth its weight in gold. This menu is a winner, also, and it won't take even eighty-nine minutes to prepare.

Summer Supper Under the Stars

♦ ♦ ♦ ♦ ♦ ♦ ♦ ♦ ♦ ♦ ♦ ♦ ♦

Peppers and Pita

Shrimp and Cream Cheese Spread with crackers

Beef Vinaigrette Salad

Port and Starboard Potato Salad

Danish Cucumbers

Nautical Knots

Tropical Dream Cake

Up and down the coast, fireworks and music fill the summer night. Waterford's Harkness Mansion, once a private estate and now a state park, is home to Summer Music. Often its open-air concerts are punctuated by colorful bursts and booms. To commemorate our country's birth, a fabulous display of fireworks fills the sky over the Thames River. Spectators line both the Groton and New London sides of the river to cheer as an explosive canopy of light reveals a river of boats filled with more sky watchers.

Dining alfresco, whether listening to a concert, or watching fireworks on a blanket or in the cockpit, means portable food. A picnic that is no problem to pack and not messy to eat will garner those "oohs" and "aahs" generally reserved for the grand finale.

FALL FEST DINNER

♦ ♦ ♦ ♦ ♦ ♦ ♦ ♦ ♦ ♦ ♦ ♦ ♦

Chutney-Bacon Brie with crackers

Golden Harvest Soup

Spiced Lamb Kabobs

Grilled Vegetables

Wild Rice with Mushrooms

Pita Toasts

Salad of mixed greens with Herbal Vinaigrette

Apple-Cranberry Crisp

Ice Cream

The transitional days between summer and fall are the most glorious on the coast. The breeze off the water is still warm and the sun is still strong. Weekends mean fairs and food fests, soccer matches and football games. For sailboat racers, Off Soundings is two days of racing and camaraderie before hauling the boat for the winter. For cruisers, a rendezvous up the Connecticut River to Lyme's Hamburg Cove is appealing. There the foliage seems more vivid against the backdrop of rock and water.

After a clear day, the air cools quickly. It's autumn again. Recall the rhythm of the day with a casual dinner that's simple to prepare and a smooth segue from soup that's golden mellow to a crisp with cool.

HAIL AND FAREWELL COCKTAIL BUFFET

◆ ◆ ◆ ◆ ◆ ◆ ◆ ◆ ◆ ◆ ◆ ◆ ◆

Marinated Cocktail Shrimp

Turkey Meatballs with Cranberry Sauce

Mystical Seafood Mousse

Sherried Stilton Cheese and assorted cheeses with crackers
Wedges of apples and pears

Sliced Baked Ham   Sliced Eye Round of Beef
Showhouse Honey Mustard
Party Rolls

Mushroom Pâté

Artichoke Squares

Coffee and Apricot Biscotti

Running between Groton and New London is the Thames River. Its harbor, the largest and deepest on the Connecticut shore, boasts an eclectic fleet. Home once to privateers who preyed on British merchant vessels, and later to a whaling fleet of world renown, the river is host to the oldest rivalry of college oarsmen, the Yale-Harvard Regatta. *Nautilus*, the first nuclear submarine, was launched at Groton's Electric Boat and her sisters continue to glide up to the U.S. Navy Submarine Base and out to sea. Docked in New London is the U.S. Coast Guard barque *Eagle*, a training vessel where cadets master the age-old art of sailing. With commercial traffic and pleasure craft also plying its waters, the Thames is a flowing connection from our maritime past to its future.

A cocktail buffet is most fun with a mix of old friends and new. Alas, for every host or hostess who harbors dreams of wow in every bite, there seems to be a guest who doesn't want to be dazzled. To keep everyone happy, the menu is best a blend of the tried and true, with a twist—it's a party—and a few surprises. A variety of textures, colors and flavors lends the buffet an energy that will spark continuous conversation and a flood of compliments.

TRADEWINDS DINNER

♦ ♦ ♦ ♦ ♦ ♦ ♦ ♦ ♦ ♦ ♦ ♦ ♦

Peanut-Pumpkin Soup

Pork Roast with Lime and Rum Sauce

Twice-Baked Sweet Potatoes

Onion Cornbread

Spicy Green Salad with Oranges

Banana Crêpes

Essex, on the shore of the Connecticut River and only a few miles from Long Island Sound, was one of the earliest trading ports of New England. Although the first settlers were farmers taken by the fertile meadows and gentle hills of the area, the proximity and possibilities of the water intrigued Robert Lay. He built a wharf in the 1650s, and in 1666 Lay's *Diligence*, a ketch, sailed to the West Indies on the first of many trading voyages from this seaport.

That West Indies trade brought sugar, molasses, rum and spices to our shores. Inspired by the passage of Mr. Lay's *Diligence*, this delightful Caribbean menu is one that will be intriguing every time it is served.

COZY DINNER FOR FRIENDS

♦ ♦ ♦ ♦ ♦ ♦ ♦ ♦ ♦ ♦ ♦ ♦ ♦

Stuffed Mushrooms

East Coast Cioppino
or
Chicken and Sausage Stew

Beer Bread

Avocado-Citrus Salad

Chocolate Cheesecake

Today in Essex, a hearty fleet of "frostbiters" sail into December. They are the few undaunted by the snow and cold winds that sometimes challenge our New England loyalties. By mid-January if we have not had the "thaw," and certainly by Groundhog Day many are itching for a shot of sun. In Essex, Essex Ed, the groundhog, is the grand marshal of a noisy children's pot-and-pan parade down Main Street. Anxious for an early spring, even those who have not enjoyed skiing, sledding, or skating come out to see if Ed sees his shadow and to revel in the playful cacophony.

"Cabin fever" is a great reason for a winter get-together. Good friends, a cozy kitchen and a hearty meal with a little spice and a lot of chocolate might even lure Ed out for another peek.

HOLIDAY TEA

♦ ♦ ♦ ♦ ♦ ♦ ♦ ♦ ♦ ♦ ♦ ♦ ♦

Fruited Cheese Logs with water biscuits

Cucumber Sandwiches

Mushroom Sandwiches

Elegant Strawberries

St. Nick's Whiskers   Sugar and Spice Roll-Ups
Cherry Meringues   Fudge Brownies
Gingerbread Cookies   Shortbread Cookies

English Scones with preserves

Lemon Glaze Cake

Percolator Punch

Tea

Successful sea captains built many of the beautiful Federal and Greek Revival homes that line the main streets of our towns. These captains returned from their voyages with wonderful gifts for their families and furnishings for their homes that still grace the private residences and museums in the area. The spices, coffee, sugar, molasses and rum from the West Indies and teas and porcelains from China forever changed the coastal kitchen.

A holiday tea is the perfect chance to use cherished family treasures—grandmother's china, some glittering silver or an heirloom tablecloth. Indulge your guests with cookies rich and buttery and splendidly spicy, luscious dark chocolate brownies and gem-colored berries stuffed with sweet cheese. Create a memory of another time.

FORMAL DINNER AT THE CAPTAIN'S TABLE

♦ ♦ ♦ ♦ ♦ ♦ ♦ ♦ ♦ ♦ ♦ ♦ ♦

Crocked Cheese with Brandy
Smoked Oyster Roll
Liver Pâté
Assorted mild crackers

Salad for Company

Beef Tenderloin with Madeira Sauce

Whipped Party Potatoes

Vegetable Medley

Charlotte Russe with Apricot Sauce

Stonington seamen sailed to the far reaches of the world in search of whales, seals and trading opportunities. In 1820, the *Hero*, a 47-foot sloop skippered by 21-year-old Nathaniel Palmer, was sealing in the Atlantic south of the Falkland Islands. Palmer ventured well beyond South America into uncharted waters. On the horizon he spied the icy mountains of Antarctica. He laid claim for the United States and the rocky peninsula now bears his name—Palmerland.

This special formal meal is perfect for every "Hero." Continental in appeal, it is a delicious dinner of discovery for friends dressed as penguins on an Antarctic-like evening.

APPETIZERS AND BEVERAGES

APPETIZERS AND BEVERAGES

♦ ♦ ♦ ♦ ♦ ♦ ♦ ♦ ♦ ♦ ♦ ♦ ♦

COLD APPETIZERS
Harvest Popcorn, 29
Marinated Cocktail Shrimp, 31
Sage-Pecan Cheese Wafers, 24
Tortilla Pinwheels, 30

HOT APPETIZERS
Artichoke Squares, 23
Bacon and Cheese Toasties, 24
Broiled Mussels on the Half Shell, 28
Caramelized Bacon, 43
China Trade Chicken Wings, 25
Crab Cheese Canapés, 26
Crispy Niantic Bay Scallops, 30
Feta Cheese Triangles, 23
Hot Olive and Cheese Canapés, 24
Mushroom Croustades, 27
Pita Toasts, 29
Sausage Tartlets, 30
Spicy Shrimp, 31
Spinach Bites, 32
Stuffed Mushrooms, 28
Turkey Meatballs with Cranberry
        Sauce, 27
Vineyard Stuffed Clams, 26

COLD DIPS
Captain's Favorite Mexican Dip, 34
Curried Cantaloupe Dip, 32
Layered Chicken Curry Dip, 33
Peppers and Pita, 35
Salsa, 35
Zesty Vegetable Dip, 36

HOT DIPS
Baked Clam Casserole, 25
Hot Artichoke Dip, 32
Hot Mexican Spinach Dip, 34
Hot Taco Dip, 36
West Cove Clam Dip, 33

COLD SPREADS
Boursin Spread, 36
Crocked Cheese with Brandy, 38
Eggplant Caponata, 40
Four-Cheese Pâté, 38
Fruited Cheese Logs, 39
Liver Pâté, 41
Mushroom Pâté, 41
Mushroom Spread, 42
Mystical Seafood Mousse, 42
Sherried Stilton Cheese, 39
Showhouse Honey Mustard, 33
Shrimp and Cream Cheese Spread, 39
Smoked Oyster Roll, 29
Sun-Drenched Brie, 37
Tomato Butter, 43

HOT SPREADS
Chutney-Bacon Brie, 37
Hot Crabmeat Spread, 40

COLD BEVERAGES
Bloody Marys, 43
Citrus Tea Punch, 45
Frozen Margaritas, 44
Graduation Punch, 45
Lime Punch, 44
Pain Killer, 44
White Sangria, 45

HOT BEVERAGES
Mocha Mix, 46
Percolator Punch, 46

NON-ALCOHOLIC BEVERAGES
Citrus Tea Punch, 45
Graduation Punch, 45
Mocha Mix, 46

ARTICHOKE SQUARES

Makes 48 servings

2 (6-ounce) jars marinated
  artichoke hearts
1 small clove of garlic, chopped
1 medium onion, chopped
4 eggs
1 cup shredded Cheddar cheese
1/4 cup minced fresh parsley
1/4 cup Italian-style bread crumbs
1/4 teaspoon salt
1/8 teaspoon pepper
1/8 teaspoon oregano
Tabasco sauce to taste
Grated Parmesan cheese

♦ Preheat the oven to 325 degrees.

♦ Drain the artichoke hearts, reserving the oil from one jar. Process the artichokes in a food processor until coarsely chopped.

♦ Sauté the garlic and onion in the reserved oil in a skillet until tender.

♦ Combine the garlic mixture, eggs, Cheddar cheese, parsley, bread crumbs, salt, pepper, oregano and Tabasco sauce in a food processor. Process using plastic blade until mixed. Fold in the artichokes. Spoon into a greased 11x17-inch baking dish.

♦ Bake at 325 degrees for 30 minutes. Sprinkle with Parmesan cheese. Cool slightly before cutting into squares.

FETA CHEESE TRIANGLES

Makes 100 servings

1 pound feta cheese, crumbled
2 egg yolks, beaten
1 egg, beaten
3 tablespoons cooked chopped
  spinach (optional)
Pepper to taste
1 (16-ounce) package phyllo
  pastry
1 1/2 cups melted butter

♦ Preheat the oven to 350 degrees.

♦ Mash the feta cheese with a fork. Stir in the egg yolks, egg, spinach and pepper.

♦ Place 1 sheet of the phyllo dough on a cutting board. (Keep remaining phyllo covered with damp cloth.) Brush with melted butter; cut into 1 1/2- to 2-inch strips.

♦ Place 1/2 teaspoon of the feta cheese mixture on each strip 1 inch from the base; fold over diagonally to form a triangle; seal edges. Place on a baking sheet. Repeat with the remaining phyllo dough and cheese mixture.

♦ Bake at 350 degrees for 20 minutes or until brown. Serve immediately.

May be prepared and frozen for future use. Thaw for 15 to 20 minutes before baking.

HOT OLIVE AND CHEESE CANAPES

Makes 15 to 20 servings

15 to 20 thin slices French bread

1 (2-ounce) can sliced black olives, drained

2 cups shredded Cheddar cheese

½ cup mayonnaise

½ teaspoon curry powder

2 green onions, finely chopped

♦ Preheat the broiler.

♦ Arrange the bread slices in a single layer on a baking sheet. Broil for 3 minutes; turn.

♦ Combine olives and remaining ingredients in a bowl; mix well.

♦ Spread the bread slices with cheese mixture. Broil for 3 minutes or until bubbly. Serve immediately.

SAGE-PECAN CHEESE WAFERS

Makes 36 servings

A savory treat that can be prepared, baked and frozen for up to two months in advance.

1 cup shredded sharp Cheddar cheese

¾ cup flour

¼ cup finely chopped pecans

1 teaspoon rubbed sage

¼ teaspoon salt

⅛ teaspoon cayenne

⅓ cup butter, cut into small pieces

♦ Preheat the oven to 350 degrees.

♦ Process the cheese, flour, pecans, sage, salt and cayenne in a food processor fitted with a steel blade for 10 seconds or until blended. Add the butter gradually, processing constantly until the mixture forms a ball.

♦ Roll ¼ inch thick on a lightly floured surface. Cut with a 1½-inch round cutter. Place on ungreased baking sheet.

♦ Bake at 350 degrees for 12 to 14 minutes or until the edges turn brown. Remove to a wire rack to cool completely.

BACON AND CHEESE TOASTIES

Makes 40 servings

1 (1-pound) package bacon, crisp-fried, crumbled

1 medium onion, finely chopped

8 ounces sharp Cheddar cheese, shredded

Mayonnaise

1 baguette French bread, cut into ¼-inch slices

♦ Preheat the broiler.

♦ Combine the bacon, onion and cheese in a bowl; mix well. Add enough mayonnaise to make of spreading consistency. Spread 1 side of each bread slice with the mixture. Place on a baking sheet.

♦ Broil until bubbly. Serve immediately.

May bake the bacon mixture in a greased baking dish at 350 degrees for 20 minutes or until light brown. Serve with assorted party crackers.

CHINA TRADE CHICKEN WINGS

Makes 16 to 18 servings

3 pounds chicken wings
1/3 cup soy sauce
2 tablespoons vegetable oil
2 tablespoons chili sauce
1/4 cup honey
1/2 teaspoon ginger
1/4 teaspoon garlic powder
1/4 teaspoon cayenne

+ Rinse the chicken and pat dry. Separate the chicken wings at the joints; discard the tips. Arrange in a shallow dish.

+ Pour a mixture of the soy sauce, oil, chili sauce, honey, ginger, garlic powder and cayenne over the chicken, turning to coat. Marinate in the refrigerator for 1 hour or longer, turning occasionally. Drain, reserving the marinade.

+ Preheat the oven to 350 degrees.

+ Arrange the chicken on a rack in a foil-lined broiler pan. Bake at 350 degrees for 30 minutes; brush with the reserved marinade. Turn the chicken.

+ Bake for 30 minutes longer, brushing occasionally with the reserved marinade.

+ Serve immediately or chill or freeze for future use.

BAKED CLAM CASSEROLE

Makes 8 to 10 servings

2 (6-ounce) cans minced clams
1/2 green bell pepper, chopped
1 medium onion, chopped
1 clove of garlic, minced
1 teaspoon lemon juice
1/2 cup unsalted butter
1 teaspoon chopped fresh parsley
1 teaspoon oregano
1/2 cup seasoned bread crumbs
Tabasco sauce to taste
4 ounces Velveeta cheese, shredded
2 tablespoons grated Parmesan cheese
Paprika to taste

+ Preheat the oven to 350 degrees.

+ Combine the undrained clams, green pepper, onion, garlic and lemon juice in a skillet; mix well. Simmer for 15 minutes, stirring occasionally.

+ Stir the butter, parsley, oregano, bread crumbs and Tabasco sauce into the clam mixture. Spoon into a baking dish. Sprinkle with the Velveeta cheese, Parmesan cheese and paprika.

+ Bake at 350 degrees for 30 minutes.

+ Serve with party rye bread or assorted crackers.

VINEYARD STUFFED CLAMS

Makes 6 to 8 servings

18 to 24 cherrystone clams
1/2 cup butter, softened
3 tablespoons chopped shallots
1 teaspoon minced garlic
1/4 cup chopped fresh parsley
1 tablespoon minced fresh basil
1 cup seasoned bread crumbs
2 tablespoons dry white wine
1/4 cup finely chopped prosciutto
1/4 teaspoon red pepper flakes
Salt and pepper to taste
1/2 cup freshly grated Asiago or
   Parmesan cheese
2 tablespoons olive oil

- Scrub and shuck the clams, reserving the shells. Process the clams in a food processor, briefly.

- Combine the clams, butter, shallots, garlic, parsley, basil, bread crumbs, white wine, prosciutto, red pepper flakes, salt and pepper in a saucepan; mix well. Cook for several minutes, stirring frequently.

- Preheat the oven to 425 degrees.

- Spoon the clam mixture into the reserved clam shells. Place on a baking sheet. Sprinkle with the cheese; drizzle with the olive oil.

- Bake at 425 degrees for 15 minutes. Broil just until golden brown.

CRAB CHEESE CANAPES

Makes 36 servings

1 (12-count) can flaky-style rolls
1 (6-ounce) can crabmeat, drained
4 ounces Swiss or Cheddar
   cheese, shredded
1 tablespoon grated onion
1/2 cup mayonnaise
1 teaspoon lemon juice
1/4 teaspoon curry powder
1 (5-ounce) can water chestnuts,
   drained, sliced

- Preheat the oven to 400 degrees.

- Separate each roll into 3 sections. Arrange on an ungreased baking sheet.

- Combine the crabmeat, cheese, onion, mayonnaise, lemon juice and curry powder in a bowl; mix well. Spread evenly on each roll section; top with the water chestnuts.

- Bake at 400 degrees for 10 to 12 minutes or until bubbly.

May substitute English muffin halves for rolls. Spread with the crabmeat mixture, place water chestnut slice in each quadrant and cut into quarters. Baking time will be slightly longer than when using rolls.

TURKEY MEATBALLS WITH CRANBERRY SAUCE

Makes 5 dozen

This is traditional cocktail party fare.

2 pounds ground fresh turkey
$1/2$ cup minced onion
$2/3$ cup fine dry bread crumbs
$1/2$ cup minced fresh parsley
$1/2$ teaspoon salt
$1/4$ teaspoon white pepper
$1/4$ teaspoon nutmeg
$1/2$ cup milk
2 eggs, beaten
1 (16-ounce) can jellied cranberry sauce
1 (12-ounce) bottle chili sauce
2 tablespoons brown sugar
1 tablespoon cider vinegar

♦ Preheat the oven to 375 degrees.

♦ Combine the turkey, onion, bread crumbs, parsley, salt, white pepper, nutmeg, milk and eggs in a bowl; mix well. Shape into 1-inch balls. Place on a rack in a baking pan sprayed with nonstick cooking spray.

♦ Bake at 375 degrees for 20 to 25 minutes or until the meatballs are cooked through; drain. May freeze the meatballs at this point for future use.

♦ Sauce: Combine the cranberry sauce, chili sauce, brown sugar and vinegar in a saucepan; mix well. Simmer for 5 minutes, stirring occasionally. Add the meatballs, tossing to coat. Cook over low heat for 15 to 20 minutes or until the meatballs are heated through. Transfer the meatballs and sauce to a chafing dish to serve.

MUSHROOM CROUSTADES

Makes 30 servings

2 tablespoons butter, softened
30 slices white bread
3 tablespoons chopped scallions
8 ounces fresh mushrooms, chopped
$1/4$ cup butter
2 tablespoons flour
1 cup whipping cream
$1/2$ teaspoon salt
$1/8$ teaspoon cayenne
$1/4$ cup chopped fresh parsley
$1/3$ cup chopped chives
$1/2$ teaspoon lemon juice
2 tablespoons grated Parmesan cheese

♦ Preheat the oven to 375 degrees.

♦ Coat bottom and sides of 2-inch muffin cups with 2 tablespoons butter. Cut $2^{1}/2$-inch rounds from bread slices; press into muffin tin. Bake at 375 degrees until brown. Let stand until cool.

♦ Sauté the scallions and mushrooms in $1/4$ cup butter in a saucepan for 8 to 10 minutes or until tender. Remove from heat; sprinkle the mixture with flour. Return to heat. Add the cream; mix well.

♦ Cook until thickened, stirring constantly. Stir in the salt, cayenne, parsley, chives and lemon juice.

♦ Place croustades on baking sheet and fill; sprinkle with the cheese.

♦ Bake at 375 degrees for 10 minutes.

STUFFED MUSHROOMS

Makes 24 servings

24 large mushrooms

Salt to taste

3 tablespoons chopped onion

1 tablespoon olive oil

½ cup butter

1 teaspoon salt

¼ teaspoon pepper

¼ cup dry red wine

2 teaspoons tomato paste

2 small cloves of garlic, minced

3 tablespoons Italian-style bread crumbs

1 tablespoon chopped fresh parsley

1 tablespoon olive oil

♦ Preheat the oven to 425 degrees.

♦ Remove stems from mushrooms and chop the stems. Invert the caps; sprinkle with salt to taste.

♦ Sauté the chopped mushroom stems and onion in 1 tablespoon olive oil and butter in a skillet until soft. Add the salt, pepper, red wine, tomato paste and garlic.

♦ Cook over medium-high heat for 2 minutes. Remove from heat. Stir in the bread crumbs and parsley. Spoon into the mushroom caps. Place on a baking sheet. Drizzle with 1 tablespoon olive oil.

♦ Bake at 425 degrees for 10 minutes. Garnish with additional fresh parsley.

BROILED MUSSELS ON THE HALF SHELL

Makes 15 to 20 servings

An adult taste treat.

1 pound mussels, scrubbed, bearded

1 cup (or more) bread crumbs

1 stalk celery, chopped

1 small onion, chopped

1 small clove of garlic, minced

6 tablespoons butter

¼ cup dry vermouth

Worcestershire sauce to taste

Sherry pepper sauce or white pepper to taste

♦ Place mussels in a steamer. Steam for 3 to 5 minutes or until the mussels open. Discard the upper shell. Loosen the mussel; do not remove. Discard any beard remaining. Arrange in broiler pan; sprinkle the mussels with the bread crumbs.

♦ Sauté the celery, onion and garlic in the butter in a skillet for 5 minutes. Stir in the vermouth, Worcestershire sauce and sherry pepper sauce.

♦ Preheat the broiler.

♦ Sauté for 5 minutes longer. Remove from heat. Drain pan juices; squeeze moisture from vegetables. Spoon over bread crumbs.

♦ Broil for 4 to 5 minutes or until bubbly. Serve immediately.

SMOKED OYSTER ROLL

Makes 16 servings

8 ounces cream cheese, softened

1 (4-ounce) can smoked oysters, drained

1/4 teaspoon lemon juice

1 to 2 cloves of garlic, minced

1/2 cup chopped pecans

1/2 cup chopped fresh parsley, 2 tablespoons reserved

- Place the cream cheese between 2 sheets of plastic wrap. Roll into a 1/4-inch thick rectangle.

- Mash the oysters in a bowl. Stir in the lemon juice, garlic, pecans and 2 tablespoons parsley. Spread the oyster mixture evenly over the cream cheese; roll to enclose the filling. Roll in additional chopped fresh parsley. Chill, covered, until serving time.

- Serve with assorted party crackers.

PITA TOASTS

Makes 6 to 10 servings

3/4 cup butter, softened

1 tablespoon lemon juice

1 clove of garlic, crushed

3 to 4 tablespoons minced fresh herbs

1 large shallot, minced

6 pita bread rounds, split

- Beat the butter, lemon juice, garlic, herbs and shallot in a mixer bowl. Let stand at room temperature for 1 hour.

- Preheat the oven to 450 degrees.

- Spread the butter mixture on the pita halves. Place on a baking sheet. Bake at 450 degrees until brown and crisp. Break into pieces.

May substitute 1 1/2 teaspoons Italian seasoning for the fresh herbs.

HARVEST POPCORN

Makes 2 1/2 quarts

This is a mildly seasoned snack mix.

1/3 cup popcorn, popped

2 cups shoestring potato sticks

1 cup mixed nuts

1/3 cup melted butter

1 teaspoon each dillweed and lemon pepper

1 teaspoon Worcestershire sauce

1/2 teaspoon each garlic powder and onion powder

1/4 teaspoon salt

- Preheat the oven to 350 degrees.

- Mix the popcorn, potato sticks and mixed nuts in a bowl.

- Pour a mixture of the butter, dillweed, lemon pepper, Worcestershire sauce, garlic powder, onion powder and salt over the popcorn mixture, tossing to coat. Spread in a baking pan.

- Bake at 350 degrees for 6 to 8 minutes or until heated through, stirring occasionally. Let stand until cool.

- Store in an airtight container.

TORTILLA PINWHEELS

Makes 7 dozen

24 ounces cream cheese, softened

1 (6-ounce) can pitted black olives, drained, chopped

1 (4-ounce) can diced green chiles

1/2 cup minced onion

1/4 cup minced red bell pepper

1 (18-ounce) package 10-inch flour tortillas

♦ Combine the cream cheese, olives, undrained chiles, onion and red pepper in a bowl; mix well. Spread approximately 1 heaping tablespoon of the cream cheese mixture on each tortilla; roll tightly to enclose the filling.

♦ Chill, wrapped in plastic wrap, for 8 to 10 hours. Cut into 1-inch slices.

Serve with favorite jalapeño salsa.

CRISPY NIANTIC BAY SCALLOPS

Makes 50 servings

5 slices white bread, crusts trimmed

1 1/2 pounds scallops

Salt and pepper to taste

1/4 cup melted butter

1/4 cup fresh basil leaves, shredded

Juice of 1 lime

♦ Preheat the broiler.

♦ Process the bread in a food processor until finely crumbled.

♦ Sprinkle the scallops with salt and pepper; dredge in the bread crumbs. Place on baking sheet. Drizzle with butter.

♦ Broil 4 to 5 inches from the heat source for 7 minutes or until golden brown. Arrange the scallops on a serving platter. Sprinkle with basil, lime juice, salt and pepper.

SAUSAGE TARTLETS

Makes 24 servings

1 recipe (2-crust) pie pastry

5 brown-and-serve sausage patties, chopped

4 ounces mushrooms, finely chopped

1 small onion, finely chopped

1 egg, lightly beaten

1/2 cup milk

1/2 cup shredded Cheddar cheese

1/2 teaspoon salt

1/2 teaspoon marjoram, crushed

1/4 teaspoon freshly ground pepper

♦ Preheat the oven to 400 degrees.

♦ Pat pastry into bottom and sides of miniature muffin tins. Bake at 400 degrees for 5 to 8 minutes or until brown. Let stand until cool. Reduce oven temperature to 375 degrees.

♦ Sauté sausage in skillet until brown and crisp; drain. Sauté mushrooms and onion in pan drippings until tender; drain. Layer sausage and mushroom mixture in prepared muffin tins. Pour mixture of egg, milk, cheese, salt, marjoram and pepper over layers.

♦ Bake at 375 degrees for 15 to 20 minutes or until set.

May freeze the baked tartlets and reheat just before serving.

SPICY SHRIMP

Makes 2 or 3 servings

1 (12-ounce) can beer
1/4 cup cider vinegar
1/2 teaspoon peppercorns
2 bay leaves
1 tablespoon (heaping) Old Bay seasoning
1 pound unpeeled shrimp, rinsed, drained

♦ Bring the beer, vinegar, peppercorns, bay leaves and Old Bay seasoning to a boil in a saucepan.

♦ Boil for 10 minutes, stirring occasionally. Add the shrimp; mix well.

♦ Boil for 1 to 2 minutes or until the shrimp turn pink; drain. Arrange the shrimp on a serving platter. Serve immediately with a large supply of napkins.

MARINATED COCKTAIL SHRIMP

Makes 10 servings

An elegant centerpiece for your next cocktail party or buffet.

2 1/2 pounds shrimp, steamed, peeled
1 sweet onion, thinly sliced
7 or 8 bay leaves
1 1/4 cups corn oil
3/4 cup vinegar
2 1/2 tablespoons capers with juice
2 1/2 teaspoons celery seeds
1 1/2 teaspoons salt
Tabasco sauce to taste

♦ Combine the shrimp and onion in a bowl. Pour a mixture of the bay leaves, corn oil, vinegar, capers, celery seeds, salt and Tabasco sauce over the shrimp mixture, tossing to coat.

♦ Marinate, covered, in the refrigerator for 24 hours, stirring occasionally. Drain, discarding the marinade.

♦ Arrange the shrimp on a serving platter.

May add whole fresh mushrooms and artichoke hearts to the marinade for variety.

SPINACH BITES

Makes 50 to 60 servings

2 (10-ounce) packages frozen chopped spinach, cooked, drained
1 small onion, finely chopped
1 small clove of garlic, minced
2 cups herb-seasoned stuffing mix
1/2 cup grated Parmesan cheese
4 eggs, beaten
3/4 cup melted butter
1/2 teaspoon thyme
1/2 teaspoon pepper

♦ Squeeze the moisture from the spinach. Combine the spinach, onion, garlic, stuffing mix, cheese, eggs, butter, thyme and pepper in a bowl; mix well. Shape into 1-inch balls. Arrange on a baking sheet.

♦ Chill until just before baking.

♦ Preheat the oven to 350 degrees.

♦ Bake at 350 degrees for 15 minutes or until light brown. Serve with Showhouse Honey Mustard (page 33).

May prepare and freeze spinach balls before baking for future use. Let stand at room temperature for 20 minutes before baking.

HOT ARTICHOKE DIP

Makes 2 1/2 cups

1 (14-ounce) can artichoke hearts, drained, coarsely chopped
1 cup sour cream
1 cup mayonnaise
1/2 cup crumbled Montrachet cheese with chives
1/4 cup freshly grated Parmesan cheese
Paprika to taste

♦ Preheat the oven to 350 degrees.

♦ Combine the artichoke hearts, sour cream, mayonnaise, Montrachet cheese and Parmesan cheese in a bowl; mix well. Spoon into a shallow baking dish; sprinkle with paprika.

♦ Bake at 350 degrees for 20 minutes or until bubbly.

♦ Serve hot with assorted crackers or Italian bread sticks.

CURRIED CANTALOUPE DIP

Makes 32 servings

1 large ripe cantaloupe
2 cups sour cream
2 tablespoons mayonnaise
1/4 to 1/2 teaspoon curry powder
1 teaspoon ketchup
1 teaspoon minced onion
1/2 teaspoon salt
White pepper to taste

♦ Cut the cantaloupe into halves; discard seeds. Scoop the pulp into balls with a melon ball scoop. Invert the shells to drain.

♦ Combine the sour cream, mayonnaise, curry powder, ketchup, onion, salt and white pepper in a bowl; mix well. Spoon into the melon shells. Arrange on a serving platter. Surround the shells with the melon balls.

May substitute any type of fresh fruit or raw vegetable for the melon balls.

WEST COVE CLAM DIP

Makes 6 cups

3 (7-ounce) cans minced clams
24 ounces cream cheese
2 cloves of garlic, crushed
4 1/2 teaspoons Worcestershire sauce
1 1/2 teaspoons lemon juice
3/4 teaspoon paprika

♦ Drain the clams, reserving 2 tablespoons clam juice.

♦ Heat the cream cheese in a double boiler over hot water, stirring until smooth. Add the clams, reserved clam juice, garlic, Worcestershire sauce, lemon juice and paprika; mix well.

♦ Cook until heated through, stirring constantly. Transfer to a chafing dish.

♦ Serve with assorted crackers.

May prepare in advance, store in the refrigerator and serve chilled.

LAYERED CHICKEN CURRY DIP

Makes 4 cups

1/3 cup chopped green onions
8 ounces cream cheese, softened
1 cup cottage cheese
1/4 cup sour cream
2 teaspoons curry powder
1/2 cup chutney
1/3 cup raisins
1/3 cup grated coconut
1 cup chopped cooked chicken
1/2 cup salted peanuts, chopped

♦ Reserve 2 tablespoons of the green onions for garnish.

♦ Process the cream cheese, cottage cheese, sour cream and curry powder in a food processor until smooth. Spread over the bottom of a platter or quiche pan. Layer the chutney, remaining green onions, raisins, coconut, chicken and peanuts in the order listed over the cream cheese layer.

♦ Chill, covered, for 3 to 10 hours. Sprinkle with the reserved green onions.

♦ Serve with assorted crackers.

SHOWHOUSE HONEY MUSTARD

Makes 1 1/2 cups

1 cup packed brown sugar
2 tablespoons flour
1/3 cup dry mustard
2 eggs
1/2 cup white vinegar
1 tablespoon honey

♦ Combine the brown sugar, flour and dry mustard in a double boiler over hot water; mix well.

♦ Beat the eggs, vinegar and honey in a bowl until blended. Stir into the brown sugar mixture.

♦ Cook for 30 minutes or until thickened, stirring occasionally.

♦ Let stand until cooled to room temperature. Ladle into hot sterilized jars; seal with 2-piece lids.

CAPTAIN'S FAVORITE MEXICAN DIP

Makes 10 to 12 servings

3 ripe avocados, mashed

2 tablespoons lemon juice

Salt and pepper to taste

1 cup sour cream

½ cup mayonnaise

1 envelope taco seasoning mix

2 (10-ounce) cans jalapeño bean dip

1 bunch green onions, chopped

2 medium tomatoes, peeled, drained, chopped

1 (4-ounce) can chopped green chiles, drained

1 (6-ounce) can black olives, sliced

3 cups shredded Cheddar cheese

♦ Combine the avocados, lemon juice, salt and pepper in a bowl; mix well. Combine the sour cream, mayonnaise and taco seasoning mix in a bowl; mix well.

♦ Layer, in order, the bean dip, avocado mixture, sour cream mixture, green onions, tomatoes, green chiles, olives and cheese on a large serving platter.

♦ Serve with tortilla chips or corn chips.

May substitute frozen avocado dip for the mashed avocados, chunky salsa for the tomatoes, one 24-ounce can refried beans mixed with 1 envelope taco seasoning mix for the jalapeño dip or may omit the taco seasoning mix from the sour cream mixture.

HOT MEXICAN SPINACH DIP

Makes 12 servings

1 medium onion, chopped

2 tablespoons vegetable oil

2 tomatoes, chopped

2 tablespoons canned chopped green chiles

1 (10-ounce) package frozen chopped spinach, thawed

2 cups shredded Monterey Jack cheese

8 ounces cream cheese, cut into chunks, softened

1 cup half-and-half

2 (2-ounce) cans sliced black olives, drained

1 tablespoon red wine vinegar

Salt, pepper and hot pepper sauce to taste

♦ Preheat the oven to 350 degrees.

♦ Sauté the onion in the oil in a skillet until tender. Stir in the tomatoes and green chiles.

♦ Drain spinach well. Combine with the onion mixture, Monterey Jack cheese, cream cheese, half-and-half, olives and wine vinegar in a bowl; mix well. Season with salt, pepper and hot pepper sauce. Spoon into a baking dish.

♦ Bake at 350 degrees for 30 minutes or until bubbly.

♦ Serve with tortilla chips.

PEPPERS AND PITA

Makes 14 servings

1 (9-ounce) jar pepper salad

1 (9-ounce) jar sliced cherry peppers, drained, seeded

1/4 cup red wine vinegar

1/4 cup olive oil

1/8 to 1/4 teaspoon basil

1/8 to 1/4 teaspoon garlic powder

1/8 to 1/4 teaspoon oregano

Pita bread

♦ Combine the pepper salad, cherry peppers, wine vinegar, olive oil, basil, garlic powder and oregano in a bowl; mix well.

♦ Let stand at room temperature for 1 hour, stirring occasionally.

♦ Serve with pita bread cut into wedges.

SALSA

Makes 3 cups

1 (4-ounce) can chopped black olives, drained

1 (4-ounce) can chopped green chiles, drained

3 large tomatoes, chopped

6 green onions, chopped

1 tablespoon chopped fresh cilantro

2/3 cup vinegar

1/3 cup vegetable oil

1/2 teaspoon garlic powder

1/2 teaspoon coarsely ground pepper

1 tablespoon sugar (optional)

♦ Combine the olives, chiles, tomatoes, green onions and cilantro in a bowl; mix well.

♦ Combine the vinegar, oil, garlic powder, pepper and sugar in a jar with a tight-fitting lid, shaking to blend. Pour over the tomato mixture, tossing to coat.

♦ Chill, covered, for 3 hours or longer; drain.

♦ Serve with tortilla chips.

HOT TACO DIP

Makes 8 servings

8 ounces cream cheese, softened

Tabasco sauce to taste

1 (6-ounce) can sliced black olives, drained

6 to 8 scallions, chopped

1½ cups shredded Monterey Jack cheese

1 (15-ounce) can chili without beans

♦ Preheat the oven to 350 degrees.

♦ Spread the cream cheese in a pie plate or quiche pan. Dot with Tabasco sauce; spread evenly over the cream cheese. Sprinkle with the olives, scallions and ½ of the Monterey Jack cheese. Spoon the chili over the prepared layers; top with the remaining Monterey Jack cheese.

♦ Bake at 350 degrees for 20 minutes.

♦ Serve with tortilla chips.

ZESTY VEGETABLE DIP

Makes 1½ cups

1 cup mayonnaise

½ teaspoon thyme

2 tablespoons chili sauce

2 teaspoons tarragon vinegar

¼ teaspoon curry powder

2 tablespoons grated onion

Salt and pepper to taste

♦ Combine the mayonnaise, thyme, chili sauce, tarragon vinegar, curry powder, onion, salt and pepper in a bowl; mix well.

♦ Chill, covered, until serving time.

♦ Serve with fresh vegetables or shrimp.

BOURSIN SPREAD

Makes 1¾ cups

8 ounces cream cheese, softened

¼ cup unsalted butter, softened

¼ cup sour cream

1 clove of garlic, crushed, or ¼ teaspoon garlic powder

1 teaspoon oregano

1 teaspoon basil

½ teaspoon dillweed

¼ teaspoon salt

½ teaspoon white pepper

Lemon pepper to taste

♦ Line a 3-inch diameter ramekin with plastic wrap.

♦ Beat the cream cheese and butter in a mixer bowl until light and fluffy. Stir in the sour cream, garlic, oregano, basil, dillweed, salt and white pepper. Spoon into the prepared ramekin. Chill, covered, for 8 to 10 hours.

♦ Invert onto a serving platter; sprinkle with lemon pepper.

♦ Serve with assorted party crackers.

Use Boursin Spread to stuff celery, cherry tomatoes or pea pods. May be used to enhance the flavor of your favorite chicken dish.

CHUTNEY-BACON BRIE

Makes 12 servings

Deceivingly simple, yet elaborately delicious.

1 (15-ounce) round Brie cheese
1/2 cup mango chutney
5 slices crisp-fried bacon,
  crumbled

♦ Preheat the oven to 325 degrees.

♦ Remove the top rind of the Brie cheese, leaving a 1/2-inch rim. Spread the chutney evenly over the top; sprinkle with the bacon.

♦ Place in a baking dish.

♦ Bake at 325 degrees for 20 minutes.

♦ Serve with assorted crackers and fresh fruit.

May microwave on High for 1 1/2 to 2 minutes or until of the desired consistency.

SUN-DRENCHED BRIE

Makes 6 servings

1 (15-ounce) round Brie cheese,
  chilled
2 cloves of garlic, minced
2 1/2 tablespoons minced fresh
  parsley
2 1/2 tablespoons freshly grated
  Parmesan cheese
5 sun-dried tomatoes, minced
2 tablespoons minced fresh basil
1 tablespoon vegetable oil

♦ Remove the rind from the Brie. Place on a serving platter.

♦ Mash the garlic in a bowl to a paste consistency. Stir in the parsley, Parmesan cheese, sun-dried tomatoes, basil and oil. Spread evenly over the top of the Brie.

♦ Let stand at room temperature for 1 hour.

♦ Serve with assorted party crackers or toasted French bread slices.

CROCKED CHEESE WITH BRANDY

Makes 1½ cups

1 or 2 cloves of garlic

8 to 10 ounces Cheddar cheese, chopped

3 ounces cream cheese, softened, cut into chunks

¼ cup butter, softened

1 teaspoon prepared mustard

1 tablespoon brandy or cognac

♦ Process the garlic in a food processor until minced. Add the Cheddar cheese, cream cheese and butter; pulse until coarsely chopped. Process until creamy. Add the prepared mustard and brandy. Process until smooth.

♦ Spoon the cheese mixture into a covered crock. Store in the refrigerator.

♦ Let stand at room temperature for 1 hour before serving.

♦ Serve with assorted party crackers.

May use low-fat Cheddar cheese, low-fat cream cheese and low-fat margarine for a lighter hors d'oeuvre.

FOUR-CHEESE PATE

Makes 4½ cups

24 ounces cream cheese, softened

2 tablespoons milk

2 tablespoons sour cream

¾ cup chopped pecans

4 ounces Camembert cheese with rind, at room temperature

1 cup shredded Swiss cheese, at room temperature

4 ounces bleu cheese, crumbled, at room temperature

½ cup pecan halves

2 red apples, cut into wedges

2 green apples, cut into wedges

♦ Line a 9-inch pie plate with plastic wrap.

♦ Beat 8 ounces of the cream cheese with milk and sour cream in mixer bowl until smooth. Spread evenly in the prepared pie plate. Sprinkle with chopped pecans.

♦ Beat the remaining 16 ounces cream cheese, Camembert cheese, Swiss cheese and bleu cheese in a mixer bowl until blended. Spread evenly over the pecans. Chill, covered with plastic wrap, for up to 1 week.

♦ Invert onto a platter just before serving; discard the plastic wrap. Arrange the pecan halves over the top; surround the pâté with the apple wedges.

FRUITED CHEESE LOGS

Makes 2 (8-inch) logs

16 ounces cream cheese, softened

1/2 cup finely chopped dried apricots

1/2 cup dried currants

2 teaspoons grated orange rind

2 tablespoons orange liqueur

1 teaspoon freshly grated gingerroot

1 1/2 cups chopped pecans

- Combine the cream cheese, apricots, currants, orange rind, liqueur and gingerroot in a bowl; mix well. Shape into two 8-inch logs. Roll in chopped pecans.
- Chill, wrapped in plastic wrap, until firm.
- Arrange cheese logs on a serving platter. Garnish with grapes and apple slices.
- Serve with gingersnaps or assorted party crackers.

SHRIMP AND CREAM CHEESE SPREAD

Makes 2 1/2 cups

16 ounces cream cheese, softened

3/4 cup cocktail sauce

1 tablespoon prepared horseradish, drained

4 ounces chopped cooked shrimp

- Beat cream cheese and cocktail sauce in mixer bowl. Add horseradish. Beat until blended. Stir in the shrimp.
- Chill, covered, until serving time. Best made 1 day in advance to enhance flavor.
- Serve with corn chips or assorted party crackers.

SHERRIED STILTON CHEESE

Makes 1 1/2 cups

8 ounces Stilton cheese, crumbled, at room temperature

8 ounces cream cheese, softened

1 to 2 tablespoons green peppercorns packed in wine vinegar, rinsed, drained

1/4 cup medium-dry sherry

- Process the Stilton cheese, cream cheese, peppercorns and sherry in a food processor until blended. Spoon into a covered crock.
- Chill, covered, until serving time.
- Serve with sliced apples, sliced pears and assorted party crackers.

HOT CRABMEAT SPREAD

Makes 6 to 8 servings

8 ounces cream cheese, softened
1½ cups flaked crabmeat
2 tablespoons finely chopped onion
1 tablespoon milk
½ teaspoon prepared horseradish
½ teaspoon salt
Worcestershire sauce to taste
Pepper to taste
⅓ cup sliced almonds, toasted

♦ Preheat the oven to 375 degrees.

♦ Combine the cream cheese, crabmeat, onion, milk, horseradish, salt, Worcestershire sauce and pepper in a bowl; mix well.

♦ Spoon into an 8-inch baking dish. Sprinkle with the almonds.

♦ Bake at 375 degrees for 15 to 20 minutes or until bubbly.

♦ Serve with assorted party crackers or chips.

EGGPLANT CAPONATA

Makes 2½ cups

May use as a spread or as an accompaniment to lamb, pork or chicken.

1 unpeeled eggplant, finely chopped
⅔ cup chopped onion
¾ cup chopped green bell pepper
2 cloves of garlic, minced
¼ cup olive oil
½ teaspoon oregano
1½ teaspoons sugar
1 cup tomato sauce
2 tablespoons wine vinegar
1 tablespoon capers, drained
½ cup chopped pitted calamata olives
Salt and pepper to taste

♦ Combine 4 cups of the chopped eggplant, onion, green pepper, garlic and olive oil in a saucepan; mix well.

♦ Simmer, covered, for 10 minutes, stirring occasionally. Stir in the oregano, sugar, tomato sauce, wine vinegar, capers, olives, salt and pepper.

♦ Simmer, covered, for 25 minutes or until the eggplant is tender but firm. Chill, covered, for 8 to 10 hours or freeze for future use.

♦ Serve at room temperature with toasted French bread slices or crackers.

LIVER PATE

Makes 32 servings

1 pound chicken livers

2 tablespoons minced shallots

1 cup butter

¼ cup brandy

2 teaspoons dry mustard (optional)

½ teaspoon nutmeg (optional)

¼ teaspoon ground cloves (optional)

Chopped fresh parsley for garnish

Grated peppercorns for garnish

- Rinse the chicken livers and pat dry.
- Sauté the shallots in ¼ cup of the butter in a skillet over medium heat until tender and light in color. Add the remaining butter and livers.
- Cook over low heat for 10 minutes or until the livers are cooked through, stirring frequently. Cool slightly.
- Process the liver mixture, brandy, dry mustard, nutmeg and cloves in a food processor until smooth. Spoon into a 3 or 4-cup serving dish. Smooth the surface of the pâté.
- Chill, covered, for 4 hours or longer. Let stand at room temperature for 30 minutes before serving. Garnish with chopped fresh parsley and grated peppercorns.
- Serve with assorted party crackers.

MUSHROOM PATE

Makes 10 to 12 servings

2 pounds mushrooms, cut into halves

4 cups water

16 ounces cream cheese, softened

½ cup unsalted butter, softened

1 tablespoon chopped fresh rosemary

1 teaspoon white pepper

½ teaspoon salt

1 teaspoon minced garlic

2 tablespoons marsala (optional)

Chopped fresh parsley for garnish

Paprika for garnish

- Process the mushrooms and water in a food processor or blender until puréed. Transfer to a saucepan. Bring to a boil; reduce heat.
- Simmer for 30 minutes, stirring occasionally. Strain the mushroom mixture, pressing to squeeze dry. Reserve both the liquid and mushroom portions. Let the mushroom purée stand until cool.
- Simmer the reserved liquid in a saucepan until reduced to ¼ to ½ cup. Let stand until cool.
- Combine the cream cheese, butter, rosemary, white pepper, salt and garlic in a mixer bowl, beating until blended. Stir in the mushroom liquid, mushroom purée and wine.
- Chill, covered, until serving time. Garnish with finely chopped parsley and a dusting of paprika.
- Serve with assorted party crackers.

May store in the refrigerator for up to 7 days.

MUSHROOM SPREAD

Makes 1½ cups

For those who love stuffed mushrooms without the work of stuffing individual caps!

1 large onion, finely chopped

4 cloves of garlic, minced

6 tablespoons unsalted butter

2 pounds fresh mushrooms, coarsely chopped

¾ teaspoon salt

½ teaspoon freshly ground pepper

3 tablespoons chopped fresh dillweed

1 teaspoon sherry

♦ Sauté the onion and garlic in the butter in a skillet for 3 to 5 minutes. Add the mushrooms.

♦ Cook for 10 to 15 minutes or until most of the liquid has been absorbed, stirring occasionally. Stir in the salt, pepper, dillweed and sherry.

♦ Let stand until room temperature. Spoon into a serving bowl.

♦ Serve with assorted party crackers, cocktail rye bread or toast points.

Can be used as a sandwich filling.

MYSTICAL SEAFOOD MOUSSE

Makes 12 servings

Elegant addition to a cocktail buffet table.

1 envelope unflavored gelatin

¼ cup cold water

1 (10-ounce) can tomato bisque or tomato soup

8 ounces cream cheese

1 cup mayonnaise

½ cup finely chopped celery

¼ cup finely chopped onion

12 ounces cooked crabmeat, lobster or shrimp (or any combination), chopped

1 unpeeled cucumber, thinly sliced

2 to 4 tablespoons chopped red bell pepper or tomato (optional)

♦ Soften the gelatin in the cold water.

♦ Combine the bisque and cream cheese in a saucepan. Cook until blended, stirring frequently. Add the gelatin; heat until gelatin dissolves, stirring constantly. Blend in the mayonnaise.

♦ Chill, covered, until slightly thickened. Fold in the celery, onion and seafood. Spoon into a lightly oiled 2-quart mold.

♦ Chill until set. Invert onto a serving platter. Surround the mousse with the cucumber slices and chopped red pepper.

♦ Serve with assorted party crackers.

TOMATO BUTTER

Makes 2½ cups

8 ounces cream cheese, softened
½ cup unsalted butter, softened
½ cup grated Parmesan cheese
¼ to ½ cup oil-pack sun-dried
    tomatoes, drained
2 tablespoons oil from sun-dried
    tomatoes
1 tablespoon chopped fresh basil

• Process the cream cheese, butter, cheese, sun-dried tomatoes, oil and basil in a food processor until blended. Spoon into a serving bowl. Store, covered, in the refrigerator.

• Serve at room temperature; spread on grilled bread.

Top with pesto and grated Parmesan cheese, if desired.

CARAMELIZED BACON

Makes 6 servings

1 pound sliced bacon
2 cups packed brown sugar

• Preheat the oven to 350 degrees.

• Cut bacon slices into thirds. Press both sides of each bacon piece into the brown sugar to coat. Place slices on the rack of a broiler pan.

• Bake at 350 degrees for 30 minutes or until the bacon is crisp and brown. Drain on paper towels.

For easy cleanup, line the bottom of the broiler pan with foil.

BLOODY MARYS

Makes 4 to 6 servings

1 (46-ounce) can vegetable juice
    cocktail
2 teaspoons sugar
½ teaspoon salt
¼ teaspoon pepper
6 tablespoons lemon juice
6 teaspoons Worcestershire sauce
6 drops of Tabasco sauce
6 to 9 ounces vodka
Lemon slices for garnish

• Combine the vegetable juice cocktail, sugar, salt, pepper, lemon juice, Worcestershire sauce and Tabasco sauce in a large pitcher; mix well. Pour into ice-filled glasses. Add vodka. Garnish with lemon slices.

May rub the rims of the glasses with lemon juice and dip into seasoned salt.

FROZEN MARGARITAS

Makes 2 to 4 servings

1 (6-ounce) can frozen limeade
  concentrate, thawed
6 ounces tequila
3 ounces Triple Sec
1 tablespoon lime juice
10 ice cubes
Lime juice to taste
Salt

♦ Combine the limeade concentrate, tequila, Triple Sec and
1 tablespoon lime juice in a blender container. Add the ice
cubes one at a time, processing constantly just until
thickened.

♦ Rub the rims of 2 to 4 glasses with lime juice and dip in the
salt. Pour the Margaritas into the prepared glasses.

PAIN KILLER

Makes 4 servings

1 cup cream of coconut
1 cup pineapple juice
1 cup orange juice
¾ cup dark rum
Grated nutmeg for garnish
Orange slices for garnish

♦ Combine the cream of coconut, pineapple juice, orange
juice and rum in a pitcher; mix well.

♦ Pour into ice-filled glasses. Garnish with nutmeg and orange
slices.

LIME PUNCH

Makes 1 gallon

1 (3-ounce) package lime gelatin
2 cups boiling water
½ cup lime juice
2 (12-ounce) cans frozen limeade
  concentrate, thawed
1 teaspoon almond extract
3 (32-ounce) bottles lemon-lime
  soda
3 to 4 cups vodka
Fresh strawberries for garnish

♦ Dissolve the gelatin in the boiling water in a large heatproof
container; mix well. Cool.

♦ Stir in the lime juice, limeade concentrate, almond flavoring,
soda and vodka; mix well.

♦ Pour into ice-filled glasses. Garnish with fresh strawberries.

WHITE SANGRIA

Makes 6 servings

26 ounces chablis

4 ounces Triple Sec

Sliced seasonal fruit such as orange, lemon, lime, pear, kiwifruit or peaches

10 ounces club soda

Fresh mint for garnish

♦ Combine the wine and Triple Sec in a large pitcher; mix well. Add the fruit in any combination and amount.

♦ Chill, covered, for several hours. Add the club soda just before serving. Pour into ice-filled glasses. Garnish with mint sprigs.

CITRUS TEA PUNCH

Makes 12 servings

A cookbook committee meeting favorite.

4 cups boiling water

6 tea bags

$1/2$ cup fresh mint leaves

$1/2$ cup sugar

4 cups cold water

$1/2$ cup lemon juice

1 cup orange juice

Lemon slices for garnish

Mint sprigs for garnish

♦ Pour the boiling water over the tea bags and mint in a heatproof container.

♦ Steep, covered, for 10 minutes. Strain, discarding the tea bags and mint. Add the sugar to the tea, stirring until dissolved. Add the cold water, lemon juice and orange juice; mix well.

♦ Pour into ice-filled glasses. Garnish with lemon slices and additional mint sprigs.

GRADUATION PUNCH

Makes 25 servings

1 quart orange juice, chilled

1 quart ginger ale, chilled

1 quart cranberry juice, chilled

$1^1/2$ quarts rainbow sherbet

1 quart fresh strawberries, hulled and cut into halves

Ice cubes

♦ Combine the orange juice, ginger ale and cranberry juice in a punch bowl.

♦ Drop the sherbet by spoonfuls into the punch just before serving. Add the strawberries and desired amount of ice cubes.

May substitute ice ring for ice cubes if desired. Make ice especially for the punch, using additional fruit juice if desired.

MOCHA MIX

Makes 15 servings

A gift of holiday warmth from your kitchen.

1 cup dry nondairy creamer
1 cup hot cocoa mix
3/4 cup instant coffee powder
1/2 cup sugar
1/2 teaspoon cinnamon
1/4 teaspoon nutmeg

+ Combine the creamer, cocoa mix, coffee powder, sugar, cinnamon and nutmeg in a bowl; mix well.

+ Store in an airtight container.

+ Combine 3 to 4 heaping teaspoons of the mocha mix with 1 cup hot water for each serving.

PERCOLATOR PUNCH

Makes 17 servings

Simple and wonderful! Serve during the holidays at cookie swap get-togethers, open-houses or skating parties.

2 (32-ounce) bottles cranberry
   juice cocktail
1 (46-ounce) can unsweetened
   pineapple juice
1 cup packed brown sugar
4 teaspoons whole cloves
12 inches stick cinnamon, broken
Rind of 1/4 orange, cut into strips
1 fifth of light rum (3 1/4 cups)
Lemon slices for garnish

+ Combine the cranberry juice cocktail, pineapple juice and brown sugar in a 24-cup electric percolator; mix well. Place the cloves, cinnamon stick pieces and orange rind in the basket. Assemble the coffee maker. Percolate using manufacturer's directions.

+ Remove the basket and stir in the rum just before serving. Pour into mugs; garnish with lemon slices.

Just as delicious without the rum.

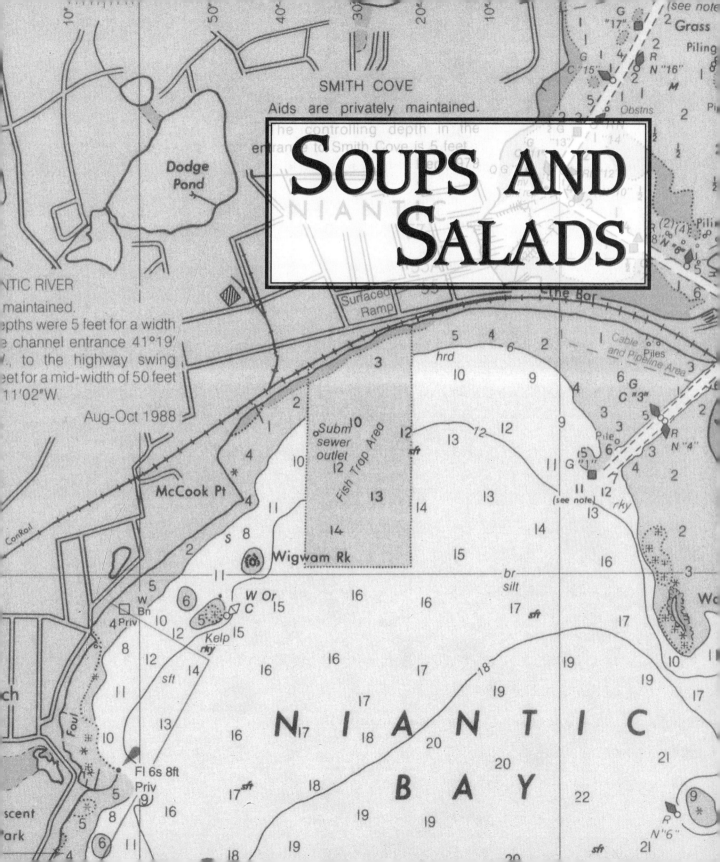

SOUPS AND SALADS

SOUPS AND SALADS

◆ ◆ ◆ ◆ ◆ ◆ ◆ ◆ ◆ ◆ ◆ ◆ ◆

BLACK BEAN VEGETARIAN CHILI

Makes 6 servings

1 eggplant
1 tablespoon coarse salt
$1/4$ cup olive oil
2 zucchini, chopped
1 red bell pepper, chopped
1 yellow bell pepper, chopped
2 medium onions, chopped
4 cloves of garlic, minced
$1/4$ cup olive oil
8 plum tomatoes, chopped
1 cup vegetarian broth
$1/2$ cup chopped fresh parsley
$1/2$ cup slivered fresh basil
3 tablespoons chili powder
$1 1/2$ teaspoons ground cumin
1 tablespoon oregano
$1/2$ teaspoon red pepper
1 teaspoon black pepper
Salt to taste
2 cups cooked black beans
$1 1/2$ cups fresh corn kernels
$1/2$ teaspoon minced dill
$1/4$ cup lemon juice
$1/2$ cup chopped fresh parsley

♦ Cut the eggplant into $1/2$-inch cubes. Toss the eggplant with the salt in a colander. Set aside for 1 hour.

♦ Pat the eggplant dry. Sauté in $1/4$ cup olive oil in a large skillet. Remove with a slotted spoon.

♦ Sauté the zucchini, red and yellow peppers, onions and garlic in the remaining $1/4$ cup olive oil over medium heat. Add the eggplant, tomatoes, broth, $1/2$ cup parsley, basil, chili powder, cumin, oregano, red pepper, black pepper and salt; mix well.

♦ Cook over low heat for 30 minutes, stirring occasionally. Add the black beans, corn, dill and lemon juice. Cook for 15 minutes. Add $1/2$ cup parsley and mix well.

♦ Ladle into soup bowls.

Serve hot with toppings of sour cream, shredded Monterey Jack cheese and sliced green onions.

CREAM OF BROCCOLI AND HERB SOUP

Makes 4 to 6 servings

1 cup chopped onion
1 cup chopped celery
2 tablespoons butter
1 teaspoon sweet basil
1/2 teaspoon marjoram
1/4 teaspoon thyme
1/4 teaspoon pepper
3 vegetable bouillon cubes
3 cups water
4 cups chopped broccoli
2 small potatoes, peeled, cubed
1 cup light cream

♦ Sauté the onion and celery in butter in a large saucepan for 5 minutes or until tender. Add the basil, marjoram, thyme and pepper. Cook for 2 minutes, stirring constantly.

♦ Add the bouillon cubes, water, broccoli and potatoes.

♦ Simmer, covered, for 30 minutes.

♦ Purée in batches in a blender. Return to the saucepan over low heat. Add the cream and stir until blended. Heat to serving temperature; do not boil.

♦ Ladle into soup bowls and serve hot.

FARMHOUSE CHEESE SOUP

Makes 6 servings

4 small carrots, chopped
3 stalks celery, chopped
1 1/2 cups chicken broth
2 tablespoons finely chopped onion
2 tablespoons butter
1/4 cup flour
3 cups hot chicken broth
1 cup shredded sharp Cheddar cheese
1 (8 1/2-ounce) can whole tomatoes, undrained, chopped
6 to 10 drops of Tabasco sauce
1/8 teaspoon nutmeg
Salt to taste
1 1/2 cups hot half-and-half

♦ Combine the carrots and celery in 1 1/2 cups chicken broth in a saucepan over high heat. Bring to a boil and reduce heat. Simmer for 15 minutes or until the vegetables are tender; set aside.

♦ Sauté the onion in the butter in a large saucepan until tender. Add the flour. Cook for 5 to 7 minutes, stirring constantly; do not brown.

♦ Add the hot broth gradually to the flour mixture, whisking constantly. Cook until thickened, whisking constantly. Add the cheese; stir until completely melted. Add the tomatoes and mix well.

♦ Add the undrained vegetables, Tabasco sauce, nutmeg and salt; mix well. Heat to serving temperature.

♦ Stir in hot half-and-half just before serving. Ladle into soup bowls.

Garnish with freshly popped popcorn. May substitute 1/4 cup white wine for 1/4 cup of the half-and-half.

GAZPACHO

Makes 8 servings

3 large tomatoes, peeled, chopped

1 large cucumber, peeled, chopped

1 medium onion, chopped

1 green bell pepper, chopped

1 red bell pepper, chopped

2 avocados, chopped

1 cup chopped celery

4 cups tomato juice

6 tablespoons red wine vinegar

4 tablespoons olive oil

1/4 teaspoon Tabasco sauce

2 teaspoons salt

1/2 teaspoon pepper

♦ Combine the tomatoes, cucumber, onion, green pepper, red pepper, avocados and celery in a food processor. Pulse until the vegetables are finely minced.

♦ Pour the mixture into a large glass or plastic container. Add the tomato juice, vinegar, olive oil, Tabasco sauce, salt and pepper and mix well.

♦ Chill, covered, for 4 hours. Mix well and ladle into soup cups.

Garnish with sour cream or croutons. Add 1/4 cup fresh dill or 1/2 teaspoon cumin for a change of pace.

CHICKEN AND VEGETABLE SOUP

Makes 4 servings

6 cups chicken broth

1 mild red onion, chopped

2 leeks, chopped

3 carrots, chopped

2 stalks celery, chopped

1 turnip or parsnip, cubed

2 cloves of garlic, crushed

2 teaspoons chopped fresh basil

1/4 cup chopped fresh parsley

1 boneless skinless chicken breast

1/2 cup orzo

Juice of 1/2 lemon

1 tablespoon chopped fresh dill

♦ Combine the chicken broth, onion, leeks, carrots, celery, turnip, garlic, basil and parsley in a large saucepan over medium heat. Simmer, covered, for 30 minutes.

♦ Add the chicken breast. Simmer for 20 to 30 minutes or until tender.

♦ Remove the chicken and cut into bite-size pieces.

♦ Bring the soup mixture to a boil. Add the orzo, lemon juice and dill; mix well. Cook for 10 minutes or until pasta is tender.

♦ Add the chicken and heat to serving temperature.

♦ Ladle into soup bowls.

Serve with a fresh fruit salad and crisp crackers for a quick, casual lunch.

Clam Digger's Chowder

Makes 8 servings

1/4 pound salt pork, chopped
2 large onions, chopped
1 cup water
2 cups clam juice
2 stalks celery, sliced
3 cups chopped peeled potatoes
1/4 teaspoon ground oregano
1/4 teaspoon ground thyme
1 bay leaf, broken
Freshly ground pepper to taste
1 quart clams, coarsely chopped
Tabasco sauce to taste
2 tablespoons unsalted butter
1 quart half-and-half

♦ Cook the salt pork in a large stockpot over medium heat until the fat is rendered and the pork is crisp.

♦ Add the onions. Sauté until tender. Add the water, clam juice, celery, potatoes, oregano, thyme, bay leaf and pepper and mix well.

♦ Simmer, covered, for 15 minutes or until the potatoes are tender.

♦ Add the undrained clams. Simmer for 3 minutes. Add the Tabasco sauce, butter and half-and-half. Cook over low heat until heated through; do not boil. Discard the bay leaf.

♦ Ladle into serving bowls and serve at once.

Crab Bisque

Makes 8 servings

1/2 cup chopped green bell pepper
1/2 cup chopped onion
2 green onions, chopped
1/4 cup chopped fresh parsley
3 cups sliced fresh mushrooms
1/2 cup butter
1/4 cup flour
2 cups milk
2 teaspoons salt
1/8 to 1/4 teaspoon white pepper
Tabasco sauce to taste
3 cups half-and-half
3 cups crabmeat
6 tablespoons dry sherry or 4 tablespoons cognac

♦ Sauté the green pepper, onion, green onions, parsley and mushrooms in the butter in a large saucepan over medium heat for 5 minutes.

♦ Add the flour. Cook for 1 to 2 minutes, stirring constantly. Add the milk. Cook until thickened, stirring constantly.

♦ Add salt, white pepper, Tabasco sauce, half-and-half and crabmeat; mix well. Cook over low heat until heated through, stirring frequently.

♦ Add the sherry just before serving. Ladle into soup bowls.

CORN CHOWDER

Makes 6 to 8 servings

1/4 pound bacon, chopped
3/4 cup chopped celery
1 large onion, chopped
2 large potatoes, chopped
2 cups water
1 1/2 teaspoons thyme
1 teaspoon salt
1/4 teaspoon pepper
1 (16-ounce) can cream-style corn
1 (16-ounce) can whole kernel
  corn, drained
1 cup milk

♦ Sauté the bacon in a large stockpot over medium heat until crisp-fried. Remove the bacon with a slotted spoon.

♦ Sauté the celery and onion in the reserved drippings until the onion is tender; drain off excess drippings.

♦ Add the potatoes, water, thyme, salt and pepper and mix well. Cook for 15 minutes or until the potatoes are tender. Add the corn and milk and stir well. Heat through; do not boil.

♦ Ladle the hot chowder into soup bowls. Top with the bacon.

May add one 6 1/2-ounce can drained minced clams or 1/2 pound bay scallops. Add 5 minutes to the cooking time.

CATCH-OF-THE-DAY CHOWDER

Makes 6 to 8 servings

This is an easy, relaxed way to prepare chowder after a long day on the water.

2 pounds haddock or cod fillets,
  cubed
4 potatoes, peeled, sliced
3 onions, sliced
1/2 cup butter, cubed
1/2 cup dry white wine
2 cups boiling water
1 bay leaf
1 clove of garlic, crushed
Chopped celery leaves to taste
1/4 teaspoon dillseeds
2 1/2 teaspoons salt
1/4 teaspoon white pepper
3 or 4 whole cloves
2 cups light cream, scalded
Fresh dill

♦ Preheat the oven to 375 degrees.

♦ Place the fish, potatoes, onions, butter, wine and boiling water in a large casserole. Add the bay leaf, garlic, celery, dillseeds, salt, white pepper and cloves.

♦ Bake, covered, at 375 degrees for 1 hour.

♦ Remove the cloves and bay leaf. Stir the cream gently into the fish mixture.

♦ Ladle into soup bowls. Garnish with fresh dill.

FISH CHOWDER

Makes 4 servings

This recipe is especially delicious when made with garden fresh tomatoes and herbs.

1 large mild onion, chopped

2 tablespoons butter

2 to 4 large tomatoes, chopped,
  or 1 (28-ounce) can whole
  tomatoes

1/2 cup finely chopped celery

1/4 cup shredded carrot

1/4 cup chopped parsley

4 cups water

1/2 teaspoon dried thyme

1/4 teaspoon dried sweet basil

Salt and freshly ground pepper
  to taste

1 pound cod fillets or pollock,
  cut up

♦ Sauté the onion in the butter in a Dutch oven until golden brown. Add the tomatoes, celery, carrot and parsley and mix well.

♦ Cook, covered, over low heat for 5 minutes, adding a small amount of liquid if necessary to keep the mixture from browning.

♦ Add water, thyme, basil, salt and pepper.

♦ Add the fish. Simmer for 15 to 20 minutes or until the fish flakes easily.

♦ Ladle the chowder into soup bowls and serve with hot garlic bread.

May triple the recipe using just 2 cups water and omitting the fish for a soup base that may be frozen for later use.

LENTIL SOUP WITH SAUSAGE

Makes 6 to 8 servings

1 pound dry lentils

4 slices bacon, chopped

2 carrots, chopped

2 stalks celery, chopped

3 (10-ounce) cans condensed
  chicken broth

3 soup cans water

1/2 teaspoon marjoram

1 bay leaf

1 pound smoked sausages, sliced

2 tablespoons balsamic or red
  wine vinegar

Salt to taste

1/2 teaspoon pepper

♦ Sort and rinse the lentils. Soak in 2 or more quarts water to cover overnight (or simmer lentils in covered saucepan for 35 minutes).

♦ Cook the bacon in a soup pot until it starts to brown. Add the carrots and celery. Sauté until the vegetables are light brown.

♦ Add the drained lentils, chicken broth, water, marjoram and bay leaf. Simmer for 1 hour.

♦ Add the sausages, vinegar, salt and pepper and heat through. Remove the bay leaf. Ladle into soup bowls.

Substitute split peas for the lentils and omit the vinegar for a great pea soup.

LOBSTER STEW

Makes 4 servings

Extravagant simplicity. Forget about cholesterol!

2 cups sliced fresh lobster meat
Paprika to taste
1 cup butter
1 quart milk
1 cup whipping cream
Salt and pepper to taste

♦ Sauté the lobster with paprika in the butter in a large saucepan over medium-low heat.

♦ Bring the milk and cream almost to the boiling point in a saucepan over medium heat. Add to the lobster. Season with salt and pepper.

♦ Ladle the hot stew into soup bowls.

MULLIGATAWNY STEW

Makes 6 servings

¼ cup chopped carrot
¼ cup chopped green bell pepper
1 onion, chopped
1 tart apple, chopped
1 tablespoon vegetable oil
5 cups hot water
3 chicken bouillon cubes
1 whole chicken breast
1 (16-ounce) can tomatoes
½ teaspoon sugar
½ teaspoon curry powder
1 teaspoon salt
2 whole cloves
2 sprigs of parsley
Mace or nutmeg to taste
Pepper to taste

♦ Sauté the carrot, green pepper, onion and apple in the oil in a large soup pot over low heat for 15 minutes.

♦ Add the hot water, bouillon cubes, chicken breast, tomatoes, sugar, curry powder, salt, cloves, parsley, mace and pepper. Simmer, covered, for 1 hour.

♦ Remove the chicken. Cut into bite-size pieces; discard bones and skin. Return to soup pot.

♦ Heat to serving temperature. Discard cloves.

Serve over hot cooked rice or with corn bread.

MUSHROOM AND LEEK BISQUE

Makes 8 servings

A rich and delicately flavored soup.

1 pound fresh mushrooms, sliced
Whites of 1 bunch leeks, sliced
1/2 cup butter
4 tablespoons flour
1 teaspoon salt
1/4 teaspoon white pepper
3 (12³/4-ounce) cans chicken broth
1 cup light cream
Parsley for garnish

♦ Sauté the mushrooms and leeks in the butter in a large saucepan for 5 minutes or until tender. Add the flour, salt and white pepper; mix well. Stir in 2 cans of the chicken broth gradually. Cook until thickened and mixture comes to a boil, stirring constanty. Reduce heat and simmer, covered, for 20 minutes.

♦ Remove from heat and cool slightly. Process in batches in a blender until puréed.

♦ Combine the puréed mixture with the remaining can of the chicken broth and cream in a large saucepan. Heat to serving temperature; do not boil.

♦ Ladle into soup bowls. Garnish with fresh chopped parsley.

CREAMY CURRIED PEA SOUP

Makes 4 servings

Elegant enough for special occasions, easy enough for everyday.

1 cup cooked peas
1 medium onion, sliced
1 small carrot, sliced
1 stalk celery, sliced
1 medium potato, peeled, sliced
1 clove of garlic, minced
1 teaspoon salt
1 teaspoon curry powder
2 cups chicken broth
1 cup cream

♦ Combine the peas, onion, carrot, celery, potato, garlic, salt, curry powder and 1 cup of the chicken broth in a large saucepan. Bring to a boil; reduce heat. Simmer, covered, for 15 minutes.

♦ Process in a blender until puréed. With the motor running, add the remaining 1 cup chicken broth and the cream, processing constantly.

♦ Serve soup hot or chilled.

When reheating, be sure that soup is not allowed to boil.

PEANUT-PUMPKIN SOUP

Makes 6 to 8 servings

This recipe has been developed to recreate the memorable soup served at the Sugar Mill restaurant in Tortola, British Virgin Islands. It is an interesting way to use fresh cooked pumpkin or squash with the delicious peanut flavor.

1/2 cup chopped onion

2 tablespoons butter

2 tablespoons flour

4 cups chicken stock

1 3/4 cups puréed cooked pumpkin

1/2 cup creamy peanut butter

1/2 teaspoon sugar

3/4 teaspoon nutmeg

1 cup light cream

Tabasco sauce to taste

Salt and pepper to taste

Peanuts and parsley for garnish

♦ Sauté the onion in butter in a large saucepan until tender. Add the flour. Cook for 3 minutes, stirring constantly.

♦ Add the chicken stock, pumpkin and peanut butter gradually, stirring until well blended. Add the sugar and nutmeg. Simmer, covered, for 15 to 20 minutes

♦ Add the cream, Tabasco sauce, salt and pepper. Heat to serving temperature, stirring frequently; do not boil.

♦ Ladle into soup bowls. Garnish with chopped peanuts and chopped fresh parsley.

May substitute milk for cream for everyday meals; use 15-ounce can pumpkin or substitute 1 3/4 cups puréed cooked butternut squash for the fresh pumpkin.

PEAR AND PARSNIP SOUP

Makes 8 servings

1 large onion, chopped

1/4 cup butter

1 1/4 pounds parsnips, peeled, cubed

4 1/2 cups chicken broth

1/2 teaspoon allspice

1/2 teaspoon white pepper

2 (16-ounce) cans pear halves in juice

1/2 cup whipping cream (optional)

♦ Sauté the onion in the butter in a 4- to 5-quart saucepan until lightly browned. Add the parsnips, broth, allspice and white pepper. Cook, covered, until mixture boils; reduce the heat. Simmer for 15 minutes or until the parsnips are tender.

♦ Process the soup and pears in a blender or food processor. Return to the saucepan. Heat to serving temperature over medium heat, sitrring constantly.

♦ Add the cream and blend well.

This soup is especially good as a first course with game.

CURRIED PARSNIP SOUP

Makes 8 servings

A treasure with wonderful texture and flavor. Don't let the word "parsnips" put you off.

4 large parsnips, peeled, sliced
4 large onions, sliced
2 to 4 tablespoons margarine
4 tablespoons flour
2 teaspoons curry powder
8 cups chicken broth

♦ Sauté the parsnips and onions in the margarine in a large saucepan until tender. Add the flour and curry and mix well. Add chicken broth gradually, stirring until well mixed. Simmer for 30 minutes.

♦ Drain the vegetables, reserving liquid. Purée in a blender or food processor. Combine the puréed vegetables and the reserved liquid in the saucepan. Heat to serving temperature.

♦ Ladle into soup bowls.

Soup may be served chilled, garnished with plain yogurt, sour cream or chopped parsley.

ITALIAN SAUSAGE SOUP

Makes 8 servings

1 pound Italian sausage
1 cup chopped onion
2 cloves of garlic, sliced
5 cups beef broth
½ cup water
½ cup dry red wine or water
2 cups chopped, seeded peeled tomatoes
1 cup thinly sliced carrots
½ teaspoon each chopped basil and oregano leaves
1 (8-ounce) can tomato sauce
1½ cups sliced zucchini
8 ounces cheese tortellini
3 tablespoons chopped parsley
1 green bell pepper, chopped

♦ Cut sausage into pieces. Brown in a Dutch oven. Drain the sausage, reserving 1 tablespoon drippings. Set aside.

♦ Sauté the onion and garlic in the reserved drippings until tender. Add the broth, water, wine, tomatoes, carrots, basil, oregano and tomato sauce.

♦ Bring to a boil and reduce heat. Simmer, uncovered, for 30 minutes.

♦ Skim the soup. Add the sausage, zucchini, tortellini, parsley and pepper; mix well.

♦ Simmer, covered, for 35 to 40 minutes or until tortellini is tender.

♦ Ladle the hot soup into soup bowls.

Garnish with a sprinkle of Parmesan cheese. Serve with Italian bread.

ORIENTAL SCALLOP AND SNOW PEA SOUP

Makes 4 to 6 servings

1½ tablespoons peeled gingerroot

1 large clove of garlic, crushed

5 black peppercorns

7 cups chicken stock

1 teaspoon soy sauce

1½ tablespoons medium dry sherry

1 teaspoon sesame oil

½ cup scallions, chopped

½ pound snow peas, diagonally sliced

½ cup thinly sliced scallions

1 (7½-ounce) can water chestnuts, sliced

1 carrot, julienned into 1-inch pieces

1 pound sea scallops, thinly sliced

- Combine the gingerroot, garlic, peppercorns, stock, soy sauce, sherry, oil and ½ cup scallions in a saucepan. Simmer for 10 minutes; strain.

- Bring strained stock to a boil in a large saucepan. Add the snow peas, remaining scallions, water chestnuts, carrot and scallops. Cook for 3 to 4 minutes or until scallops are tender.

Serve this colorful hot soup in an oriental-style soup cup accompanied by thin rice wafers.

SCOTCH BROTH

Makes 4 to 8 servings

8 cups water

1 (1-pound) lamb shank

¼ cup pearl barley

¼ cup dried peas, rinsed

1 bay leaf

½ teaspoon ground cloves

1 large onion, chopped

1 leek, chopped

1 carrot, coarsely grated

1 small turnip, finely chopped

½ teaspoon curry powder

1½ teaspoons salt

¼ teaspoon pepper

- Combine the water, lamb shank, barley, peas, bay leaf and cloves in a large stockpot. Simmer for 1½ hours.

- Discard the bay leaf. Set lamb shank aside.

- Add the onion, leek, carrot and turnip to the stockpot. Simmer for 45 minutes or until the vegetables are tender.

- Cut the lamb meat into bite-size pieces and add to the soup. Add the curry powder, salt and pepper. Heat to serving temperature.

- Ladle into soup bowls.

SEAFOOD CHOWDER SUPREME

Makes 8 servings

2 medium onions, chopped

1 cup chopped celery

4 cloves of garlic, crushed

3 tablespoons butter

4 potatoes, peeled, chopped

2 tablespoons mustard seeds

1 cup water

1/3 cup dark rum

1/3 cup brandy

5 tablespoons butter

2 (15-ounce) cans New England
   clam chowder

2 tablespoons horseradish

1/2 teaspoon Tabasco sauce

1 tablespoon Worcestershire
   sauce

1 tablespoon dried or 3
   tablespoons fresh basil

1 pound firm fish fillets, cut into
   chunks

Paprika and pepper to taste

1 pound clams

1 pound scallops

4 cups light cream

♦ Sauté the onions, celery and garlic in 3 tablespoons butter in a large stockpot until the vegetables are tender.

♦ Add the potatoes, mustard seeds, water, rum and brandy. Simmer, covered, for 15 to 20 minutes or until the potatoes are tender but firm.

♦ Add 5 tablespoons butter, clam chowder, horseradish, Tabasco sauce, Worcestershire sauce and basil; mix well. Season the fish with paprika and pepper. Add fish, clams and scallops to stockpot. Simmer for 15 to 20 minutes or until fish flakes easily.

♦ Add the cream and heat to serving temperature. Ladle into soup bowls.

May substitute crab meat or other shellfish for all or part of the scallops. The total amount of seafood should be 2 to 3 pounds. The soup can be prepared ahead but do not add cream until reheating just before serving.

GOLDEN HARVEST SOUP

Makes 6 to 8 servings

1 cup sliced celery

2 onions, chopped

3 tablespoons butter

1 cup sliced carrots

2½ pounds butternut squash, peeled, cubed

3 tart green apples, peeled, sliced

6 cups chicken broth

½ teaspoon nutmeg

½ teaspoon crushed rosemary

½ teaspoon rubbed sage

Salt to taste

Sour cream for garnish

- Sauté the celery and onion in the butter in a large saucepan until tender.
- Add the carrots, squash, apples and chicken broth; mix well. Simmer, covered, for 40 minutes or until the vegetables are tender. Add the nutmeg, rosemary, sage and salt.
- Purée the mixture in a food processor or blender.
- Return to the saucepan. Simmer for 10 minutes longer.
- Ladle into soup bowls. Garnish with a dollop of sour cream.

TOMATO BISQUE

Makes 6 servings

1 medium onion, chopped

1 tablespoon butter

2 pounds ripe tomatoes, peeled, chopped

1 bay leaf

1 tablespoon brown sugar

2 teaspoons finely chopped fresh or 1 teaspoon dried basil

2 whole cloves

1 teaspoon salt

½ teaspoon pepper

2 cups half-and-half

1 cup milk

Fresh chopped chives for garnish

- Sauté the onion in butter in a saucepan until tender. Add the tomatoes, bay leaf, brown sugar, basil, cloves, salt and pepper.
- Simmer for 25 minutes or until the tomatoes are tender, stirring occasionally.
- Remove the bay leaf and cloves. Purée the mixture in a food processor or blender. Return to the saucepan.
- Add the half-and-half and milk. Heat to serving temperature, stirring frequently; do not boil.
- Ladle into soup bowls. Garnish with a sprinkle of fresh chopped chives.

CHILLED SPINACH AND PEA SOUP

Makes 8 servings

1/2 bay leaf

1 sprig parsley

1/4 teaspoon chervil

1/4 teaspoon tarragon

1 (10-ounce) package frozen peas

1 (10-ounce) package frozen
   spinach

1 small onion, chopped

2 1/2 cups chicken broth

2 cups half-and-half

Salt and white pepper to taste

Sour cream and chopped mint
   for garnish

• Combine the bay leaf, parsley, chervil and tarragon in a
  piece of cheesecloth and tie with string to make a bouquet
  garni.

• Combine the bouquet garni, peas, spinach, onion and 1
  cup of the chicken broth in a saucepan. Simmer for 20 to
  25 minutes or until the vegetables are tender.

• Purée the soup in a blender or food processor. Add the
  half- and-half, remaining 1 1/2 cups broth, salt and white
  pepper and mix well. Chill, covered, until serving time.

• Ladle into soup bowls. Garnish with sour cream and
  chopped fresh mint.

VEGETABLE AND CHEESE SOUP

Makes 4 servings

1 leek, chopped

2 carrots, sliced

1 small onion, chopped

1 stalk celery, chopped

2 tablespoons butter

1 tablespoon cornstarch

3 tablespoons flour

2 cups milk

1 (14-ounce) can chicken broth

2 cups shredded Cheddar cheese

1/2 teaspoon salt

2 tablespoons minced parsley

2 tablespoons chopped chives

Cayenne to taste

1/8 teaspoon baking soda

• Sauté the leek, carrots, onion and celery in the butter in a
  large saucepan until the vegetables are tender. Add the
  cornstarch and flour and mix well.

• Heat the milk and broth in a saucepan. Add to the vegetables. Cook over medium heat until thickened, stirring
  constantly.

• Purée in a food processor. Return to the saucepan.

• Add the cheese, salt, parsley, chives and cayenne. Cook
  until cheese melts, stirring constantly.

• Add the baking soda and mix well. Ladle into soup bowls.

Serve with a fresh fruit salad and whole wheat muffins.

Cheesy Vegetable Chowder

Makes 6 servings

10 slices bacon, chopped

1 cup chopped onion

1 cup sliced carrots

2½ cups finely chopped potatoes

1 cup water

2 chicken bouillon cubes

3 cups milk

1 (17-ounce) can whole kernel corn, drained

3 cups shredded Cheddar cheese

3 tablespoons flour

Salt to taste

Minced parsley for garnish

♦ Sauté the bacon in a 4-quart Dutch oven until crisp; remove with a slotted spoon.

♦ Sauté the onion in the bacon drippings until tender; drain.

♦ Add the bacon, carrots, potatoes, water and bouillon cubes. Simmer for 15 to 20 minutes or until the carrots and potatoes are just tender. Add the milk and corn and heat through, stirring frequently.

♦ Toss the cheese with the flour to coat. Stir into the soup mixture gradually. Cook until the cheese melts, stirring constantly.

♦ Ladle into soup bowls. Garnish with fresh minced parsley.

Serve with crusty bread.

Winter Vegetable Beef Soup

Makes 6 to 8 servings

3 onions, chopped

2 tablespoons butter

1 pound lean ground beef

1 clove of garlic, minced

3 cups beef broth

1 (28-ounce) can tomatoes, chopped

1 cup chopped potatoes

1 cup chopped carrots

1 cup chopped celery

1 (10-ounce) package frozen green beans

1 cup dry red wine

2 tablespoons chopped parsley

1 teaspoon basil

¼ teaspoon thyme

Salt and pepper to taste

♦ Sauté the onions in butter in a large stockpot until tender and golden brown. Add the ground beef and garlic. Cook until ground beef is brown, stirring until crumbly.

♦ Add the beef broth, tomatoes, potatoes, carrots, celery, green beans, wine, parsley, basil, thyme, salt and pepper; mix well. Simmer for 30 minutes or until the vegetables are tender.

♦ Ladle into soup bowls.

Serve with Italian bread for the perfect one-dish meal.

ZESTY ZUCCHINI SOUP

Makes 4 servings

½ cup finely chopped shallots
3 tablespoons butter
5 cups coarsely chopped zucchini
6 cups chicken broth
1½ teaspoons wine vinegar
¾ teaspoon dillweed
1 teaspoon (or more) curry powder
Salt and pepper to taste
½ cup sour cream or yogurt

- Sauté the shallots in the butter in a large saucepan until tender but not brown. Add the zucchini, broth, vinegar, dillweed, curry powder, salt and pepper and mix well. Simmer, partially covered, for 25 to 30 minutes or until the zucchini is tender.
- Purée in a blender or food processor. (May freeze at this point.) Return to saucepan. Blend in the sour cream. Heat to serving temperature.
- Ladle into soup bowls. Top with a dollop of sour cream.

May substitute 2 bunches of fresh broccoli for the zucchini and omit the vinegar and dillweed. Garnish each serving with 1 cooked and chilled broccoli floret.

AVOCADO-CITRUS SALAD

Makes 6 to 8 servings

3 avocados, peeled, sliced
Juice of 1 lemon
3 oranges, peeled, sectioned
2 grapefruit, peeled, sectioned
1 head Bibb lettuce, torn
Sweet Vinaigrette Dressing

- Sprinkle the avocado slices with lemon juice to prevent discoloring.
- Arrange the avocado slices, orange and grapefruit sections on lettuce-lined salad plates.
- Drizzle the dressing over each salad.

Sprinkle salad with pomegranate seeds for added color.

Sweet Vinaigrette Dressing

½ cup vegetable oil
2 tablespoons cider vinegar
2 tablespoons lemon juice
½ teaspoon salt
¼ teaspoon dry mustard
¼ teaspoon paprika
3 tablespoons confectioners' sugar

- Combine the oil, vinegar, lemon juice, salt, mustard, paprika and confectioners' sugar in a covered container and shake well.
- Chill, covered, until serving time.

BROCCOLI SALAD

Makes 6 servings

½ cup mayonnaise

3 tablespoons sugar

3 tablespoons cider vinegar

1 head of broccoli, cut into florets

1 medium red onion, chopped

¼ cup slivered almonds or
    sunflower kernels

1 cup golden raisins (optional)

¼ pound bacon, crisp-fried,
    crumbled

• Combine the mayonnaise, sugar and vinegar in a bowl and mix well. Chill, covered, overnight.

• Combine the broccoli, onion, almonds and raisins in a large serving bowl. Pour the dressing over the salad just before serving.

• Sprinkle the bacon over top and toss to mix.

BEEF VINAIGRETTE SALAD

Makes 4 to 6 servings

1½ pounds London broil

1 medium sweet onion

8 ounces mushrooms

⅓ cup red wine vinegar

1 cup salad oil

1 tablespoon Dijon mustard

2 cloves of garlic

2 tablespoons fresh chopped
    parsley

2 tablespoons minced chives

2 teaspoons salt

Freshly ground pepper to taste

Cherry tomatoes for garnish

Parsley sprigs for garnish

• Cook and slice London broil as desired. Slice onion and mushrooms thinly.

• Combine the vinegar, oil, mustard, garlic, parsley, chives, salt and pepper in a blender; process well.

• Combine the beef, onion and mushrooms in a shallow dish. Add the vinaigrette. Marinate for 2 to 4 hours.

• Place marinated beef and vegetables on a large salad plate. Arrange cherry tomatoes and parsley around the edge as garnish.

May substitute cooked roast beef or other tender beef for the London broil.

CAROLINA COLESLAW

Makes 8 to 12 servings

This slaw improves in flavor when prepared ahead of time. It is a good basic recipe for a popular dish.

1 (3-pound) head red cabbage

1 green bell pepper, finely chopped

1 medium sweet onion, finely chopped

1/2 to 3/4 cup sugar

1 teaspoon salt

1 teaspoon dry mustard

1 teaspoon celery seeds

1 cup cider vinegar

1/2 cup vegetable oil

♦ Shred the cabbage. Combine with the green pepper and onion in a large bowl; toss to mix.

♦ Combine the sugar, salt, mustard, celery seeds, vinegar and oil in a saucepan over medium heat. Bring to a boil, stirring until the sugar dissolves.

♦ Pour dressing over the cabbage mixture; toss to coat well. Cool to room temperature.

♦ Chill, covered, until serving time.

SHRIMP CAESAR SALAD

Makes 4 servings

2 tablespoons red wine vinegar

1/2 cup olive oil

1 tablespoon Dijon mustard

1 coddled egg, chopped

2 anchovy fillets, chopped, or 2 inches anchovy paste

1/2 teaspoon freshly ground pepper

1/2 teaspoon oregano

1 clove of garlic

1 large head romaine, torn

Croutons to taste

Freshly grated Parmesan cheese to taste

1 pound shrimp, cooked, peeled, chilled

♦ Combine the vinegar, olive oil, mustard, egg, anchovies, pepper and oregano in a small bowl and mix well.

♦ Rub a wooden salad bowl with garlic; discard the garlic. Place the lettuce in the bowl. Sprinkle with the croutons and cheese.

♦ Pour the dressing over the salad. Sprinkle the shrimp on top; toss to mix.

May grill boneless skinless chicken breasts; chill, slice and substitute for the shrimp.

CAESAR SALAD

Makes 8 to 10 servings

1 egg

1/2 teaspoon salt

1 tablespoon olive oil

1 clove of garlic

2 large heads romaine

1/2 pound bacon, crisp-fried

2 tomatoes, cut into wedges

1/3 cup chopped scallions

1 to 2 tablespoons minced fresh mint

1/2 cup grated Parmesan cheese

1/2 teaspoon freshly ground pepper

1/4 teaspoon oregano

1 cup croutons

1/3 cup lemon juice

1/3 cup extra-virgin olive oil

+ Place egg in saucepan with cold water to cover. Bring to a boil; remove from heat. Let stand for 1 minute. Remove from water; place in refrigerator.

+ Sprinkle a large wooden salad bowl with the salt and 1 tablespoon olive oil. Rub the garlic around the inside of the bowl until garlic disintegrates.

+ Tear the romaine into large pieces. Crumble the bacon. Layer the tomatoes, lettuce, scallions, mint, bacon, cheese, pepper, oregano and croutons in the bowl.

+ Scoop soft-cooked egg from shell; place in small bowl. Whisk the egg with the lemon juice and 1/3 cup olive oil in a bowl until smooth.

+ Pour over salad just before serving; toss to mix.

Note that there are no anchovies in this dressing. For those who like Caesar salad with the traditional anchovies, serve the little fish on the side.

DANISH CUCUMBERS

Makes 12 servings

4 to 5 cucumbers, peeled, very thinly sliced

3 tablespoons salt

1 1/2 cups white vinegar

1/2 cup water

1 cup sugar

1/4 teaspoon white pepper

Thinly sliced onions (optional)

+ Place the cucumbers and salt in a bowl with ice water to cover. Let stand for 10 minutes; drain and rinse.

+ Combine the vinegar, water, sugar, pepper and onions in a bowl and mix well. Pour the mixture over the cucumbers.

+ Chill, covered, until serving time or for up to 24 hours.

FIESTA SALAD

Makes 6 to 8 servings

1 (19-ounce) can black beans

2 ears of corn, cooked

1 tomato, seeded, chopped

1/3 cup chopped sweet onion

1 red bell pepper, finely chopped

1/4 cup red wine vinegar

2 tablespoons each lime juice and honey

1 teaspoon cumin

2 tablespoons chopped cilantro or parsley

1/8 teaspoon salt (optional)

♦ Rinse and drain the beans well. Scrape the corn from the cobs.

♦ Combine the beans, corn, tomato, onion and red pepper in a bowl and toss to mix well.

♦ Whisk the vinegar, lime juice, honey, cumin, cilantro and salt in a bowl until blended. Pour the dressing over the salad and toss to coat well.

♦ Chill, covered, for 1 hour or for up to 2 days.

SALAD FOR COMPANY

Makes 6 servings

1/2 cup olive oil

3 tablespoons red wine vinegar

1 tablespoon each balsamic vinegar and Dijon mustard

1 clove of garlic

2 shallots

1 head each radicchio and romaine, torn

2 heads endive, torn

8 ounces mushrooms, sliced

♦ Combine the olive oil, red wine vinegar, balsamic vinegar, mustard, garlic and shallots in a blender; process until well mixed.

♦ Combine the greens and mushrooms in a salad bowl.

♦ Pour the dressing over the vegetables; toss to mix.

Serve with Gorgonzola cheese and crackers.

MUSHROOM TARRAGON SALAD

Makes 4 servings

1 tablespoon Dijon mustard

2 tablespoons tarragon vinegar

1/4 teaspoon dried tarragon leaves

1/2 cup vegetable or olive oil

30 large mushrooms, sliced

Cracked black pepper to taste

♦ Mix the mustard, vinegar and tarragon leaves in a small bowl. Add the oil gradually, whisking until blended.

♦ Arrange the mushroom slices on individual salad plates. Drizzle 2 tablespoons of the dressing over each serving. Sprinkle with the pepper.

Circle each plate with a garnish of fresh tarragon leaves.

CRUNCHY PEA SALAD

Makes 6 servings

4 cups shelled fresh peas

1 (8-ounce) can sliced water chestnuts, drained

1¼ cups honey-roasted cashews

1 tablespoon chopped fresh mint

1 cup sour cream

2 tablespoons soy sauce

½ to 1 teaspoon sesame oil

2 teaspoons brown sugar

♦ Blanch the peas until tender-crisp; drain. Plunge into ice water; drain well. Combine with water chestnuts, cashews and mint in a large salad bowl.

♦ Blend the sour cream with soy sauce, oil and brown sugar. Pour over the salad; toss to coat.

♦ Chill, covered, until serving time.

Serve with fresh grilled salmon and roasted new potatoes.

PICNIC POTATO SALAD

Makes 6 servings

This potato salad is perfect for picnics because it does not have to be kept cold.

8 tablespoons olive oil

2 tablespoons vinegar

1 teaspoon Dijon mustard

4 tablespoons dry sherry

3 tablespoons chopped onion

2 tablespoons chopped parsley

2 teaspoon salt

½ teaspoon freshly ground pepper

¼ teaspoon cayenne

3 pounds potatoes

♦ Combine the olive oil, vinegar, mustard, sherry, onion, parsley, salt, ground pepper and cayenne in a bowl and mix well.

♦ Boil the potatoes. Peel and slice.

♦ Place the potatoes in a warm salad bowl and pour dressing over top; toss to coat. Serve warm or cold.

The flavor is enhanced when prepared ahead.

PORT AND STARBOARD POTATO SALAD

Makes 6 servings

5 large red potatoes

1 (9-ounce) package frozen whole green beans

1 red onion, thinly sliced

½ cup Italian salad dressing

1 to 2 teaspoons fresh chopped dill

♦ Cook and slice the potatoes. Cook the beans according to package directions and drain.

♦ Place the warm potatoes and beans in a serving bowl. Add the onion, dressing and dill and toss to coat. Chill.

Garnish with chopped Niçoise olives.

SHRIMP SALAD MASTERPIECE

Makes 4 servings

1 (6-ounce) package curried rice
  mix
2 cups cooked peeled shrimp,
  halved lengthwise
1 cup finely chopped celery
1/2 cup finely chopped mixed
  green and red bell pepper
4 slices bacon, crisp-fried,
  crumbled
1/2 cup whipping cream, whipped
1/2 cup mayonnaise
1 teaspoon curry powder

- Cook the rice according to package directions and cool.

- Reserve 6 shrimp for garnish. Combine remaining shrimp, rice, celery, peppers and bacon in a large salad bowl.

- Blend the whipped cream, mayonnaise and curry powder in a small bowl. Add to the shrimp mixture and toss to coat well. Arrange reserved shrimp on top.

- Chill, covered, until serving time.

Serve on lettuce-lined plates with an array of garnishes such as shredded coconut, cashews, raisins, sliced cucumbers and chutney.

May substitute chicken for shrimp.

SWEET AND SASSY SALAD

Makes 8 servings

1/2 cup sugar
1 1/2 teaspoons celery salt
1 teaspoon paprika
1 teaspoon dry mustard
1 cup vegetable oil
1/2 cup vinegar
1 teaspoon finely minced onion
1/2 teaspoon garlic powder
1/4 pound bacon, crisp-fried
1 (11-ounce) can mandarin
  oranges
8 ounces sliced water chestnuts
1 head Bibb lettuce, torn
1 head romaine, torn
1 pound fresh spinach, torn
2 hard-cooked eggs, chopped
1 small red onion, sliced

- Combine the sugar, celery salt, paprika, mustard, oil, vinegar, onion and garlic powder in a bowl and blend well. Let stand for 30 minutes.

- Crumble the bacon; drain the oranges and water chestnuts well.

- Combine the Bibb lettuce, romaine, spinach, eggs and red onion in a large salad bowl. Add the bacon, oranges and water chestnuts.

- Add the dressing; toss to mix. May store extra dressing, covered, in the refrigerator for up to a week.

SPICY GREEN SALAD WITH ORANGES

Makes 4 servings

2 oranges, peeled, sectioned
1 small red onion, sliced
1 head romaine, torn
1/2 cup olive oil
1/4 cup cider vinegar
1/2 teaspoon coriander
1/4 teaspoon each cumin,
    cardamom and salt
1/8 teaspoon pepper

♦ Combine the oranges, onion and romaine in a salad bowl and mix well.

♦ Blend the oil, vinegar, coriander, cumin, cardamom, salt and pepper in a bowl until well mixed. Pour the dressing over the salad and toss to mix.

TROPICAL SALAD

Makes 4 servings

1 head Boston lettuce, torn
1 pound fresh spinach, torn
1 red onion
1 each red and green bell peppers
8 ounces mushrooms
1 cup fresh strawberries, halved
1 (11-ounce) can mandarin oranges
1 or 2 kiwifruit, sliced
Key Lime Dressing

♦ Combine the lettuce and spinach in a large salad bowl. Slice the onion, peppers and mushrooms. Combine with the strawberries, oranges and kiwifruit and toss to mix.

♦ Chill, covered, for 1 hour or until serving time.

♦ Add the Key Lime Dressing and toss to coat well. Garnish with shredded coconut.

Key Lime Dressing

1 small shallot, minced
2 cloves of garlic, minced
1/2 cup chopped fresh chives
2 teaspoons honey
1 teaspoon Dijon mustard
2 tablespoons Key lime juice
1/2 cup vegetable oil
2 tablespoons each balsamic and
    red wine vinegar
Cayenne and pepper to taste

♦ Combine the shallot, garlic, chives, honey, mustard, lime juice, oil, balsamic vinegar, red wine vinegar, cayenne and pepper in a covered container and shake well.

♦ Chill, covered, until serving time.

CURRIED SPINACH SALAD

Makes 12 servings

1/2 cup white wine vinegar
2/3 cup vegetable oil
1 tablespoon Major Grey chutney
1 teaspoon each curry powder
  and dry mustard
1 teaspoon salt
1/4 teaspoon Tabasco sauce
2 pounds fresh spinach
2 large Red Delicious apples
1/2 cup raisins
1/3 cup thinly sliced green onions
2 tablespoons sesame seeds,
  toasted

♦ Combine the vinegar, oil, chutney, curry, mustard, salt and Tabasco sauce in a bowl and mix well. Let stand for 2 hours to blend flavors.

♦ Rinse the spinach well, discard stems and tear into bite-size pieces. Chop the apples into bite-size pieces and place in a salad bowl with the spinach, raisins, green onions and sesame seeds and toss well.

♦ Pour the dressing over the salad and toss just before serving.

SPINACH PECAN SALAD

Makes 8 servings

1 pound fresh spinach
1 (11-ounce) can mandarin oranges
2 stalks celery, thinly sliced
2 scallions, thinly sliced
1 cup white mushrooms, sliced
1/3 cup shredded coconut
1/2 cup pecans
Poppy Seed Dressing

♦ Rinse spinach well; discard stems and tear into bite-size pieces. Drain mandarin oranges.

♦ Combine the spinach, celery, scallions, mushrooms and oranges in a large salad bowl; toss to mix. Sprinkle the coconut and pecans on top.

♦ Serve with Poppy Seed Dressing.

This salad is nice to serve with poultry.

Poppy Seed Dressing

1/2 cup sugar
1 tablespoon dry mustard
1 teaspoon salt
1/4 onion, grated
1/2 cup white vinegar
2 cups vegetable oil
1 1/2 tablespoons poppy seeds

♦ Blend the sugar, mustard, salt, onion and vinegar in a small bowl. Add the oil in a fine stream, whisking constantly. Stir in the poppy seeds.

STRAWBERRY AND SPINACH SALAD

Makes 4 servings

1/2 pound fresh spinach
1 pint fresh strawberries, sliced
Sesame Seed Dressing
2 ounces slivered almonds, toasted

♦ Rinse spinach well, discard stems and tear into bite-size pieces. Place the spinach and strawberries on individual salad plates or in a glass salad bowl. Drizzle the Sesame Seed Dressing over top.

♦ Top with the almonds.

May substitute or add kiwifruit. Substitute cashews or macadamia nuts for almonds.

Sesame Seed Dressing

1/2 cup sugar
2 tablespoons sesame seeds
1 tablespoon poppy seeds
1 1/2 teaspoons minced onion
1/4 teaspoon Worcestershire sauce
1/4 teaspoon paprika
1/4 cup cider vinegar
1/2 cup vegetable oil

♦ Process the sugar, sesame seeds, poppy seeds, onion, Worcestershire sauce, paprika and vinegar in a blender.

♦ Add the oil in a fine stream, blending constantly at low speed until the dressing is thick.

TORTELLINI SALAD

Makes 4 to 6 servings

1 pound fresh cheese-filled tortellini
1/4 cup olive oil
1/2 pound (3/8-inch) prosciutto slices
1/2 pound (3/8-inch) smoked turkey slices
2 carrots
1 red bell pepper
1 cup frozen baby peas, thawed
1/2 cup chopped Italian parsley
2 cloves of garlic, minced
1/2 cup olive oil
1 head red leaf lettuce

♦ Cook the tortellini in a generous amount of boiling water for 5 minutes or just until tender; drain and rinse with cold water. Drain for 5 to 10 minutes. Toss with 1/4 cup olive oil in a large bowl. Chill, covered, in the refrigerator.

♦ Cut the prosciutto and turkey into bite-size pieces. Cut the carrots and red pepper into julienned strips. Add carrots, red pepper and peas to the tortellini.

♦ Combine the parsley, garlic and 1/2 cup olive oil and mix well. Pour the dressing over the salad and toss to mix.

♦ Line salad plates with the red leaf lettuce. Spoon salad onto lettuce.

ROASTED VEGETABLE PASTA SALAD

Makes 8 servings

1/4 cup olive oil

1/4 teaspoon each garlic powder and pepper

3 red bell peppers, cut into pieces

3 small zucchini, julienned

10 ounces mushrooms, sliced in thirds

1 pint cherry tomatoes, halved

1 pound spiral macaroni

1 cup sliced Greek olives

8 ounces feta cheese, crumbled

1 (8-ounce) bottle Italian dressing

♦ Preheat the oven to 400 degrees.

♦ Combine the oil, garlic powder, pepper, red peppers, zucchini, mushrooms and tomatoes in a small baking pan.

♦ Bake at 400 degrees for 10 minutes. Broil 6 inches from heat source for 10 minutes, tossing once. Cool.

♦ Cook macaroni using package directions. Drain well.

♦ Combine vegetables, macaroni, olives, cheese and desired amount of salad dressing; toss to mix.

♦ Chill, covered, until serving time.

WINTER SALAD

Makes 4 servings

1 (10-ounce) package each frozen artichokes and chopped broccoli

3/4 cup chick-peas

1 red onion, halved, thinly sliced

1/2 cup mayonnaise

2 tablespoons white wine vinegar

1 teaspoon Dijon mustard

♦ Cook the artichokes and broccoli in 1/2 cup water according to package directions; drain and squeeze dry. Combine with chick-peas and onion in a large salad bowl.

♦ Blend the mayonnaise, vinegar and mustard in a small bowl. Pour over the vegetables and toss to coat well.

♦ Chill, covered, for several hours before serving.

CHICKEN SALAD WITH GARLIC MAYONNAISE

Makes 8 servings

8 boneless skinless chicken breasts

1 cup white wine

Salt to taste

2 (6-ounce) jars marinated artichoke hearts

2 cups mayonnaise

3 teaspoons minced garlic

1 (7-ounce) can hearts of palm, drained, sliced

♦ Rinse the chicken and pat dry. Poach the chicken in white wine and salt for 12 minutes or until cooked through. Drain and cut into bite-size pieces.

♦ Drain artichokes, reserving marinade; slice artichokes. Combine the mayonnaise, garlic and artichoke marinade in a bowl and blend well. Add the chicken, artichokes and hearts of palm; mix well. Chill, covered, until serving time.

Spoon salad onto lettuce-lined salad plates. Garnish with cherry tomato halves.

CHICKEN AVOCADO SALAD

Makes 8 servings

3 pounds cooked chicken
$1/2$ pound bacon, crisp-fried
$1/2$ cup minced fresh parsley
1 cup finely chopped celery
$1/2$ cup minced scallions
3 avocados, chopped
Lime and Mustard Dressing

+ Cut chicken into bite-size pieces. Crumble the bacon.
+ Combine the chicken, bacon, parsley, celery, scallions and avocados in a large salad bowl. Add the Lime and Mustard Dressing and mix gently to coat.
+ Spoon onto lettuce-lined salad plates.

Garnish with cherry tomatoes.

Lime and Mustard Dressing

2 teaspoons Dijon mustard
2 teaspoons minced shallots
1 egg
2 tablespoons lime juice
1 tablespoon white wine vinegar
$1/8$ teaspoon salt
$1/4$ teaspoon white pepper
$1/2$ cup vegetable oil
2 tablespoons bacon drippings

+ Combine the mustard, shallots, egg, lime juice, vinegar, salt and pepper in a blender and process until well mixed.
+ Add the oil and bacon drippings in a fine stream, blending until smooth.
+ Chill, covered, until serving time.

TARRAGON CHICKEN SALAD

Makes 6 servings

3 pounds boneless skinless
   chicken breasts
1 cup white wine
Celery leaves
$1/2$ teaspoon dried tarragon
2 stalks celery, sliced
$1/2$ cup sour cream
$1/2$ cup mayonnaise
1 tablespoon dried tarragon
Salt and pepper to taste

+ Rinse the chicken and pat dry. Poach the chicken in the wine with celery leaves and $1/2$ teaspoon tarragon for 20 minutes or until cooked through. Drain, cool and cut into bite-size pieces. Combine with the sliced celery in a large bowl.
+ Blend the sour cream, mayonnaise, 1 tablespoon tarragon, salt and pepper in a small bowl. Add to chicken; mix well. Chill overnight.
+ Serve on lettuce-lined salad plates.

CURRIED CHICKEN SALAD

Makes 4 servings

1 (2¹/₂-pound) chicken
1 cup green grape halves
¹/₂ cup chopped celery
¹/₄ cup sliced water chestnuts
¹/₄ cup toasted slivered almonds
3 tablespoons chicken broth
1 teaspoon curry powder
³/₄ cup mayonnaise
2 teaspoons soy sauce
2 teaspoons lemon juice
¹/₄ cup toasted slivered almonds
Pineapple chunks for garnish

♦ Cook chicken with salt and pepper in 3 cups water until tender; drain, bone and chop. Combine with grapes, celery, water chestnuts and ¹/₄ cup almonds in a salad bowl.

♦ Simmer the chicken broth and curry powder in a saucepan over medium heat until mixture forms a paste. Cool. Blend with the mayonnaise, soy sauce and lemon juice.

♦ Pour the curried mayonnaise over the salad and toss to coat well. Chill, covered, until serving time.

♦ Spoon the salad onto lettuce-lined plates; top with the remaining ¹/₄ cup almonds. Garnish with pineapple chunks.

Use the curried mayonnaise for open-face cucumber sandwiches. Spread on 2-inch firm white bread rounds, add thin cucumber slices and dust with fresh chopped dill.

CHICKEN AND PASTA SALAD

Makes 8 to 10 servings

1 (12-ounce) package twist pasta, cooked
2 stalks celery, chopped
¹/₂ cucumber, quartered, sliced
1 green onion, chopped
2 cups green grape halves
¹/₂ cup raisins
3 whole chicken breasts, cooked, chopped
1 cup snow peas, blanched
1 kiwifruit, peeled, sliced
1 (11-ounce) can mandarin oranges, drained
²/₃ cup mayonnaise
¹/₂ cup grated Parmesan cheese
¹/₃ cup fresh lemon juice
Salt and pepper to taste
1 pound of spinach, torn

♦ Combine the pasta, celery, cucumber, green onion, grapes, raisins and chicken in a large bowl and toss to mix well. Add the snow peas, kiwifruit slices and oranges, reserving a few of each item for garnish.

♦ Blend the mayonnaise, cheese, lemon juice and salt and pepper in a bowl. Pour the dressing over the salad and toss well. Spoon onto spinach-lined salad plates. Garnish with the reserved snow peas, kiwifruit slices and mandarin oranges.

LOBSTER AND MELON SALAD

Makes 8 servings

2 teaspoons yogurt

1/2 cup olive oil

1/2 tablespoon white wine

Vinegar to taste

1/3 teaspoon Dijon mustard

Tarragon and chives to taste

2 pounds cooked lobster meat

1 melon, peeled, cubed

2 tangerines, peeled, seeded, sectioned

1/4 cup chopped fresh parsley

Seedless grapes for garnish

♦ Combine the yogurt, olive oil, wine, vinegar, mustard, tarragon and chives in a large bowl and mix well.

♦ Add the lobster meat to the dressing. Chill, covered, overnight.

♦ Add melon, tangerines and parsley; toss to mix.

♦ Spoon onto lettuce-lined salad plates. Garnish with green and purple grapes.

Serve with fresh steamed asparagus and hot rolls.

RAJAH'S SALAD

Makes 4 servings

1 pound peeled cooked shrimp

2 cups green grape halves

2 cups cashews

1/2 cup sour cream

1/2 cup mayonnaise

2 tablespoons minced onion

2 tablespoons minced green bell pepper

1 tablespoon lemon juice

1 1/2 teaspoons curry powder

1/2 teaspoon salt

1/8 teaspoon ginger

♦ Cut the shrimp into bite-size pieces and mix with the grapes and cashews in a large bowl.

♦ Blend the sour cream, mayonnaise, onion, green pepper, lemon juice, curry powder, salt and ginger in a small bowl.

♦ Pour the dressing over the shrimp mixture and toss to coat well.

♦ Chill, covered, until serving time.

Serve on crisp chilled salad greens and garnish with grape clusters.

TUNA PASTA SALAD

Makes 6 to 8 servings

1 pound small pasta shells
1 tablespoon olive oil
1/2 cup frozen baby peas
1 cup Pesto
1 (12 1/2-ounce) can water-pack
   white tuna, drained
1 red bell pepper, chopped

- Cook the pasta according to the package directions until al dente, adding 1 tablespoon oil. Add the peas and drain immediately.
- Add the Pesto to the warm pasta in large bowl; toss to mix. Cool.
- Add the tuna and red pepper; mix well. Serve at room temperature to enhance flavor.

Pesto

2 cups fresh basil leaves
3 tablespoons pine nuts
1 to 2 cloves of garlic, sliced
3/4 cup grated Parmesan cheese
1/4 teaspoon salt
1/8 teaspoon pepper
2/3 cup olive oil

- Process the basil, pine nuts, garlic, cheese, salt and pepper in a food processor. Add the oil in a fine stream, processing at low speed until mixed well. Makes 1 3/4 cups.
- Store in the refrigerator for up to 1 week. Freeze in ice cube trays to store for up to 6 months.

Other Uses: Blend 2 tablespoons Pesto with 1 cup sour cream for a dip. Blend 2 tablespoons Pesto with 1/2 cup unsalted butter for a bread spread or as a topping on hot vegetables. Melt the butter mixture for dipping sauce for shrimp and lobster.

BLUE CHEESE DRESSING

Makes 3 1/4 cups

1 cup mayonnaise
1 cup sour cream
4 tablespoons olive oil
1 tablespoon cider vinegar
1/4 teaspoon garlic powder
1 teaspoon Worcestershire sauce
1 cup crumbled blue cheese
Salt and pepper to taste

- Combine the mayonnaise, sour cream, olive oil, vinegar, garlic, Worcestershire sauce, cheese, salt and pepper in a bowl; mix well.
- Chill, covered, until serving time.

GREEK BASIL DRESSING

Makes 2 cups

1 medium tomato, chopped
2 scallions, chopped
12 black olives
4 cloves of garlic
6 tablespoons fresh chopped basil
6 tablespoons fresh chopped
  parsley
2 teaspoons Dijon mustard
2 tablespoons balsamic vinegar
2 tablespoons lemon juice
$^1/_8$ teaspoon salt
$^1/_2$ teaspoon pepper
$^2/_3$ cup olive oil

♦ Combine the tomato, scallions, olives, garlic, basil, parsley, mustard, vinegar, lemon juice, salt and pepper in a food processor. Process just until chunky.

♦ Add the oil in a fine stream, processing constantly.

♦ Chill, covered, until serving time.

Serve over a salad of cold chicken, new potatoes, green beans and cherry tomatoes or on grilled fish fillets.

HERBAL VINAIGRETTE

Makes 1 cup

$^1/_2$ cup olive oil
2 tablespoons chopped onion
1 tablespoon freshly grated
  Parmesan cheese
1 teaspoon salt
$^3/_4$ teaspoon Worcestershire sauce
$^3/_4$ teaspoon each dry mustard,
  basil, oregano, sugar and
  pepper
$^1/_4$ cup red wine vinegar
1 tablespoon lemon juice

♦ Combine the oil, onion, cheese, salt, Worcestershire sauce, mustard, basil, oregano, sugar and pepper in a blender. Process for 30 seconds.

♦ Add the vinegar and lemon juice and blend well.

♦ Chill until serving time.

LEDGE LIGHT DRESSING

Makes 1/2 cup

1/2 cup olive oil

2 tablespoons each white wine vinegar and Dijon mustard

2 teaspoons lemon juice

1 teaspoon each minced garlic and fresh minced parsley

1/2 teaspoon each dry mustard and white pepper

1/4 teaspoon salt

♦ Combine the oil, vinegar, Dijon mustard, lemon juice, garlic, parsley, dry mustard, white pepper and salt in a blender. Process at high speed for 1 minute.

95 HOUSE SALAD DRESSING

Makes 2¾ cups

2 cups sour cream

1/2 cup mayonnaise

3/4 teaspoon vegetable oil

2 tablespoons red wine vinegar

1 teaspoon lemon juice

1 teaspoon Worcestershire sauce

2 teaspoons mustard seeds

2 cloves of garlic or 2 teaspoons garlic powder

Salt and pepper to taste

♦ Combine the sour cream, mayonnaise, oil, vinegar, lemon juice, Worcestershire sauce, mustard seeds, garlic, salt and pepper in a bowl; blend well.

♦ Chill, covered, until serving time.

Serve over a mixed green salad of half Chinese cabbage and half lettuce.

RASPBERRY POPPY SEED DRESSING

Makes 2½ cups

1/4 cup sugar

1/2 cup raspberry vinegar

1½ teaspoons dry mustard

3/4 teaspoon salt

2 tablespoons minced onion

1¾ cups vegetable oil

2 tablespoons poppy seeds

♦ Process the sugar, vinegar, mustard, salt and onion in a food processor. Add the oil in a fine stream, processing constantly until smooth. Add the poppy seeds and process just to distribute the seeds.

♦ Chill, covered, until serving time or for up to 2 weeks.

For a more liquid dressing do not process; just combine ingredients in jar and shake well.

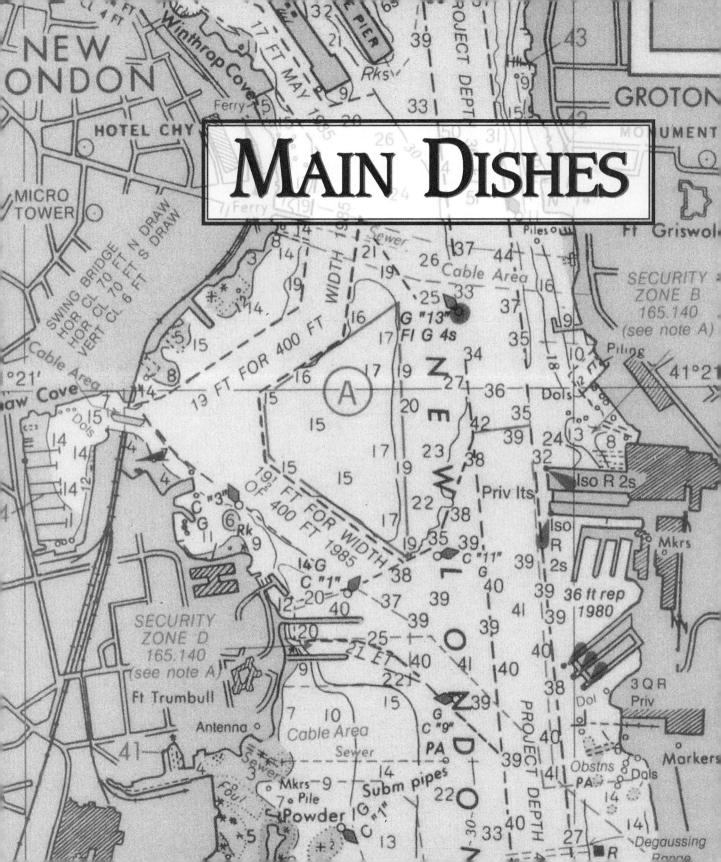

MAIN DISHES

MAIN DISHES

◆ ◆ ◆ ◆ ◆ ◆ ◆ ◆ ◆ ◆ ◆ ◆ ◆

SWEET-AND-SOUR POT ROAST

Makes 6 to 8 servings

1 (4 to 5-pound) beef roast
Vegetable oil
2 large onions, sliced
1 clove of garlic, minced
2 cups water or consommé
2 bay leaves
1/4 cup lemon juice
2 tablespoons brown sugar
5 tablespoons ketchup
1/2 cup raisins
1/2 teaspoon salt

♦ Brown the beef in oil in a heavy stockpot. Add the onions and garlic. Cook until brown. Add water and bay leaves.

♦ Simmer, covered, for 1 hour. Add lemon juice, brown sugar, ketchup, raisins and salt.

♦ Cook, covered, for 30 minutes. Remove the bay leaves.

Serve with potatoes or noodles with thickened pan juices.

MARINATED EYE OF ROUND

Makes 4 servings per pound

This do-ahead recipe is a lovely addition to a buffet table when thinly sliced and served with finger rolls.

1 (4 to 5-pound) eye of round
1 tablespoon soy sauce
1 clove of garlic, minced
1 cup vegetable oil
1/2 cup bourbon

♦ Marinate round in a mixture of soy sauce, garlic, oil and bourbon in refrigerator for 24 to 48 hours.

♦ Preheat the oven to 500 degrees.

♦ Roast 4 minutes per pound for rare, 5 minutes per pound for medium.

♦ Turn off oven. Let stand in closed oven for 2 hours.

GRILLED EYE OF ROUND

Makes 4 servings per pound

1 (any size) eye of round
Kosher salt
Waxed paper

♦ Prepare the charcoal.

♦ Sprinkle round with water; coat thinly with salt. Wrap in 3 layers of waxed paper, twisting the ends tightly.

♦ Place directly on the hot gray coals. Cook for 11 minutes on each of the three sides. Remove any remaining waxed paper.

♦ Let rest for 10 minutes. Slice very thinly.

STOPWATCH RIB-EYE ROAST

Makes 4 servings per pound

1 (4 to 8-pound) rib-eye, at room
  temperature
1/2 teaspoon each seasoned salt
  and seasoned pepper
1/4 teaspoon garlic salt
3 tablespoons melted butter
1 tablespoon Worcestershire
  sauce

- Preheat the oven to 500 degrees.
- Rub the roast with seasonings; place in a shallow roaster. Drizzle with butter and Worcestershire sauce.
- Roast for exactly 5 minutes per pound for rare or 6 minutes per pound for medium. Turn off oven. Let stand in closed oven for 10 minutes per pound. Remove from oven. Cover with foil until ready to slice.

BEEF TENDERLOIN WITH MADEIRA SAUCE

Makes 6 servings

1 (3-pound) beef tenderloin
Madeira Sauce
Radish blossoms for garnish
Parsley sprigs for garnish

- Preheat the oven to 425 degrees.
- Place tenderloin in a shallow roasting pan. Roast for 15 minutes. Reduce the oven heat to 350 degrees. Roast for 20 minutes for rare or 30 minutes for medium.
- Let rest for 10 minutes. Slice thinly; arrange on a heated platter. Pour 1/3 cup of Madeira Sauce over the slices.

  Garnish with radish blossoms and parsley. Serve remaining sauce in sauceboat to be passed.

Madeira Sauce

1/2 cup sliced shiitake mushrooms
1/4 cup unsalted butter
2 tablespoons flour
2 cups beef stock
6 tablespoons madeira
1 tablespoon tomato paste
Salt and pepper to taste

- Sauté the mushrooms in 2 tablespoons of the butter in a skillet until soft. Remove with a slotted spoon and set aside.
- Melt the remaining butter in a medium saucepan. Whisk in the flour. Cook over low heat for 3 minutes, stirring constantly. Blend in beef stock, 4 tablespoons of the madeira and the tomato paste. Bring just to the boiling point over medium-high heat, stirring constantly; reduce the heat. Simmer for 30 minutes or until reduced to 1 cup.
- Add mushrooms and remaining 2 tablespoons madeira, whisking gently. Simmer for 2 minutes. Add salt and pepper.

  May prepare sauce ahead of the point before adding the mushrooms. Reheat and complete at serving time.

PENINSULA STEAK WITH HERBED BUTTER

Makes 4 servings

This recipe comes from the famed Peninsula Hotel in Hong Kong.

1/4 cup butter, softened
1 clove of garlic, minced
1 egg yolk
2 teaspoons minced parsley
1 teaspoon minced onion
1/8 teaspoon thyme
1/8 teaspoon tarragon
1 teaspoon lemon juice
1 teaspoon Dijon mustard
1/2 teaspoon brandy
1/4 teaspoon madeira
2 (8-ounce) sirloin steaks

♦ Preheat a heavy skillet and the broiler.

♦ Cream butter, garlic, egg yolk, parsley, onion, thyme and tarragon in a small bowl. Whisk in the lemon juice, mustard, brandy and madeira.

♦ Trim fat from steaks; reserve a small amount for greasing skillet.

♦ Rub the reserved fat over the bottom and side of a hot skillet. Brown the steaks quickly on both sides.

♦ Place on cutting board and cut lengthwise into 1/3-inch slices.

♦ Arrange the slices in individual gratin dishes, overlapping slightly. Spread with herbed butter.

♦ Broil for 3 minutes or until brown.

KOREAN BEEF

Makes 4 servings

This quick and easy dish served over rice will be popular with the whole family. Buy Chinese vinegar in Asian markets or specialty stores.

1 (1-inch) piece of fresh ginger, peeled, shredded
3 scallions, sliced
1 tablespoon sesame seeds
3 tablespoons soy sauce
1 tablespoon sugar
1 tablespoon Chinese vinegar or dry sherry
1 tablespoon vegetable oil
1 teaspoon sesame oil
1 1/2 pounds flank steak

♦ Mix the ginger, scallions, sesame seeds, soy sauce, sugar, vinegar, vegetable oil and sesame oil in a medium bowl.

♦ Slice the steak into 1/2-inch strips. Add to the ginger sauce and coat completely. Let stand at room temperature for 45 minutes to 2 hours.

♦ Preheat broiler or stovetop grill.

♦ Arrange steak strips in a single layer on rack of broiler pan or grill.

♦ Broil or grill for 1 to 2 minutes on each side.

May cook in 1 tablespoon vegetable oil in a frying pan on the stove.

BEEF PIQUANT

Makes 6 servings

2 pounds chuck or round steak, cubed

1 tablespoon vegetable oil

1 (10-ounce) can consommé

1 tablespoon curry powder

1 cup red wine

2 large onions, thinly sliced

½ teaspoon salt

¼ teaspoon pepper

2 cups sour cream

1 tablespoon horseradish, or to taste

♦ Brown the chuck in the oil in a large skillet. Add the consommé, curry powder, wine, onions, salt and pepper; mix well.

♦ Simmer, covered, for 2 hours.

♦ Pour off and reserve the pan juices.

♦ Stir the sour cream and horseradish into the skillet. Add ½ cup of the reserved liquid or enough to make sauce of the desired consistency.

♦ Heat to serving temperature but do not boil.

Serve over long grain and wild rice.

STIR-FRIED ORANGE BEEF WITH PISTACHIOS

Makes 4 to 6 servings

1 pound lean beef (round or sirloin)

1 tablespoon dry sherry

1 tablespoon soy sauce

2 tablespoons honey

2 tablespoons cornstarch

1 teaspoon grated fresh gingerroot

⅛ teaspoon dried red pepper flakes

Freshly ground black pepper to taste

Zest of 1 whole orange, sliced into julienne strips

¾ cup shelled pistachios

2 scallions, sliced diagonally

6 tablespoons peanut oil

♦ Thinly slice the beef across the grain.

♦ Combine sherry, soy sauce, honey, cornstarch, gingerroot and red and black pepper in a bowl. Stir in the beef.

♦ Stir-fry the orange zest, pistachios and scallions in oil in a wok or skillet for 1 minute. Remove with a slotted spoon.

♦ Stir-fry the beef in the hot oil for 2 to 3 minutes.

♦ Return the pistachio mixture to the wok. Stir-fry for 30 seconds. Arrange on a serving platter.

Serve with rice.

BEEF AND SAUTEED VEGETABLES

Makes 4 servings

This colorful, spicy beef and vegetable dish can be made ahead of time.

2 pounds flank steak or London broil chuck
2 tablespoons soy sauce
1 tablespoon sherry or vermouth
2 tablespoons sugar
2 tablespoons oyster sauce
Florets of 1 bunch broccoli
Mushroom caps (optional)
3 tablespoons vegetable oil
Salt to taste
2 tablespoons water

♦ Slice steak cross grain 1/8 to 1/4-inch thick. Add to mixture of soy sauce, sherry and sugar in a shallow bowl. Marinate for 3 hours. Stir in the oyster sauce.

♦ Sauté the broccoli and mushrooms in oil in a skillet until tender. Add salt and water; set aside.

♦ Sauté the beef with the marinade in a large skillet. Add additional oyster sauce to taste. Serve over sautéed vegetables.

May thicken pan juices if desired. Add 1 teaspoon cornstarch dissolved in 2 teaspoons cold water. Cook until clear and thickened, stirring constantly.

BEEF BARBECUE

Makes 24 sandwiches

Make this recipe ahead of time to take to the ski lodge, the beach or to tailgate picnics.

6 pounds boneless chuck roast, cut into chunks
3 stalks celery, chopped
3 medium onions, chopped
1 green bell pepper, chopped
1 (28-ounce) bottle ketchup
3 tablespoons barbecue sauce
3 tablespoons vinegar
2 tablespoons salt
1 teaspoon pepper
1 teaspoon Tabasco sauce
2 teaspoons chili powder
1 1/2 cups water

♦ Preheat the oven to 250 degrees.

♦ Place the beef with the celery, onions and green pepper in a large Dutch oven.

♦ Blend the ketchup, barbecue sauce, vinegar, salt, pepper, Tabasco sauce, chili powder and water in a bowl. Pour over the beef and vegetables.

♦ Bake, covered, at 250 degrees for 4 to 5 hours or until the beef pulls apart with a fork.

♦ Remove the beef; shred, discarding fat and gristle. Cool and skim sauce.

♦ Mix the shredded beef and the sauce together. Reheat.

Serve the barbecue and sauce on hard rolls.

BERMUDA RACE STEW

Makes 4 servings

A winning combination of a beef burgundy and a beef stew, this can be done ahead of time and frozen. Undercook the vegetables if stew is to be frozen so they won't get mushy when reheated.

6 slices bacon
1 pound (½-inch) beef cubes
½ cup flour
1 teaspoon salt
1 cup dry red wine
2 tablespoons parsley
½ clove of garlic, minced
½ teaspoon thyme
1 (10-ounce) can beef broth
6 medium potatoes, peeled
12 small white onions
3 or 4 carrots
1 (4-ounce) can mushroom stems
   and pieces, chopped

♦ Preheat the oven to 350 degrees.

♦ Cook the bacon in a large skillet until tender. Drain on paper towels, reserving the pan drippings.

♦ Coat beef cubes with a mixture of flour and salt. Brown in the reserved bacon drippings in the skillet over medium heat. Place in 2-quart casserole.

♦ Process the wine, parsley, garlic, thyme and beef broth in a blender until puréed. Pour over the beef.

♦ Bake, covered, at 350 degrees for 1 hour.

♦ Cut the potatoes, onions and carrots into 2-inch chunks. Add to the casserole.

♦ Bake, covered, for 1 hour longer. Stir in the mushrooms.

♦ Crumble the bacon over the top. Add additional chopped parsley, if desired.

FLEMISH BEEF STEW

Makes 4 to 6 servings

2 large onions, sliced
1 clove of garlic, minced
3 tablespoons vegetable oil
2 pounds stew beef cubes
2 tablespoons seasoned flour
2 teaspoons sugar
½ teaspoon thyme
1 or 2 bay leaves
1 to 2 tablespoons wine vinegar
1 (12-ounce) can beer
½ cup beef broth
4 carrots, peeled, cut into chunks
4 medium potatoes, peeled, cubed

♦ Sauté the onions and garlic in oil in a Dutch oven until golden brown. Remove and set aside.

♦ Coat the beef with seasoned flour. Brown in the pan drippings. Add the sautéed onions, sugar, thyme, bay leaves, vinegar, beer and beef broth.

♦ Simmer, covered, for 1 hour.

♦ Add the carrots and potatoes. Cook, covered, for 30 minutes longer, adding additional beer if necessary.

♦ Adjust the seasonings. Thicken pan juices with flour if desired. Remove the bay leaves.

♦ Ladle into soup bowls and garnish with fresh chopped parsley.

Serve with salad, warm rye or pumpernickle bread and the apple dessert of your choice.

BEEF TERIYAKI

Makes 5 servings

2 pounds London broil chuck, cut 1 inch thick

1 small onion, sliced

1 to 2 teaspoons chopped fresh gingerroot

1 tablespoon sugar

1/2 cup soy sauce

1/2 cup orange juice

1/2 cup vegetable oil

1 clove of garlic

♦ Slice the beef into 1/4-inch pieces. Place beef and onion in a shallow bowl. Add mixture of gingerroot, sugar, soy sauce, orange juice, oil and garlic.

♦ Marinate in the refrigerator for 24 to 72 hours.

♦ Preheat the broiler or grill.

♦ Drain the beef, reserving the marinade. Thread onto skewers. Broil for 4 to 6 minutes on each side, basting occasionally with the reserved marinade.

OLD-FASHIONED TAMALE PIE

Makes 4 servings

2 onions, finely chopped

2 cloves of garlic, minced

1 green bell pepper, seeded, chopped

1 tablespoon peanut oil

3/4 pound ground chuck or round

1 tablespoon chili powder

1/2 teaspoon ground cumin

2 cups tomato sauce

1 (12-ounce) can whole kernel corn, drained

1 teaspoon sugar (optional)

Salt and pepper to taste

1 1/2 cups shredded sharp Cheddar cheese

2 cups water

3/4 cup cornmeal

1/2 teaspoon salt

2 tablespoons butter

♦ Sauté the onions, garlic and green pepper in oil in a large skillet until wilted.

♦ Add the ground beef. Cook until brown, stirring until crumbly. Add chili powder, cumin, tomato sauce, corn, sugar, salt and pepper to taste. Simmer for 30 minutes. Cool slightly.

♦ Preheat the oven to 375 degrees.

♦ Alternate layers of ground beef mixture and shredded cheese in a 1 1/2-quart baking dish.

♦ Crust: Bring water to a boil in saucepan. Stir in the cornmeal and 1/2 teaspoon salt. Cook over low heat until thickened, stirring constantly. Stir in the butter.

♦ Spoon over the casserole; smooth with the back of a spoon.

♦ Bake at 375 degrees for 40 minutes.

Top the casserole with shredded lettuce, chopped onions and tomatoes to make a truly one-dish meal. Serve with salsa.

APRICOT-GLAZED PORK ROAST

Makes 8 servings

2 tablespoons dry mustard

2 teaspoons whole thyme leaves

1/2 cup dry sherry

1/2 cup soy sauce

2 cloves of garlic, minced

1 teaspoon ground ginger

1 (4 to 5-pound) boneless pork loin, rolled, tied

1 (12-ounce) jar apricot preserves

1 tablespoon soy sauce

2 tablespoons dry sherry

♦ Combine the mustard, thyme, sherry, soy sauce, garlic and ginger in a shallow dish. Add the pork loin, rolling to coat. Marinate, covered, in the refrigerator for 3 to 24 hours, turning occasionally.

♦ Preheat the oven to 325 degrees.

♦ Remove the pork loin from the marinade. Place on a rack in a shallow roasting pan. Bake, uncovered, at 325 degrees for 2½ to 3 hours or to 170 degrees on meat thermometer inserted into the thickest part.

♦ Sauce: Combine the preserves, soy sauce and sherry in a small saucepan. Cook over low heat until the preserves melt, stirring occasionally.

♦ Serve sliced roast, hot or cold, with warm sauce.

PORK ROAST WITH LIME AND RUM SAUCE

Makes 6 servings

Spicy flavors of the islands.

1 (3-pound) boneless pork loin

1 large clove of garlic, minced

1 teaspoon ginger

1/2 teaspoon cumin

1/2 teaspoon coriander

1/4 teaspoon nutmeg

1/2 cup packed brown sugar

1/2 cup dark rum

1 cup chicken broth

1/2 cup lime juice

1 tablespoon soy sauce

1 tablespoon cornstarch

2 tablespoons water

♦ Preheat the oven to 325 degrees.

♦ Trim fat on the roast to no more than 1/2 inch; place in a roasting pan. Roast at 325 degrees for 1 hour. Drain.

♦ Mix the garlic, ginger, cumin, coriander, nutmeg, brown sugar and rum in a small bowl; spread over the roast. Combine the broth, lime juice and soy sauce in a separate small bowl; mix well and pour into the roaster.

♦ Roast for 1 hour and 20 minutes longer or to 160 degrees on meat thermometer, basting every 20 minutes. Remove from the oven. Let stand, covered, for 10 minutes.

♦ Bring the pan juices to a boil. Whisk in cornstarch dissolved in water. Cook until slightly thickened, whisking constantly.

♦ Carve the roast in thin slices and spoon part of the sauce over the top. Serve the remaining sauce on the side.

PORK TENDERLOINS WITH FRUIT SAUCE

Makes 4 to 8 servings

This tangy do-ahead dish is lovely served with orange slices on top, rice pilaf and mixed sautéed vegetables.

1/4 cup olive oil

2 tablespoons soy sauce

1/3 cup apricot jam

1 teaspoon rosemary

1 1/2 teaspoons minced garlic

1 1/2 teaspoons grated orange rind

1/2 cup orange juice

1 1/2 teaspoons Dijon mustard

2 to 4 whole pork tenderloins

1/3 cup red wine vinegar

- Blend the olive oil, soy sauce, jam, rosemary, garlic, orange rind, juice and mustard in a food processor.

- Place the tenderloins in a shallow glass dish and pour the marinade over the top. Marinate, covered, in the refrigerator for 8 to 24 hours.

- Bring tenderloins to room temperature. Drain, reserving the marinade. Place the tenderloins in a roaster.

- Preheat the oven to 450 degrees.

- Roast the tenderloins at 450 degrees for 20 to 25 minutes or until tender, turning once. Remove to serving platter.

- Sauce: Add vinegar to roaster. Deglaze over medium heat. Add the reserved marinade. Cook for 3 to 5 minutes, stirring frequently.

- Slice the tenderloins 1/3 inch thick and serve with the sauce.

GRILLED ORIENTAL PORK TENDERLOIN

Makes 10 servings

There is no substitute for fresh cilantro, which gives the meat its "oriental" flavor.

1/2 cup soy sauce

1/4 cup sesame oil

1/4 cup rice vinegar

1 (2-inch) piece fresh gingerroot, sliced

1 bunch cilantro, chopped

2 tablespoons minced garlic

2 tablespoons brown sugar

1/2 cup water

3 pounds pork tenderloin

- Combine the soy sauce, sesame oil, vinegar, ginger, cilantro, garlic, brown sugar and water in a bowl; mix well.

- Pour over the pork in a shallow dish. Marinate, covered, in the refrigerator for 8 hours or longer.

- Preheat the grill.

- Remove the pork from the marinade. Grill for 40 minutes, turning occasionally and basting with marinade. Let stand for 10 minutes before slicing.

GRILLED PORK TENDERLOIN WITH PLUM SAUCE   Makes 4 to 6 servings

2 (1-pound) pork tenderloins
1/2 cup vegetable oil
1/3 cup soy sauce
1/4 cup red wine vinegar
2 tablespoons Worcestershire
  sauce
1 clove of garlic, minced
1 tablespoon chopped fresh parsley
1 tablespoon dry mustard
1 1/2 teaspoons pepper
1 cup plum preserves
1/2 cup mango chutney
1 tablespoon cider vinegar

♦ Combine the tenderloins with the oil, soy sauce, vinegar, Worcestershire sauce, garlic, parsley, mustard and pepper in a large sealable plastic bag. Marinate in the refrigerator for 6 to 8 hours, turning occasionally.

♦ Preheat the grill.

♦ Place the tenderloins on the grill 6 inches above hot coals. Grill, covered, for 15 minutes on each side or to 165 to 170 degrees on a meat thermometer.

♦ Sauce: Combine the preserves, chutney and cider vinegar in a blender container; process until smooth.

♦ Serve the tenderloins with the sauce on the side.

PORK CHOPS WITH CARAMELIZED ONIONS   Makes 8 servings

8 (3/4-inch thick) center-cut pork
  chops
Salt and pepper to taste
1 cup flour
1/2 cup vegetable oil
4 cups sliced onions
1/2 teaspoon sugar
4 teaspoons minced garlic
4 cups beef stock
1 cup shredded Gouda cheese
Chopped parsley for garnish

♦ Trim the chops. Sprinkle with salt and pepper; coat with flour. Heat 3 tablespoons of the oil in a skillet over medium-high heat. Brown 4 chops at a time for 4 minutes on each side. Place in large baking dish.

♦ Add the remaining 2 tablespoons oil to skillet. Add the onions. Cook over medium heat until browned, stirring frequently. Sprinkle with sugar. Cook for 10 minutes longer or until well browned, stirring frequently. Add the garlic. Cook for 2 minutes longer. Arrange the onions and garlic over the chops. Add enough beef stock to just cover the chops.

♦ Preheat the oven to 350 degrees.

♦ Bake, covered with foil, at 350 degrees for 45 to 60 minutes or until the chops are tender.

♦ Remove the foil. Sprinkle the cheese over the chops. Bake, uncovered, for 5 minutes or until the cheese melts and is slightly crusty. Remove to platter. Garnish with parsley.

May thicken the pan juices by whisking in mixture of 3 tablespoons melted butter and 5 tablespoons flour and simmering for 5 minutes.

COUNTRY RIBS AND KRAUT

Makes 8 servings

6 to 7 pounds country-style pork spareribs

Salt and pepper to taste

3 pounds sauerkraut, rinsed and drained

1½ cups coarsely chopped cooking apples

¾ cup chopped onion

8 whole cloves

2 to 4 tablespoons brown sugar

¼ teaspoon pepper

1½ cups chicken broth or combination of chicken broth and vermouth

Chopped fresh parsley

♦ Preheat the broiler.

♦ Arrange the ribs in a shallow roasting pan. Season with salt and pepper to taste. Broil 6 inches from heat source for about 30 minutes, browning all sides.

♦ Reduce the oven temperature to 325 degrees.

♦ Combine the sauerkraut, apples, onion, cloves, brown sugar, ¼ teaspoon pepper and broth in a large ovenproof casserole. Bury ribs in mixture. Bake, covered, for 2 hours. Baste twice by spooning juices over all.

♦ Transfer to a large platter and sprinkle with parsley.

PORK CURRY HOT POT

Makes 4 to 6 servings

2 pounds boneless pork

2 tablespoons vegetable oil

1½ cups sliced onion

1 cup chopped peeled apples

3 tablespoons flour

1 to 2 teaspoons curry powder

1 teaspoon salt

¼ teaspoon pepper

½ teaspoon nutmeg

Dash of Tabasco sauce

1 (19-ounce) can Italian tomatoes, drained

1 (10-ounce) can beef broth

½ cup seedless raisins

2 tablespoons brown sugar

♦ Cut the pork into 1-inch cubes. Brown the pork in the oil in a 4-quart stockpot, stirring frequently.

♦ Add the onion and apples. Cook over low heat until the onion is soft.

♦ Stir in the flour, curry powder, salt, pepper, nutmeg, Tabasco sauce, tomatoes, broth, raisins and brown sugar.

♦ Simmer for 1½ hours or until pork is tender.

Serve with customary condiments for curry.

PEARL STREET PORK PIE

Makes 6 servings

6 large potatoes, scrubbed
Skim milk
6 tablespoons margarine
1 cup sliced celery
1 tablespoon margarine
1½ pounds boneless pork cubes
1 large onion, chopped
2 tablespoons margarine
2 apples, chopped
1 teaspoon ground thyme
1 tablespoon steak sauce
Sprig of parsley
1½ cups sliced carrots, cooked
2 tablespoons cornstarch
¼ cup sherry
1 (9-inch) unbaked pie shell

- Preheat the oven to 400 degrees.
- Bake the potatoes at 400 degrees for 1¼ hours or until tender. Scoop out pulp and whip with the skim milk and 6 tablespoons margarine until fluffy; set aside.
- Sauté celery in 1 tablespoon margarine in small skillet until tender-crisp; set aside.
- Brown pork with onion in 2 tablespoons margarine in a large deep skillet over medium heat. Simmer for 30 minutes.
- Stir in the apples, thyme, steak sauce and parsley. Cook for 15 minutes longer. Add the sautéed celery and carrots.
- Dissolve the cornstarch in the sherry. Stir into the pork mixture. Cook until thickened, stirring constantly.
- Reduce oven temperature to 350 degrees.
- Spoon the mixture into the pie shell. Spread the whipped potatoes over the top.
- Bake at 350 degrees for 30 minutes.

LEMON BARBECUED SPARERIBS

Makes 4 servings

3 to 4 pounds spareribs, cut into serving pieces
½ cup lemon juice
2 teaspoons Worcestershire sauce
1 teaspoon salt
⅓ cup ketchup
¼ teaspoon chili powder
¼ cup packed brown sugar
1 clove of garlic, minced
1 lemon, thinly sliced

- Preheat the oven to 450 degrees.
- Place the ribs on a rack in a roasting pan.
- Bake at 450 degrees for 15 minutes or until the ribs are lightly browned; drain. Reduce the oven temperature to 350 degrees.
- Blend the lemon juice, Worcestershire sauce, salt, ketchup, chili powder, brown sugar and garlic in a small bowl.
- Brush the spareribs generously with the sauce. Place a lemon slice on each rib portion and return to the oven.
- Bake at 350 degrees for 1 hour, basting frequently with the sauce.

RICH AND TANGY PORK (Szèkely Galyas)

Makes 6 servings

Those who like the tang of sauerkraut and other Eastern European flavors will enjoy this unusual dish.

3 medium onions, sliced

2 tablespoons vegetable oil

2½ pounds lean pork, cubed

Salt to taste

3 cloves of garlic, minced

4 teaspoons caraway seeds

2 tablespoons minced fresh dill

1 cup tomato sauce

1 cup water, chicken stock or red wine

16 ounces sauerkraut, rinsed, drained

1 tablespoon paprika

1 cup sour cream

½ cup chopped parsley

♦ Sauté the onions in oil in a medium skillet until soft. Remove with a slotted spoon.

♦ Sprinkle the pork with salt; add to the skillet. Cook until brown, stirring frequently.

♦ Add the sautéed onions, garlic, caraway seeds, dill, tomato sauce and water; mix well. Simmer for 1 hour.

♦ Stir in the sauerkraut and paprika. Cook for 1 hour longer or until the pork is tender.

♦ Add the sour cream and heat through. Do not boil. Sprinkle with parsley.

Serve over noodles. Add a salad, dark bread and a fruit dessert to round out this hearty meal.

VEAL CASSEROLE

Makes 8 servings

3 pounds boneless veal, cut into pieces

2 to 4 tablespoons butter or oil

½ cup minced onion

1 pound mushrooms, sliced

2 (10-ounce) cans cream of mushroom soup

1 cup sour cream

1 cup white wine

1 teaspoon oregano, or to taste

Salt and pepper to taste

♦ Preheat the oven to 350 degrees.

♦ Brown the veal in butter in a large skillet. Remove to ovenproof casserole.

♦ Sauté the onion in the pan drippings. Set aside. Sauté mushrooms. Add the onion, soup, sour cream, wine, oregano, salt and pepper; mix well. Bring to a simmer. Pour over veal.

♦ Bake, covered, at 350 degrees for 1 hour.

VEAL WITH FRESH SPINACH

Makes 2 servings

1 bunch fresh spinach
8 ounces fresh mushrooms
3/4 pound (1/4-inch) veal cutlets
1/2 teaspoon salt
1/4 teaspoon pepper
2 tablespoons flour
4 tablespoons margarine
1/3 cup port or red wine
1/4 teaspoon instant chicken
    bouillon
1/4 teaspoon dried thyme leaves
1 teaspoon flour
1/2 cup water

- Rinse the spinach and pat dry. Chop enough spinach to yield 2 tablespoons and reserve the remaining spinach.

- Cut mushrooms into halves or quarters; set aside.

- Slice cutlets into halves. Coat with mixture of salt, pepper and 2 tablespoons flour.

- Cook the veal in 2 tablespoons of margarine in a medium skillet over medium-high heat for 2 minutes on each side. Remove to a warm plate; keep warm.

- Add the remaining 2 tablespoons of margarine to the skillet. Add the mushrooms. Sauté until golden brown.

- Sauce: Mix the wine, bouillon, thyme, 1 teaspoon flour and 1/2 cup water in a small bowl. Add to the mushrooms. Stir in the chopped spinach. Cook over high heat until the sauce boils and is slightly thickened, stirring constantly.

- Line a warmed serving platter with the reserved spinach. Arrange the veal over the spinach and top with the sauce.

VEAL TENDERLOIN IN MOREL SAUCE

Makes 8 servings

1 (4-pound) veal tenderloin
2 tablespoons butter
1 clove of garlic, minced
1/4 cup minced green onions
1/3 pound morels, trimmed,
    washed, chopped
1/4 cup butter
1/2 teaspoon rosemary
1/2 teaspoon thyme
1/8 teaspoon white pepper
1/2 cup blanc de noir sparkling
    wine
1 1/2 cups whipping cream

- Preheat the oven to 325 degrees.

- Brown the veal on all sides in 2 tablespoons butter in a large skillet over medium-high heat. Place in roasting pan.

- Roast at 325 degrees for 45 minutes or to 170 degrees on meat thermometer.

- Sauce: Sauté garlic, green onions and mushrooms in remaining 1/4 cup butter in skillet. Add the rosemary, thyme and pepper. Sauté for 1 minute longer.

- Add the wine. Simmer for 4 to 5 minutes, stirring to deglaze skillet. Stir in the whipping cream. Simmer until the sauce is reduced to desired consistency.

- Slice the veal. Serve the sauce over the veal.

GRILLED BUTTERFLIED LAMB

Makes 8 servings

This dish is flavorful and easy. The grilling time will vary; allow about 20 minutes for each side.

1 teaspoon pepper
4 cloves of garlic, sliced
2 tablespoons red wine vinegar
1/2 cup red wine
2 bay leaves
1/2 teaspoon tarragon
2 teaspoons salt
1/2 cup olive oil
1 (6 to 7-pound) leg of lamb,
    butterflied

• Combine the pepper, garlic, vinegar, wine, bay leaves, tarragon, salt and olive oil in a bowl. Place the lamb in a rectangular glass baking dish. Pour the marinade over the lamb.

• Marinate, covered, in the refrigerator for 8 hours or longer, turning several times.

• Preheat the grill.

• Mound the coals in the middle of the grill. Sear the lamb over the hot coals for 10 minutes on each side to seal in the juices.

• Spread out the coals and grill for 6 to 10 minutes on each side, basting frequently with the marinade.

• Slice the meat diagonally into thin slices.

ROSEMARY GRILLED LAMB

Makes 6 servings

1 (6-pound) leg of lamb,
    butterflied
3 cloves of garlic, sliced
1/2 cup fresh rosemary or
    1 tablespoon dried rosemary
2 cups red wine
1/2 cup olive oil (optional)

• Cut several slits in the lamb. Rub the lamb with the fresh garlic and insert the garlic slices into the slits. Crush the rosemary; rub over the lamb. Place in a shallow pan and drizzle with wine and olive oil.

• Marinate in the refrigerator for 8 hours or longer, turning frequently.

• Preheat the grill.

• Spread out the coals. Grill for 15 to 20 minutes on each side.

Serve with mint sauce, parsley rice and buttered carrots.

INDONESIAN SATAY KAMBING MADERA

Makes 6 servings

½ cup soy sauce

1 teaspoon molasses

½ cup roasted peanuts, ground

1 teaspoon hot red pepper flakes

⅓ cup peanut butter

1 clove of garlic, minced

Juice of 1 lemon

3 pounds lamb or chicken, cut into 1-inch cubes

1 cup tomato sauce

¼ cup water

Juice of 1 lemon

1 teaspoon Tabasco sauce

♦ Mix the soy sauce and molasses in a medium saucepan. Add the peanuts, red pepper flakes, peanut butter, garlic and lemon juice. Bring to a boil, stirring constantly. Cool to room temperature.

♦ Place the lamb in a shallow dish. Pour half the sauce over the lamb; mix well. Reserve the remaining peanut sauce. Let stand for 1 hour.

♦ Preheat the broiler or the grill.

♦ Thread the lamb onto small bamboo skewers. Broil for about 3 minutes on each side in the oven or grill over hot coals.

♦ Sauce: Combine the reserved peanut sauce, tomato sauce, water, lemon juice and Tabasco sauce in a saucepan. Bring to a boil, stirring until smooth. Remove from the heat.

Serve the lamb with the hot sauce for dipping.

SPICED LAMB KABOBS

Makes 6 servings

Juice of 2 limes or lemons

½ cup olive oil

4 cloves of garlic, crushed

1½ teaspoons turmeric

1 teaspoon ground cumin

Chopped cilantro or parsley

2½ to 3 pounds cubed lamb

Bite-size vegetables

♦ Combine the lime juice, oil, garlic, turmeric, cumin and a generous amount of cilantro in a shallow bowl.

♦ Add the lamb cubes and mix to coat.

♦ Marinate in the refrigerator for several hours.

♦ Preheat the grill.

♦ Thread lamb cubes onto skewers, adding your choice of bite-size vegetables if desired. Grill for 5 minutes on each side.

Serve with couscous or rice.

CHICKEN BASQUE SAUTE

Makes 6 to 8 servings

8 boneless skinless chicken
   breasts, cut into ½-inch strips

½ cup flour

2 tablespoons vegetable oil

2 medium zucchini, cut into thin
   strips

2 cloves of garlic, minced

¾ pound sweet sausage, sliced,
   cooked, drained

½ pound mushrooms, sliced

¼ cup white wine

1 cup chicken broth

1 green bell pepper, sliced

Salt and pepper to taste

♦ Rinse the chicken and pat dry. Dredge in the flour to coat.

♦ Sauté the chicken in 1 tablespoon of the vegetable oil in a
  skillet until browned; remove with a slotted spoon. Sauté
  the zucchini and the garlic in the remaining 1 tablespoon oil
  in the skillet.

♦ Combine the chicken, zucchini, garlic, sausage, mushrooms,
  wine, chicken broth, green pepper, salt and pepper in the
  skillet. Simmer for 10 minutes.

♦ Garnish with chopped parsley.

Serve with rice or noodles.

CHICKEN CAN-CAN

Makes 6 to 8 servings

An easy dish to prepare for unexpected guests.

10 boneless skinless chicken
   breasts

Salt and pepper to taste

1 (4-ounce) can mushroom caps,
   drained

1 (14-ounce) can artichoke
   hearts, drained, quartered

1 (7-ounce) jar hearts of palm,
   cut into thirds

1 (8-ounce) can sliced water
   chestnuts, drained

1 (10-ounce) can cream of
   mushroom soup or cream of
   asparagus soup

½ cup sherry or dry white wine

1 cup sour cream

Paprika to taste

♦ Preheat the oven to 350 degrees.

♦ Rinse the chicken and pat dry. Arrange in a shallow
  9x13-inch baking dish. Season with the salt and pepper.
  Layer the mushrooms, artichokes, hearts of palm and water
  chestnuts over the chicken.

♦ Spoon the soup into a small bowl. Add the sherry and sour
  cream and stir to blend well.

♦ Pour the soup mixture over the layers. Sprinkle with paprika.

♦ Bake, covered, at 350 degrees for 30 minutes.

♦ Bake, uncovered, for 30 minutes longer or until the chicken
  is tender.

Serve with rice or noodles.

HONEY AND CURRY CHICKEN

Makes 8 servings

Use the specified amount of curry powder. It's not too much.

4 whole chicken breasts, split

Salt and freshly ground pepper to taste

2 tablespoons lemon juice

1/4 cup melted butter

1 to 1 1/2 tablespoons curry powder

6 tablespoons Dijon mustard

1 teaspoon soy sauce

1/2 cup honey

♦ Preheat the oven to 350 degrees.

♦ Rinse the chicken and pat dry. Arrange in a shallow greased baking dish and season with salt and pepper. Sprinkle the chicken with the lemon juice.

♦ Combine the butter, curry powder, mustard and soy sauce in a small saucepan. Add the honey in a fine stream. Cook over low heat until blended.

♦ Pour the curry mixture over the chicken.

♦ Bake at 350 degrees for 1 hour or until chicken is tender, basting every 15 minutes.

May be refrigerated before baking. Leftovers make a delicious chicken salad.

CHICKEN BREASTS STUFFED WITH CHEESE

Makes 6 servings

6 boneless skinless chicken breasts

6 chunks feta cheese or boursin cheese

1/2 cup dry bread crumbs

1/2 cup freshly grated Parmesan cheese

2 tablespoons freshly chopped parsley

1/4 cup melted butter or margarine

♦ Preheat the oven to 350 degrees.

♦ Rinse the chicken and pat dry. Pound each piece into a 5-inch square with a meat mallet.

♦ Roll each piece of chicken around 1 chunk of the cheese; tuck in the sides. Secure with wooden picks if necessary.

♦ Combine the bread crumbs, Parmesan cheese and parsley in a small bowl. Dip the chicken rolls into the butter and roll in the crumb mixture to coat.

♦ Place the chicken in a shallow 9-inch baking pan. Drizzle the remaining butter over the top.

♦ Bake, covered, at 350 degrees for 25 minutes.

♦ Bake, uncovered, for 20 minutes longer.

CHICKEN BREASTS ON EGGPLANT

Makes 4 servings

4 (1/4-inch) eggplant slices, peeled

Nonstick olive oil cooking spray

4 boneless chicken breasts, with skin

Freshly ground black pepper to taste

2 teaspoons minced garlic

1 1/2 cups crushed canned tomatoes

1/4 teaspoon crushed hot red pepper flakes

1 teaspoon dried oregano

1/4 cup dry white wine

1/2 cup crumbled feta cheese

♦ Preheat the broiler.

♦ Spray the eggplant slices with the nonstick olive oil cooking spray and place on rack in broiler pan. Broil until browned; watch carefully. Turn the slices over; spray and broil. Place in single layer in a baking dish.

♦ Rinse the chicken and pat dry. Pound with a meat mallet to double its original size.

♦ Decrease the oven temperature to 400 degrees.

♦ Sauté the chicken in a large nonstick skillet until golden brown. Place 1 chicken breast skin side up on each eggplant slice.

♦ Drain the skillet, reserving 1 tablespoon of the pan drippings. Add the garlic. Sauté briefly. Add the tomatoes, red pepper flakes, oregano and wine. Cook over medium heat for 5 to 10 minutes, stirring frequently.

♦ Spoon the sauce over the chicken. Sprinkle with the feta cheese. Bake at 400 degrees for 30 minutes.

CHICKEN INDIENNE

Makes 8 servings

8 whole chicken breasts, split

4 tablespoons butter or margarine

Salt and pepper to taste

1 1/2 cups orange juice

1/4 teaspoon Tabasco sauce

1/2 teaspoon cinnamon

1/2 teaspoon curry powder

1/4 teaspoon thyme

1/2 cup raisins

2 tablespoons mango chutney

12 blanched almonds, split

Orange sections

♦ Preheat the oven to 425 degrees.

♦ Rinse the chicken; pat dry. Arrange in a greased shallow baking dish. Dot with the butter. Season with salt and pepper.

♦ Bake at 425 degrees for 15 minutes or until golden brown. Reduce oven temperature to 350 degrees.

♦ Combine the orange juice, Tabasco sauce, cinnamon, curry powder and thyme in a medium bowl; mix well. Add the raisins, chutney and almonds, tossing to coat. Pour over the chicken.

♦ Bake at 350 degrees for 45 minutes or until the chicken is tender, basting occasionally.

♦ Garnish with orange sections sautéed in butter.

Serve with condiments of sliced green onions, crumbled crisp-fried bacon and shredded coconut.

CHICKEN IN MUSHROOM AND WINE SAUCE

Makes 12 servings

12 boneless skinless chicken breasts

6 tablespoons flour

1 1/2 teaspoons salt

1/4 teaspoon pepper

3 tablespoons vegetable oil

8 tablespoons butter

3 shallots, minced

1 (10-ounce) can golden mushroom soup

3/4 cup water

3/4 cup dry white wine

1/2 teaspoon lemon juice

1 (10-ounce) package frozen green peas, thawed

1 pound mushrooms, sliced

♦ Rinse the chicken and pat dry.

♦ Shake chicken in a mixture of the flour, 1 teaspoon salt and pepper in a sealable plastic bag until coated.

♦ Sauté in oil and 2 tablespoons butter in a large skillet over medium-high heat for 2 to 3 minutes on each side or until browned. Remove the chicken from the skillet.

♦ Sauté the shallots in the pan drippings until translucent. Add the soup, water, 1/2 cup wine, lemon juice and 1/2 teaspoon salt. Bring to a boil. Return the chicken to the skillet. Simmer, covered, for 10 minutes or until tender.

♦ Stir in the peas. Cook, covered, for 5 minutes.

♦ Sauté the mushrooms in the remaining 6 tablespoons butter in a small skillet for 5 minutes. Stir the mushrooms and the remaining 1/4 cup wine into the skillet with the chicken. Cook until heated through.

Serve over rice.

CHICKEN BREASTS WITH PECAN SAUCE

Makes 8 servings

3/4 cup pecan halves

1 tablespoon butter

8 chicken breasts, split, skinned

Salt and pepper to taste

1/2 cup flour

2 tablespoons each butter and vegetable oil

1 cup dry white wine

1 tablespoon Dijon mustard

3 tablespoons light corn syrup

2 tablespoons fresh lemon juice

1/2 cup whipping cream

1 teaspoon chopped fresh parsley

♦ Sauté pecans in 1 tablespoon butter in a large skillet over medium heat for 4 minutes. Remove the pecans; wipe skillet with a paper towel.

♦ Rinse the chicken and pat dry. Season with salt and pepper and dredge in the flour, shaking off the excess.

♦ Sauté the chicken, one-half at a time, in the remaining butter and the oil in the skillet over medium-high heat for 3 minutes on each side or until golden brown. Return all the chicken to the skillet. Pour mixture of wine and mustard over top. Simmer, covered, for 10 to 15 minutes or until chicken is tender.

♦ Arrange the chicken on a serving platter.

♦ Stir the corn syrup and lemon juice into the pan drippings. Add the whipping cream. Cook over medium heat until the sauce thickens slightly. Add the pecans and parsley. Pour over the chicken.

NORWEGIAN STUFFED CHICKEN

Makes 6 servings

1 (10-ounce) package frozen chopped spinach, thawed
1 1/2 cups shredded Jarlsburg cheese
1/2 cup fresh bread crumbs
1/2 cup shredded carrot
1/2 cup sliced green onions
1/4 cup chopped parsley
2 tablespoons chopped fresh dill
1/2 teaspoon salt
1/8 teaspoon pepper
1 egg, beaten
3 whole chicken breasts, split
1/4 cup melted butter or margarine
2 tablespoons lemon juice
2 tablespoons chopped parsley

- Preheat the oven to 375 degrees.

- Drain spinach well. Combine with cheese, bread crumbs, carrot, green onions, parsley, dill, salt, pepper and egg in a large bowl; mix well.

- Rinse the chicken and pat dry.

- Spoon the spinach mixture between the breast meat and the skin of each chicken piece. Place skin side up in a shallow baking dish.

- Combine the butter, lemon juice and parsley in a small bowl and drizzle over the chicken.

- Bake at 375 degrees for 50 to 60 minutes or until the chicken is tender, basting frequently with the pan drippings.

Serve with a medium white sauce with 1 cup shredded Jarlsburg cheese and 1 tablespoon chopped fresh dill added.

POLLO SCARPARIELLO

Makes 6 servings

Pollo Scarpariello is Italian for Shoemaker's Chicken.

2 pounds boneless chicken breasts
1/2 cup flour
1/4 cup (or more) olive oil
5 shallots, minced
2 cloves of garlic, minced
1 (14-ounce) can artichoke hearts, drained, quartered
1 cup sliced white mushrooms
3/4 cup dry white wine
1 1/2 cups veal or beef broth
1 to 2 teaspoons dried rosemary, crumbled
1/4 teaspoon each salt and pepper
4 tablespoons melted butter

- Rinse the chicken and pat dry. Cut each chicken breast into 3 pieces. Pound with a meat mallet until all pieces are of the same thickness.

- Dredge lightly in the flour and shake off the excess. Sauté in the olive oil in a large skillet for 7 to 10 minutes or until lightly browned. Remove with a slotted spoon; drain.

- Sauté the shallots, garlic, artichokes and mushrooms in the pan drippings until softened.

- Return the chicken to the skillet. Add the wine. Bring to a boil over medium-high heat, stirring to deglaze the skillet. Add the broth, rosemary, salt and pepper.

- Cook for 10 minutes or until the sauce thickens.

- Remove from the heat and stir in the butter.

Serve over noodles with plenty of crusty bread.

STIR-FRIED CHICKEN WITH CASHEWS

Makes 8 servings

2 pounds boneless skinless
   chicken breasts
1/3 cup sesame oil
1/3 cup rice vinegar
1/4 cup dry sherry
2 cloves of garlic, minced
1 1/2 teaspoons cornstarch
1/3 cup soy sauce
8 ounces snow peas
2 tablespoons peanut oil
1/3 cup hoisin sauce
1 tablespoon sugar (optional)
2 tablespoons grated fresh ginger
1 (7-ounce) can water chestnuts,
   thinly sliced
2 cups cashews, lightly toasted
8 ounces white mushrooms, sliced
1 cup thinly sliced scallions,
   including green parts

- Rinse the chicken and pat dry. Marinate in a mixture of sesame oil, rice vinegar, sherry and garlic in refrigerator for 1 hour.

- Blend cornstarch and soy sauce; set aside.

- Remove the tips and strings from the snow peas. Blanch for 30 seconds in boiling water; drain and set aside.

- Heat the peanut oil in a wok or a large heavy skillet until very hot. Transfer the chicken from the marinade to the wok with a slotted spoon, reserving the marinade. Stir-fry the chicken for 3 to 4 minutes or until no longer pink.

- Add the cornstarch mixture, hoisin sauce, sugar and ginger to the reserved marinade; mix well. Pour over the chicken and reduce the heat to medium-low.

- Add the snow peas, water chestnuts, cashews and mushrooms. Stir-fry for 5 to 6 minutes or until heated through.

- Sprinkle the scallions over the chicken mixture and toss to mix. Stir-fry for 1 minute longer.

Serve over rice.

CHICKEN SALTIMBOCCA

Makes 6 servings

Except that it calls for white wine instead of marsala, this is like the classic veal version of Saltimbocca.

6 boneless skinless chicken
   breasts
Freshly ground pepper to taste
1/2 cup flour
1 tablespoon butter
1 tablespoon olive oil
12 fresh sage leaves or 1
   tablespoon dried sage
6 (1/8-inch) slices lean prosciutto
   or Canadian bacon
3/4 cup dry white wine

- Rinse the chicken and pat dry. Pound each piece with a meat mallet until very thin.

- Sprinkle with pepper. Coat with flour, shaking off the excess.

- Cook the chicken pieces in butter and oil in a large nonstick skillet over medium heat until brown on just 1 side; turn the chicken. Place 2 sage leaves on each piece. Cover with a prosciutto slice. Add the wine.

- Cook, covered, over low heat for about 15 minutes. Turn chicken. Cook for 10 minutes longer, adding additional wine or water if necessary.

- Serve immediately, pouring pan juices over each serving.

CHICKEN AND SAUSAGE STEW

Makes 4 to 6 servings

This hot and spicy stew is perfect for a cold winter's night. It can be frozen for up to one month.

8 boneless skinless chicken breasts

2 tablespoons vegetable oil

1/2 pound sweet Italian sausage

1 (4-ounce) can chopped green chiles, drained

1 large onion, chopped

1 clove of garlic, minced

1 (16-ounce) can tomatoes

2 (16-ounce) cans kidney beans, rinsed, drained

1 (15-ounce) can tomato sauce

1 (6-ounce) can tomato paste

2 cups chicken broth

2 teaspoons chili powder

1 teaspoon ground cumin

1/2 teaspoon salt

1/4 teaspoon crushed red pepper

- Rinse the chicken and pat dry. Cut into 1-inch pieces.
- Sauté the chicken in oil in a large stockpot until browned; drain and set aside.
- Slice the sausage. Cook the sausage in the stockpot until browned; drain and set aside.
- Add the chiles, onion and garlic to the pan drippings. Sauté over low heat until tender.
- Drain the tomatoes, reserving the juice.
- Stir in tomatoes, beans, tomato sauce, tomato paste, broth, chili powder, cumin, salt and red pepper. Bring to a boil. Return the chicken and sausage to the stockpot. Simmer, uncovered, for 30 minutes or until thickened.
- Add the reserved tomato juice if a thinner sauce is preferred.

Serve with a tossed green salad and a rustic peasant bread.

WEST INDIAN CHICKEN

Makes 4 servings

4 boneless skinless chicken breasts

1/4 cup dark rum

Rind and juice of 1 lime

4 tablespoons chutney

1 cup bread crumbs

4 to 6 tablespoons butter

- Rinse the chicken and pat dry.
- Flatten the chicken with a meat mallet. Place in a bowl. Pour mixture of rum, lime rind and juice over the chicken. Marinate, covered, in the refrigerator for 2 hours or longer.
- Preheat the oven to 375 degrees.
- Drain the chicken, reserving the marinade. Spoon 1 tablespoon chutney onto each piece of chicken. Roll and secure with a wooden pick. Dip into the marinade and coat with the bread crumbs. Brown in the butter in a skillet. Arrange in a shallow baking dish. Top with the remaining marinade.
- Bake at 375 degrees for 30 minutes, basting several times.

CHICKEN IN WINE SAUCE

Makes 6 servings

Allow plenty of time to prepare the thick, rich Wine Sauce after cooking the chicken and vegetables.

2 or 3 carrots, thinly sliced
1 large onion, sliced
6 mushrooms, chopped
3 tablespoons melted butter
6 to 8 boneless chicken breasts
2 cups white wine or Champagne
Salt and pepper to taste
Wine Sauce

- Preheat the oven to 325 degrees.
- Layer the carrots, onion slices and mushrooms in a 9x13-inch baking dish. Drizzle the butter over the top.
- Place the chicken on top of the vegetables. Pour the wine over the chicken and sprinkle with the salt and pepper.
- Bake, covered, at 325 degrees for 1 hour. Remove the chicken to a serving platter and keep warm, reserving the vegetables and pan juices for the sauce.
- Pour Wine Sauce over the chicken.

Wine Sauce

$1/2$ cup whipping cream
$1/4$ cup white wine or Champagne
2 tablespoons flour

- Cook reserved vegetable mixture in saucepan over medium heat until liquid is reduced by half. Stir in mixture of cream, wine and flour. Cook until thickened, stirring constantly.

YORKSHIRE CHICKEN

Makes 4 to 6 servings

$1/3$ cup flour
1 teaspoon salt
$1 1/2$ teaspoons ground sage
$1/4$ teaspoon pepper
6 boneless skinless chicken breasts
$1/4$ cup vegetable oil
1 cup sifted flour
1 teaspoon baking powder
$1/2$ teaspoon salt
$1/4$ teaspoon sage
3 eggs, beaten
$1 1/2$ cups milk
$1/4$ cup melted butter
$1/4$ cup chopped parsley

- Preheat the oven to 350 degrees.
- Combine $1/3$ cup flour, 1 teaspoon salt, $1 1/2$ teaspoons sage and pepper. Rinse the chicken and pat dry. Dredge in the flour mixture.
- Heat the oil in a skillet, add the chicken and cook until browned. Place the chicken in a 2-quart baking dish.
- Sift 1 cup sifted flour, baking powder, $1/2$ teaspoon salt and $1/4$ teaspoon sage into a medium bowl.
- Beat the eggs with milk, butter and parsley. Add to the flour mixture, stirring until smooth. Pour over the chicken.
- Bake at 350 degrees for 45 to 60 minutes or until the chicken is tender and the pastry is puffed and golden brown.

CURRIED CHICKEN AND BROCCOLI

Makes 4 to 6 servings

$^{1}/_{2}$ teaspoon hot red pepper flakes

2 cloves of garlic, minced

2 tablespoons vegetable oil

1 (16-ounce) package frozen broccoli cuts, thawed

$^{1}/_{3}$ cup water

2 cups chopped cooked chicken

4 tablespoons butter

1 tablespoon curry powder

$^{1}/_{4}$ cup flour

2 cups chicken broth

$^{1}/_{3}$ cup sliced scallions

$^{1}/_{2}$ cup bread crumbs

$^{1}/_{3}$ cup grated Parmesan cheese

1 tablespoon butter

♦ Preheat the oven to 425 degrees.

♦ Sauté red pepper and garlic in oil in skillet for 15 seconds. Add the broccoli. Sauté for 1 minute. Add the water, cover and cook for 4 minutes.

♦ Toss the chicken and broccoli mixture in a bowl.

♦ Melt 4 tablespoons butter in a skillet. Add the curry powder and cook for 30 seconds, whisking constantly. Add the flour and cook for 3 minutes. Remove from heat and add broth in a fine stream, stirring constantly. Return to heat; bring to a boil. Reduce the heat and simmer for 3 minutes or until thickened, stirring constantly. Add the scallions. Pour the mixture over the chicken and broccoli.

♦ Spoon into a greased baking dish. Sprinkle a mixture of the bread crumbs and cheese over the top. Dot with the remaining 1 tablespoon butter.

♦ Bake at 425 degrees for 20 to 30 minutes or until browned and bubbly.

CHICKEN WITH SAUSAGE AND WILD RICE

Makes 8 to 10 servings

Great for a buffet.

1 (6-ounce) package long grain and wild rice mix

1 pound Italian sweet sausage

1 pound mushrooms, sliced

2 medium onions, chopped

1 (3-pound) chicken, cooked, boned, cut into bite-size pieces

$^{1}/_{2}$ cup whipping cream or light cream

$^{1}/_{4}$ cup flour

$2^{1}/_{2}$ cups chicken broth

$^{1}/_{4}$ to $^{1}/_{2}$ cup slivered almonds

♦ Cook the rice using package directions.

♦ Sauté the sausage in a large skillet; drain and set aside. Sauté the mushrooms and onions in the pan drippings. Add the sausage and chicken.

♦ Preheat the oven to 350 degrees.

♦ Blend cream and flour in a small saucepan. Stir in the chicken broth. Cook over low heat until slightly thickened, stirring constantly. Combine with rice and chicken mixture; mix lightly.

♦ Spoon into a 9x13-inch baking dish. Sprinkle with the almonds.

♦ Bake at 350 degrees for 25 to 30 minutes.

CHICKEN TETRAZZINI

Makes 6 servings

8 ounces mushrooms, sliced

2 tablespoons butter

1 cup chicken broth

½ cup milk

2 tablespoons flour

1 (10-ounce) can cream of
  mushroom soup

2 cups chopped cooked chicken

4 cups cooked spaghetti

4 slices crisp-fried bacon,
  crumbled

½ cup grated Parmesan cheese

+ Preheat the oven to 350 degrees.

+ Sauté the mushrooms in butter in a small skillet.

+ Combine the broth, milk, flour and soup in a large bowl,
  mixing until smooth. Stir in the mushrooms, chicken and
  spaghetti.

+ Spoon into a greased 9x13-inch baking dish. Sprinkle the
  bacon and Parmesan cheese over the top.

+ Bake at 350 degrees for 30 minutes.

  May substitute turkey for the chicken.

CHICKEN POT PIE

Makes 6 servings

A great way to use leftover chicken. The beautiful golden brown crust is as appealing as the taste.

¾ cup chopped onion

1 cup sliced carrots

1 cup sliced celery

2 tablespoons butter

½ teaspoon salt

Pepper to taste

½ teaspoon thyme

1 bay leaf

2 tablespoons flour

2 cups chicken stock

1 cup frozen peas

½ cup parsley

1⅔ cups chopped cooked
  chicken

1 (9-inch) pie pastry

1 egg yolk, beaten

1 tablespoon water

+ Sauté the onion, carrots and celery in the butter in a large
  skillet just until tender. Add the salt, pepper, thyme and bay
  leaf. Stir in the flour.

+ Add the stock, stirring until well mixed. Bring to a boil,
  stirring constantly; reduce heat. Simmer, covered, for 8 to
  10 minutes.

+ Preheat the oven to 400 degrees.

+ Remove the skillet from heat; remove the bay leaf. Stir in
  the peas, parsley and chicken, tossing to mix.

+ Spoon into a shallow round baking dish. Top with the pie
  pastry. Beat egg yolk with water and brush over pastry.

+ Bake at 400 degrees for 30 to 35 minutes or until crust is
  golden brown.

CHICKEN LIVERS IN WINE SAUCE

Makes 6 servings

1 pound chicken livers
5 slices bacon
2 large onions, chopped
2 to 3 tablespoons flour
1/2 teaspoon pepper
1 1/2 cups water
2 low-sodium chicken bouillon cubes, crushed
1/4 cup vermouth or 1/3 cup dry white wine

♦ Rinse the chicken livers and pat dry.

♦ Fry the bacon in a skillet until crisp; drain and crumble. Reserve 2 tablespoons of the bacon drippings.

♦ Sauté the onions in the reserved drippings. Add the chicken livers. Cook until browned on all sides. Sprinkle with the flour and pepper and toss to mix.

♦ Stir in the water, bouillon cubes and vermouth. Bring to a boil, stirring constantly. Simmer until the livers are cooked through.

♦ Sprinkle with the bacon.

♦ Serve on rice or toast.

BAKED CORNISH HENS WITH HONEY SAUCE

Makes 6 servings

6 Cornish game hens
Salt and pepper to taste
1/2 cup white wine Worcestershire sauce
1/2 cup honey

♦ Preheat the oven to 350 degrees.

♦ Rinse the game hens and pat dry.

♦ Season with salt and pepper and place in a nonstick baking pan.

♦ Blend the Worcestershire sauce and honey in a small bowl.

♦ Bake the hens at 350 degrees for 30 minutes. Baste with honey mixture. Bake for 45 minutes longer, basting every 15 minutes with the honey mixture.

GRILLED WILD DUCK BREASTS

Makes 4 servings

Plan to have your guests at the table before the duck fillets come off the grill; they must be served immediately. Duck meat should be served rare, and continues to cook even off the grill and may toughen if not served immediately.

6 boneless skinless wild duck
   breasts
1/2 cup sherry
1/2 cup Italian salad dressing
1 teaspoon Worcestershire sauce
2 tablespoons Dijon mustard
6 slices bacon
Ground pepper to taste

♦ Rinse the duck breasts and pat dry.

♦ Combine the sherry, Italian dressing and Worcestershire sauce in a small bowl.

♦ Spread both sides of each breast with a thin coating of mustard. Place in a bowl. Pour the sherry marinade over the breasts. Chill, covered, for 1 hour.

♦ Preheat the grill.

♦ Wrap each fillet with a slice of bacon. Season with pepper. Arrange on grill in a circle above gray coals.

♦ Grill for 8 or 9 minutes on each side or until the bacon is crisp; duck should be slightly rare.

TURKEY WITH GRAINY MUSTARD AND SAGE

Makes 4 servings

1 egg
2 tablespoons water
1 pound turkey cutlets, pounded
   1/4 inch thick
3/4 cup seasoned bread crumbs
Pepper to taste
1 tablespoon vegetable oil
1/4 cup plus 1/2 tablespoon dry
   white wine
2 cups chicken broth
1 tablespoon grainy mustard
8 fresh sage leaves
1 teaspoon arrowroot
Salt to taste

♦ Beat the egg with the water in a small bowl. Dip the cutlets into the egg mixture and coat with the bread crumbs.

♦ Season the cutlets with pepper. Cook in oil in a large nonstick skillet over high heat for 1 to 2 minutes on each side or until browned. Remove to a platter and keep warm.

♦ Add the 1/4 cup wine to the skillet. Cook over medium-high heat until reduced by half, stirring to deglaze skillet. Add the chicken broth and mustard. Boil for 4 minutes. Add the sage leaves. Cook for 4 minutes or until the liquid is reduced by half.

♦ Dissolve the arrowroot in the remaining 1/2 tablespoon white wine and stir into the sauce. Return to boil and cook until thickened, stirring constantly. Season with salt and pepper.

♦ Add the turkey to the sauce, turning to coat.

♦ Place the cutlets on serving platter and spoon the sauce over the top.

SPICY TURKEY SAUSAGE

Makes 5 pounds

Great for a winter brunch. Delicious wrapped in crescent rolls.

4¹/₂ pounds freshly ground turkey

1 large onion, finely chopped

1 large clove of garlic, minced

2 teaspoons paprika

1¹/₂ tablespoons medium grind black pepper

2 tablespoons crushed dried red pepper

2 teaspoons fennel seeds

³/₄ teaspoon finely crushed bay leaves

¹/₄ teaspoon powdered thyme

¹/₄ teaspoon coriander

²/₃ cup white or red wine or ¹/₂ cup dry vermouth plus ¹/₄ cup water

♦ Place the turkey in a large bowl and sprinkle with the onion, garlic, paprika, pepper, red pepper, fennel seeds, bay leaves, thyme and coriander. Add the white wine; mix well.

♦ Divide sausage into 4 portions and shape into 2¹/₂-inch diameter logs. May slice into ¹/₄-inch thick patties. Divide into meal-size portions and freeze in sealable plastic bags.

BLUEFISH WITH ONIONS AND MUSTARD

Makes 4 servings

"Fish must swim thrice—once in water, a second time in the sauce, and a third time in the wine of the stomach." John Ray: English Proverbs (1670)

2 tablespoons butter

2 pounds filleted bluefish

¹/₂ cup finely chopped onion

¹/₂ cup seasoned bread crumbs

6 tablespoons butter or olive oil

Juice of 1 lemon

2 tablespoons Dijon mustard

1¹/₂ teaspoons Beau Monde seasoning

¹/₂ teaspoon ground pepper

♦ Preheat the broiler.

♦ Place 2 tablespoons butter in 4 portions in a broiler pan. Arrange the fillets over the butter and sprinkle with half the onion and the bread crumbs.

♦ Melt the remaining 6 tablespoons butter in a saucepan. Stir in the lemon juice, mustard, seasoning and pepper. Baste the fillets with the mustard mixture.

♦ Broil for 5 minutes. Turn fillets over and sprinkle with remaining onion and crumbs. Broil for 4 minutes longer or until the fish flakes easily with a fork.

Serve with zucchini, Italian bread, a good chardonnay and the remaining mustard sauce.

BAKED STUFFED BLUEFISH

Makes 4 servings

1¼ pounds filleted bluefish
½ cup mayonnaise
¼ cup ketchup
Garlic Topping
1 medium green bell pepper,
    sliced into rings

♦ Preheat the oven to 350 degrees.

♦ Line the bottom and sides of a baking pan with foil.

♦ Blend the mayonnaise and ketchup in a small bowl. Place half the fillets on the foil; spoon the Garlic Topping on the fillets.

♦ Top with the remaining fillets and green pepper rings. Spoon the ketchup mixture over the fish.

♦ Bake at 350 degrees for 1 hour or until the fish flakes easily.

Garlic Topping

1 onion, finely chopped
3 cloves of garlic, crushed
½ cup butter
2 cups dry bread crumbs
1 tablespoon chopped basil
2 tablespoons lemon juice
Salt and pepper to taste

♦ Sauté the onion and garlic in 2 tablespoons of the butter in a medium skillet over low heat.

♦ Add remaining butter. Stir in the bread crumbs and remaining ingredients.

BAKED FRESH COD

Makes 2 or 3 servings

1 pound cod fillets
½ cup unseasoned bread crumbs
2 tablespoons grated Parmesan
    cheese
2 teaspoons grated lemon rind
¾ teaspoon marjoram
½ teaspoon paprika
¼ teaspoon dried thyme leaves
⅛ teaspoon garlic powder
3 tablespoons lemon juice
2 tablespoons white wine
2 tablespoons vegetable oil

♦ Preheat the oven to 425 degrees.

♦ Rinse the fillets and pat dry.

♦ Combine the bread crumbs, cheese, lemon rind, marjoram, paprika, thyme and garlic powder in a shallow dish. Mix the lemon juice and wine in a shallow dish. Dip each fillet in the lemon mixture; dredge in the bread crumbs to coat.

♦ Place the fillets in a baking pan; drizzle with vegetable oil.

♦ Bake at 425 degrees for 15 to 20 minutes or until the fish flakes easily when tested with a fork.

MEXICAN BAKED FLOUNDER

Makes 4 servings

1/4 cup chopped onion

2 cloves of garlic, minced

1 tablespoon vegetable oil

1 (16-ounce) can tomatoes, drained, chopped

1 tablespoon chopped green chiles

1 teaspoon chili powder

1/8 teaspoon pepper

1 egg white

1 tablespoon skim milk

4 (4-ounce) flounder fillets

1/2 cup cornmeal

1/2 cup shredded part-skim mozzarella cheese

♦ Preheat the oven to 350 degrees.

♦ Sauté the onion and garlic in oil in a medium saucepan over medium heat for 3 minutes or until soft. Add the tomatoes, chiles, chili powder and pepper. Simmer, covered, for 15 minutes, stirring occasionally.

♦ Beat the egg white and skim milk in a shallow dish.

♦ Dip the fillets in the egg mixture and coat with cornmeal.

♦ Place in a single layer in a baking dish sprayed with nonstick cooking spray. Spoon the sauce over the fillets and sprinkle with cheese.

♦ Bake at 350 degrees for 20 minutes or until fish flakes easily.

Garnish with avocado slices and a dollop of fat-free sour cream.

MONTEREY BAKED FLOUNDER

Makes 6 servings

2 pounds flounder fillets

1 cup sliced mushrooms

2 scallions or 1 shallot, chopped

1 teaspoon marjoram

Salt and pepper to taste

2 tablespoons dry white wine

2 teaspoons lemon juice

1/2 cup shredded Monterey Jack cheese

1/4 cup bread crumbs

1/2 cup melted butter

♦ Preheat the oven to 400 degrees.

♦ Rinse the fillets and pat dry.

♦ Place the mushrooms and scallions in the bottom of a buttered 9x13-inch baking dish. Arrange the flounder fillets over the mushrooms and scallions, covering the thin part of each fillet with the thick part of another to prevent overcooking. Sprinkle with marjoram, salt, pepper, wine and lemon juice.

♦ Top with the cheese and bread crumbs and pour the melted butter over the top.

♦ Wrinkle a piece of waxed paper, wet it and spread over the fillets.

♦ Bake at 400 degrees for 7 minutes. Remove the waxed paper. Bake for 5 minutes longer.

GRILLED BARBECUED SALMON

Makes 6 servings

2¹/₂ pounds fresh salmon fillets
Salt and pepper to taste
Lemon juice to taste
Barbecue Sauce for Fish

♦ Preheat the grill.

♦ Rinse the salmon and pat dry. Sprinkle with salt, pepper and lemon juice.

♦ Baste the fillets with the Barbecue Fish Sauce. Place on 2 layers of heavy-duty foil. Place foil over medium coals.

♦ Grill just until the salmon begins to flake, basting frequently. Baste again just before serving.

Serve with fresh peas and new potatoes.

Barbecue Sauce for Fish

1 cup butter
2 or more cloves of garlic, minced
¹/₄ cup soy sauce
2 tablespoons Dijon mustard
Dash each of Worcestershire sauce and ketchup

♦ Combine the butter, garlic, soy sauce, mustard, Worcestershire sauce and ketchup in a small saucepan.

♦ Heat until well blended, stirring frequently; do not boil.

SALMON WITH LIME AND GINGER

Makes 4 servings

1¹/₄ pounds salmon fillets
3 teaspoons minced fresh gingerroot
2 teaspoons minced lime zest
3 tablespoons freshly squeezed lime juice
Freshly ground pepper to taste

♦ Preheat the oven to 500 degrees.

♦ Line a large broiler pan or baking sheet with foil; spray lightly with nonstick cooking spray.

♦ Rinse the salmon and pat dry. Remove any bones. Slice diagonally into ¹/₂ to 1-inch thick pieces. Arrange the salmon pieces in the center of the foil with pieces touching.

♦ Sprinkle with gingerroot and lime zest; drizzle with lime juice.

♦ Bake at 500 degrees for 3 to 4 minutes or until the salmon is opaque throughout.

♦ Sprinkle with pepper. Serve immediately.

CONNECTICUT RIVER BROILED SHAD

Makes 4 servings

1½ pounds boned shad fillets, unskinned
Salt and pepper to taste
5 slices bacon
Shad Roe
Lemon wedges
Chopped parsley

- Preheat the broiler.
- Place the shad fillets skin side down in baking pan sprayed with nonstick cooking spray. Sprinkle with salt and pepper. Arrange the bacon strips on top.
- Broil for 15 minutes.
- Arrange the shad and Shad Roe on a serving plate. Garnish with lemon wedges and chopped parsley. Serve with melted butter and lemon juice.

Shad Roe

2 whole shad roe
Lemon juice to taste
Salt and pepper to taste
½ cup melted butter

- Place the roe in ice water to cover in a bowl for 30 minutes before cooking; drain. Rinse; pat dry. Place roe in greased broiler pan. Sprinkle with lemon juice, salt and pepper.
- Broil for 5 minutes, basting with lemon juice and butter. Turn roe over. Broil for 5 minutes longer, basting frequently. Cut each roe into halves.

Chilling the shad roe in ice water keeps the roe sack from breaking during cooking. Shad may be grilled using the same method. Shad roe may be lightly fried in bacon drippings for 5 minutes on each side.

FILLETS OF SOLE WITH WINE

Makes 4 servings

2 shallots, chopped
8 sole or flounder fillets
¼ cup melted butter
Salt and white pepper to taste
1 cup fresh white bread crumbs
¼ cup dry vermouth
¼ cup chablis

- Preheat the oven to 400 degrees.
- Place the shallots in the bottom of a large au gratin dish.
- Rinse the sole fillets and pat dry. Dip 4 of the fillets in the melted butter. Place white side up over the chopped shallots. Sprinkle with salt and pepper. Dip the remaining fillets in the butter and arrange white side up over the other fillets.
- Sprinkle the bread crumbs on top. Pour the vermouth and chablis around the fillets, allowing the bread crumbs to remain dry.
- Bake at 400 degrees for 20 minutes or until fish flakes easily.

POACHED FILLET OF SOLE

Makes 6 servings

1 bottle white wine

1 bay leaf

1 slice lemon

1 medium onion, peeled, studded
   with cloves

1 parsley sprig

Salt and pepper to taste

12 jumbo shrimp, peeled,
   deveined

1/4 cup cold water

1 1/2 pounds sole fillets

6 tablespoons Herbed
   Mayonnaise

♦ Combine the wine, bay leaf, lemon slice, onion, parsley sprig, salt and pepper in a large skillet. Bring to a boil. Add the shrimp. Cook for 3 minutes or until the shrimp turn pink. Remove and cover the shrimp. Reserve 6 of the shrimp; chill in refrigerator. Discard the onion, bay leaf and parsley. Add 1/4 cup cold water to skillet. Bring to a simmer.

♦ Cut the fillets lengthwise and roll each half around a shrimp.

♦ Place the rolled fillets seam side down in the skillet. Poach for 4 to 5 minutes; drain. Chill until serving time.

♦ Arrange the rolled fillets on a serving platter. Spoon 1 tablespoon of the Herbed Mayonnaise over each serving.

♦ Garnish servings with fresh dill and reserved shrimp.

Herbed Mayonnaise

3 egg yolks

1 tablespoon red wine vinegar

1 chicken bouillon cube, crushed

1/2 teaspoon Dijon mustard

2 1/2 cups vegetable oil

1/4 cup boiling water

1/2 cup parsley

1/2 cup fresh dill or 1 1/2
   tablespoons dried dill

1/4 cup snipped chives

Dash of Tabasco sauce

Lemon juice to taste

Salt and white pepper to taste

♦ Beat the egg yolks with a whisk in a large bowl until creamy.

♦ Add the vinegar, bouillon powder and mustard.

♦ Add 1/2 cup of the oil in a fine stream, beating constantly. Add the remaining oil 2 tablespoons at a time until the mixture is thick. Beat in the boiling water.

♦ Measure 1 1/2 cups of the mayonnaise. Add parsley, dill and chives. Season with Tabasco sauce, lemon juice, salt and white pepper. Store remaining mayonnaise and Herbed Mayonnaise in the refrigerator.

SWORDFISH DIJON

Makes 4 servings

4 (8-ounce) swordfish or tuna steaks
2 tablespoons mayonnaise
2 tablespoons Dijon mustard
1 teaspoon basil or dill

- Preheat the oven to 400 degrees.
- Place the swordfish in a shallow baking dish. Spoon mixture of the mayonnaise and mustard over the top (or substitute ranch dressing); sprinkle with basil.
- Bake at 400 degrees for 20 to 30 minutes.

  May grill for 10 minutes on each side, over white coals. Serve with fresh asparagus and a tossed salad.

GRILLED TUNA WITH SALSA

Makes 4 servings

4 (1-inch) tuna steaks
Salt and pepper to taste
Mustard Marinade
4 sprigs of fresh dill for garnish
4 lime slices for garnish
1 cup salsa

- Rub both sides of the tuna steaks with salt and pepper; place in a large glass baking dish. Pour the Mustard Marinade over the steaks. Chill, covered, for 2 hours or longer, turning occasionally.
- Preheat the broiler or grill.
- Place tuna on rack in broiler pan or on grill. Broil or grill 6 inches from the heat source for 4 to 6 minutes on each side or until firm, basting frequently with marinade.
- Garnish with dill sprigs and lime. Serve with salsa.

  May substitute Italian dressing for Mustard Marinade.

Mustard Marinade

2 tablespoons Dijon mustard
2 cloves of garlic, minced
½ cup olive oil
Juice of 4 limes
¼ cup soy sauce
1 teaspoon freshly ground pepper
1 tablespoon chopped fresh dill

- Combine the mustard, garlic, olive oil, lime juice, soy sauce, pepper and dill in a small bowl; mix well.

EAST COAST CIOPPINO

Makes 8 servings

1 large onion, chopped
1 medium green pepper, chopped
1/2 cup sliced celery
1 carrot, shredded
3 cloves of garlic, minced
3 tablespoons vegetable oil
2 (16-ounce) cans tomatoes
1 (8-ounce) can tomato sauce
1 (8-ounce) bottle clam juice
1 teaspoon basil, crushed
1 teaspoon salt
1/4 teaspoon pepper
1 1/2 cups white wine
2 tablespoons minced parsley
1 pound cod or halibut pieces
1 pound shrimp, shelled
1 pound scallops
24 mussels or clams in shells

♦ Sauté the onion, green pepper, celery, carrot and garlic in oil in a large soup pot over medium heat until the vegetables are soft.

♦ Stir in the tomatoes, tomato sauce, clam juice, basil, salt and pepper. Simmer, covered, for 2 hours.

♦ Refrigerate overnight. Heat in a large saucepan. Stir in the wine, parsley, cod, shrimp, scallops and mussels.

♦ Steam, covered, for 10 to 15 minutes or until the mussel shells open and fish is cooked. Discard any unopened mussels.

Serve in large bowls with plenty of crusty peasant bread and a salad.

MUSSELS MARINARA

Makes 4 servings

4 pounds mussels
3 large cloves of garlic, minced
2 large tomatoes, chopped, or
   1/3 cup tomato sauce
1/2 cup dry white wine
1/2 cup chopped parsley
1/4 teaspoon dried oregano
3 tablespoons olive oil
1 teaspoon salt
1/4 teaspoon pepper

♦ Scrub the mussels, remove the beards and discard any open mussels.

♦ Combine the garlic, tomatoes, wine, parsley, oregano, oil, salt and pepper in a large stockpot.

♦ Add the mussels and steam, covered, for 10 minutes or until the mussels open, shaking the pot occasionally. Discard any unopened mussels.

♦ Ladle the mussels and broth into soup plates.

Serve with melted butter and Italian or garlic bread.

NOANK STEAMED MUSSELS

Makes 4 servings

Mussels are abundant along the New England coast. Whether bought or hand-gathered, this recipe is a delicious way to serve them.

4 pounds mussels
½ cup chopped onion
1 clove of garlic, chopped
1 stalk celery, sliced
¼ cup butter
½ to 1 cup dry white wine

♦ Scrub the mussels; remove the beards.

♦ Sauté the onion, garlic and celery in the butter in a large pot over medium heat until soft.

♦ Add the wine and the mussels. Steam, covered, for 5 to 10 minutes or until the mussels open. Discard any mussels that remain closed.

♦ Use the broth for dipping.

SEAFOOD MORNAY

Makes 8 servings

1 pound bay scallops or deep-sea scallops (cut up)
1 cup water
1 small onion, chopped
2 teaspoons lemon juice
½ teaspoon salt
1 pound mushrooms, sliced
4 tablespoons butter
6 tablespoons flour
1 cup milk
1 cup light cream or half-and-half
4 tablespoons shredded Gruyère, Swiss or Cheddar cheese
1 tablespoon snipped fresh parsley
Pepper to taste
1 pound lobster meat, cooked, cut into bite-size pieces
1 pound salad shrimp, cooked, peeled
1 cup dry white wine
16 prepared patty shells

♦ Simmer scallops in boiling water with onion, lemon juice and salt for 5 minutes. Drain, reserving the cooking liquid.

♦ Sauté the mushrooms in butter in a large saucepan. Sprinkle with flour; mix well. Stir in milk and reserved cooking liquid. Cook until thickened, stirring constantly.

♦ Fold in the light cream, cheese, parsley, pepper, scallops, lobster and shrimp. Bring to a bubbly boil, stirring constantly.

♦ Stir in the wine and remove from heat.

♦ Serve in prepared patty shells or from a chafing dish.

TRASH CAN CLAMBAKE

Makes 8 servings

A time honored summer tradition.

Metal trash can with cover

Seaweed

2 (3½ to 4-pound) chickens, quartered

Vegetable oil to taste

2 teaspoons paprika

Salt and pepper to taste

24 or more cherrystone or littleneck clams

2½ pounds new red potatoes

3 to 4 quahog clams

8 (1 to 1½-pound) lobsters

16 ears of fresh corn, unshucked

1 cup butter, melted

4 lemons, cut into wedges

Tabasco sauce (optional)

Worcestershire sauce (optional)

♦ Preheat the charcoal grill.

♦ Build wood fire and arrange rocks or cinder blocks around fire to support trash can. Gather the seaweed.

♦ Place the chicken in a large dish and coat with oil; rub with paprika, salt and pepper.

♦ Grill the chicken pieces quickly over hot coals until golden brown on each side but not cooked through.

♦ Tie 2 chicken quarters in each of 4 cheesecloth bags.

♦ Tie in each cheesecloth bag 3 or more cherrystone clams.

♦ Place a layer of stones 2 inches deep in the bottom of a new, clean garbage can. Add enough water to cover.

♦ Place a layer of seaweed (rockweed with little pods that pop) over the stones.

♦ Add the chicken. Cover with seaweed. Reserve 1 potato. Arrange the remaining potatoes over the seaweed.

♦ Alternate layers of seaweed, clams, lobsters and corn, ending with seaweed.

♦ Place the reserved potato in the center of the top layer of seaweed.

♦ Cover tightly with the clean garbage can lid and weight with heavy stones.

♦ Cook over a medium fire for 1½ hours or until the potato on top is tender but not mushy.

♦ Serve with melted butter, lemon wedges and sauces.

Chicken can be cooked entirely on grill.

BAKED STUFFED LOBSTER

Makes 6 servings

6 (1¼-pound) lobsters

2 to 3 cups fresh Italian bread crumbs

6 saltines, crumbled

6 sprigs of fresh parsley, minced

1 teaspoon grated Parmesan cheese

½ cup melted butter

Salt and pepper to taste

Lemons, sliced

- Preheat the oven to 375 degrees.

- Steam the lobsters for 5 minutes in a large stockpot of boiling water to cover over high heat.

- Place the lobsters on a cutting board with the legs and claws down. Lobster meat does not dry out using this method. Cut the heads off just behind the eyes using a very sharp knife and cut straight down the backs and tails using a sawing motion; do not cut completely through. Keep the lobster shells intact. Remove the intestinal vein, the tomalley and the coral.

- Remove the lobster claws. Cook separately in boiling water to cover in saucepan and set aside.

- Combine the bread crumbs, saltines, parsley, cheese, butter, salt and pepper. Mix until the stuffing is moist.

- Stuff the lobsters. Place on a large baking sheet. Bake at 375 degrees for 30 to 40 minutes.

- Place the lobsters and claws on serving plates.

- Serve with melted butter and lemon slices.

BOILED LOBSTER

Makes 6 servings

6 (1¼-pound) lobsters

1 tablespoon salt

½ cup cider vinegar

2 tablespoons prepared mustard or 1 tablespoon dry mustard

Pepper

Lemons, sliced

½ cup melted butter

- Bring enough water to cover lobsters to a boil in a large stockpot. Add salt, vinegar, mustard and a generous amount of pepper.

- Plunge the lobsters head first into the boiling water and allow the water to return to boiling. Reduce heat to medium. Boil for 20 minutes; drain.

- Serve hot with lemon slices and melted butter or cool and serve with mayonnaise.

BAY SCALLOPS FLORENTINE

Makes 4 servings

1 (10-ounce) package frozen chopped spinach, thawed

2 teaspoons flour

Dash each of nutmeg and ground red pepper

2 teaspoons margarine

3/4 cup milk

1/4 cup shredded Swiss cheese

1 pound fresh bay scallops

2 tablespoons grated Parmesan cheese

1 tablespoon fine dry bread crumbs

♦ Preheat the broiler.

♦ Drain and squeeze the spinach dry; set aside.

♦ Cook the flour, nutmeg and red pepper in margarine in a small saucepan over medium-low heat for 1 minute, stirring constantly. Stir in milk gradually. Cook for 5 minutes or until slightly thickened, stirring constantly. Remove from heat; stir in Swiss cheese until melted.

♦ Coat a medium skillet with nonstick cooking spray. Add the spinach and scallops. Cook for 6 minutes or until the scallops are cooked through, stirring frequently; drain.

♦ Divide mixture into four greased 8-ounce ramekins. Top with sauce, Parmesan cheese and crumbs.

♦ Broil 6 inches from heat source for 1 minute or until slightly brown.

WATERCRESS SCALLOPS

Makes 6 servings

3/4 cup (or more) dry vermouth

1/2 onion, sliced

1 sprig of parsley

1 bay leaf

Salt and lemon pepper to taste

1 pound sea scallops

Watercress Sauce

♦ Heat the vermouth, onion, parsley, bay leaf, salt and lemon pepper in a large stockpot over low heat.

♦ Add the scallops. Simmer for 6 minutes or until just cooked through; do not overcook. Drain and place in a medium bowl. Chill for 1 hour.

♦ Mix scallops with Watercress Sauce just before serving.

Watercress Sauce

4 scallions, chopped

1/2 cup mayonnaise

1/4 cup watercress leaves

2 tablespoons chopped parsley

2 tablespoons chopped chives

1 1/2 teaspoons fresh dill

Juice of 1/2 small lime

♦ Combine the scallions, mayonnaise, watercress leaves, parsley, chives, dill and lime in a blender container; process until smooth.

♦ Chill for 1 hour or longer.

May substitute 1/4 teaspoon dried dill for the fresh dill.

SCALLOP KABOBS

Makes 4 servings

1 pound scallops

2 (4-ounce) cans button
  mushrooms, drained

2 tablespoons vegetable oil

2 tablespoons soy sauce

2 tablespoons lemon juice

2 tablespoons minced parsley

½ teaspoon salt

Dash of pepper

8 slices bacon

1 (13-ounce) can pineapple
  chunks, drained

2 green bell peppers, cut in
  chunks

♦ Marinate the scallops and mushrooms in a mixture of oil, soy sauce, lemon juice, parsley, salt and pepper in a medium bowl for 30 minutes, turning once.

♦ Cut bacon slices into halves. Cook in a skillet over medium heat until limp, not crisp.

♦ Preheat the broiler or grill.

♦ Thread scallops, mushrooms, bacon, pineapple chunks and green peppers onto skewers; place on rack in broiler pan or grill.

♦ Broil for 8 to 10 minutes or until the bacon is crisp, turning once.

HOT SHRIMP

Makes 10 servings

This shrimp dish is great served in the summer for a porch supper. When served in soup bowls, it allows plenty of sauce for dipping.

2 cups butter or margarine

4 ounces Worcestershire sauce

4 tablespoons ground pepper

1 teaspoon ground rosemary

2 teaspoons Tabasco sauce

2 teaspoons sea salt

3 cloves of garlic, minced

Juice of 2 lemons

6 pounds uncooked unpeeled
  shrimp

2 whole lemons, sliced

♦ Preheat the oven to 400 degrees.

♦ Combine the butter, Worcestershire sauce, pepper, rosemary, Tabasco sauce, sea salt, garlic and lemon juice in a large saucepan. Pour half the butter mixture into a large baking dish.

♦ Alternate layers of shrimp and lemon slices in the baking dish, leaving an inch at the top of the pan. Pour the remaining butter mixture over the top.

♦ Bake, uncovered, at 400 degrees for 20 minutes or until the shrimp turn pink and firm.

Serve with hot French bread and a green salad.

SHRIMP ROCKEFELLER

Makes 4 servings

This lovely recipe is a variation of the New Orleans favorite, "Oysters Rockefeller." Serve as an appetizer or a main dish. Spinach should be about half of the vegetable mixture.

12 jumbo or 24 large shrimp
1/2 cup chopped celery
1/2 cup chopped onion
1/4 green bell pepper, chopped
2 tablespoons butter
1/2 (10-ounce) package frozen
   chopped spinach, thawed
1/4 cup mayonnaise
1 teaspoon lemon juice
Worcestershire sauce to taste
1/3 to 1/2 cup bread crumbs
1 teaspoon basil
1/2 teaspoon pepper
1/2 teaspoon fennel seeds
Grated Parmesan cheese to taste

♦ Preheat the oven to 400 degrees.

♦ Cook the shrimp in boiling water for 2 minutes; drain. Peel and devein. Split the head ends halfway to the tails.

♦ Sauté celery, onion and green pepper in butter in a medium skillet for 5 minutes.

♦ Drain the spinach; squeeze dry. Stir into the celery mixture. Cook for 5 minutes; remove from heat. Add the mayonnaise, lemon juice and Worcestershire sauce; mix well.

♦ Stir in the bread crumbs, basil, pepper and fennel seeds. Spoon 1/3 of the spinach mixture into an 8-inch round baking pan.

♦ Spread the split end of the shrimp apart. Arrange in a circle on the spinach mixture so the tails are standing against the side of the pan.

♦ Spoon the remaining spinach mixture over the split ends; sprinkle with cheese.

♦ Bake at 400 degrees for 10 minutes.

Serve over cooked rice with melted butter and lemon wedges.

SHRIMP SCAMPI

Makes 4 servings

This is a quick, fun meal to prepare after a day at the beach.

2 cloves of garlic
1/4 cup butter
1/4 cup olive oil
1/4 cup white wine
1/4 cup lemon juice
2 pounds shrimp, peeled, deveined
Salt and pepper to taste

♦ Sauté the garlic in butter and olive oil in a medium skillet or paella pan over medium-high heat until light gold in color. Stir in the wine, lemon juice and shrimp. Cook over high heat for 2 to 3 minutes or until firm and pink, stirring constantly. Sprinkle with salt and pepper.

♦ Serve informally in the skillet, accompanied by French bread to dip in the shrimp juices.

Can be served on plates accompanied by cooked rice, a green vegetable and French bread.

SHRIMP WITH SNOW PEAS BEURRE BLANC

Makes 4 servings

Providing a sweet-and-sour tang to this unusual dish are the Triple Sec, vinegar and lemon juice. A spoonful of rice under the snow peas makes a colorful and tasty presentation.

2 pounds jumbo shrimp, peeled, deveined

1/2 cup vegetable oil

15 parsley sprigs

3 or 4 cloves of garlic, lightly crushed

1/2 teaspoon salt

2 tablespoons fresh lemon juice

Salt and pepper to taste

1/2 pound snow peas

1 tablespoon unsalted butter

Beurre Blanc

+ Combine the shrimp with the oil, parsley, garlic, 1/2 teaspoon salt and lemon juice in a large bowl. Marinate, covered, in the refrigerator for 4 hours or longer, stirring occasionally.

+ Drain the shrimp, discarding the parsley sprigs and garlic.

+ Sauté the shrimp in a large heavy skillet over moderately high heat for 2 minutes or until firm and pink. Sprinkle with salt and pepper to taste.

+ Blanch the snow peas in boiling salted water in a saucepan for 1 minute; drain. Toss the snow peas with butter and salt and pepper to taste in a bowl.

+ Spoon the Beurre Blanc onto warmed dinner plates to just cover the plates. Arrange the shrimp around the edge of the plates. Mound the snow peas in the center.

Beurre Blanc

1/3 cup dry white wine

3 tablespoons Triple Sec

2 tablespoons white wine vinegar

1 tablespoon minced shallot

10 tablespoons cold unsalted butter, cut into 1/4-inch slices

3 tablespoons lemon juice

1/3 cup finely chopped parsley

Salt and pepper to taste

+ Combine the wine, Triple Sec, vinegar and minced shallot in a small heavy saucepan. Boil until reduced to about 3 tablespoons.

+ Reduce the heat to medium-low and whisk in the butter, one piece at a time, lifting the pan from the heat occasionally to prevent the mixture from overheating. Add each new piece of butter before the previous piece has melted completely.

+ Stir in the lemon juice, parsley, salt and pepper. Keep warm in a double boiler over hot water over low heat.

ELEGANT SEAFOOD ROLLS

Makes 6 servings

A rich blend of flavors for a company luncheon.

6 heads endive lettuce

¹/₄ cup butter

12 thin slices boiled ham

1 pound cooked shrimp, peeled, deveined, or 1 pound lobster meat

Béchamel Sauce

Grated Parmesan cheese to taste

♦ Preheat the oven to 250 degrees.

♦ Rinse the endive in cold water. Remove any damaged outside leaves. Trim the base, cutting so that the leaves do not fall apart. Cut each head through the center into halves. Place the endive in a casserole and dot with the butter. Braise, covered with foil, at 250 degrees for 30 minutes. Drain, reserving 3 tablespoons of the liquid for the Béchamel Sauce.

♦ Increase the oven temperature to 350 degrees.

♦ Wrap each endive with a slice of ham and place in a greased shallow baking dish. Arrange the shrimp over the endive. Spoon the Béchamel Sauce over the top; sprinkle with the Parmesan cheese.

♦ Bake at 350 degrees until heated through and golden brown.

Béchamel Sauce

2 cups milk

2 to 3 tablespoons chopped onion or shallot

1 tablespoon chopped fresh parsley

¹/₄ cup butter

¹/₄ cup flour

1 cup shredded Gruyère cheese

3 tablespoons reserved endive liquid or whipping cream

Salt and white pepper to taste

Dash of nutmeg

♦ Scald the milk with the onion and parsley, strain and set aside.

♦ Melt the butter in a medium saucepan over low heat. Blend in the flour. Whisk in the strained milk. Cook until smooth and thickened, stirring constantly.

♦ Stir in the cheese until melted. Add the reserved 3 tablespoons endive liquid, salt, white pepper and nutmeg and mix well.

SHRIMP AND ARTICHOKES

Makes 8 to 10 servings

2 (10-ounce) packages frozen artichoke hearts

2 pounds large shrimp, cooked, peeled

1 pound mushrooms, sliced

3/4 cup plus 1 tablespoon butter

1/2 cup plus 1 tablespoon flour

1 1/2 cups milk

1 1/2 cups cream

1 teaspoon salt

1/2 teaspoon pepper

1/2 cup dry sherry

1/2 tablespoon Worcestershire sauce

1/2 cup grated Parmesan cheese

1/2 teaspoon nutmeg

Paprika to taste

- Preheat the oven to 350 degrees.

- Cook the artichoke hearts according to package directions. Drain and arrange in the bottom of a buttered 10x10-inch baking dish. Layer the shrimp over the artichoke hearts.

- Sauté the mushrooms in 2 tablespoons of the butter in a skillet for 6 minutes. Spoon over the shrimp.

- Melt the remaining butter in a 2-quart saucepan over low heat. Blend in the flour. Stir in the milk and cream gradually. Cook until thickened, stirring constantly with a wire whisk. Remove from the heat. Stir in the salt, pepper, sherry and Worcestershire sauce. Pour over the mushrooms and shrimp. Sprinkle with cheese, nutmeg and paprika.

- Bake at 350 degrees for 30 minutes.

COMPANY BAKED EGGS

Makes 10 servings

1 pound sweet Italian sausage

4 ounces mushrooms, sliced

1 medium onion, chopped

1 tablespoon butter

12 eggs, beaten

1 cup milk

2 cups shredded mozzarella cheese

2 tomatoes, peeled, chopped

1/2 teaspoon salt

1/2 teaspoon pepper

1/2 teaspoon oregano

- Preheat the oven to 400 degrees.

- Brown the sausage in a small skillet, stirring until crumbly; drain.

- Sauté the mushrooms and onion in the butter in a skillet until the onion is tender. Add the sausage, eggs, milk, mozzarella cheese, tomatoes, salt, pepper and oregano; mix well.

- Spoon into a lightly greased shallow 3-quart baking dish.

- Bake at 400 degrees for 30 to 35 minutes or until eggs are set.

CHRISTMAS BREAKFAST CASSEROLE

Makes 8 servings

Can be prepared the night before and baked the next morning. If you prefer a meatless dish, substitute fresh mushrooms for the sausage or bacon.

1½ pounds lightly seasoned
  sausage or 1 pound bacon

9 eggs

3 cups milk

1½ teaspoons salt

1½ teaspoons dry mustard

Pepper to taste

12 slices white bread, crusts
  trimmed, cubed

1½ cups shredded sharp
  Cheddar cheese

Paprika to taste

♦ Brown the sausage in a skillet, stirring until crumbly; drain and let cool.

♦ Whisk the eggs and milk in a large bowl. Add the salt, mustard and pepper.

♦ Stir in the bread, cheese and sausage. Spoon into a greased 9x13-inch baking dish. Chill, covered, for 8 to 12 hours.

♦ Preheat the oven to 350 degrees.

♦ Remove the casserole from the refrigerator 30 minutes prior to baking. Sprinkle with paprika.

♦ Bake at 350 degrees for 45 minutes.

♦ Let stand for 10 to 15 minutes before cutting.

SUNDAY BRUNCH BAKE

Makes 6 servings

Increase the amount of seasonings if you like a spicier dish.

½ pound lightly seasoned pork
  sausage

½ cup chopped green bell pepper

½ cup chopped red bell pepper

½ cup sliced scallions

2 teaspoons sage

½ teaspoon garlic powder

¼ teaspoon pepper

8 eggs

1 cup milk

1 cup shredded Cheddar cheese

♦ Preheat the oven to 350 degrees.

♦ Brown the sausage with the green and red peppers, half the scallions, sage, garlic powder and pepper in a skillet, stirring until sausage is crumbly; drain.

♦ Spoon into a greased 9-inch baking dish.

♦ Whisk the eggs, milk and half the cheese in a bowl and pour over the sausage mixture.

♦ Bake at 350 degrees for 30 minutes or until a knife inserted in the center comes out clean.

♦ Top with the remaining scallions and cheese.

♦ Bake at 350 degrees for 3 minutes or until the cheese melts.

GATEAU DE CREPE FLORENTINE

Makes 6 to 8 servings

1/2 cup each water and milk

2 eggs, beaten

1/4 teaspoon salt

1 cup sifted flour

3 tablespoons melted butter

1 small onion or shallot

2 (10-ounce) packages frozen
   spinach, thawed, drained

Mornay Sauce

8 ounces each whipped cream
   cheese and whipped cream
   cheese with chives

1 egg

2 tablespoons milk (optional)

2 tablespoons Parmesan cheese

♦ Process the water, milk, eggs, salt, flour and 2 tablespoons butter in a food processor for 5 seconds. Scrape sides; process for 5 seconds. Let stand for 1 hour.

♦ Cook 12 crêpes, one at a time, in a well greased 8-inch round crepe pan over high heat until golden brown. Set aside.

♦ Sauté the onion in 1 tablespoon butter. Mix the onion, spinach, 2/3 cup of the Mornay Sauce, salt and pepper to taste in a small bowl. Set aside.

♦ Blend the cream cheeses, egg and milk in a small mixer bowl.

♦ Preheat the oven to 350 degrees.

♦ Grease a shallow round baking dish. Layer 1 crêpe, spinach mixture, another crêpe and cream cheese mixture in dish. Repeat until 12 crêpes have been used. Top with remaining Mornay Sauce and Parmesan cheese.

♦ Bake at 350 degrees for 25 to 30 minutes. Cut into wedges.

Mornay Sauce

2 tablespoons melted butter

3 tablespoons flour

1 cup milk

1/2 cup light cream

1/2 cup shredded Swiss cheese

1/2 cup Parmesan cheese

♦ Blend the butter and flour in a small saucepan. Stir in milk and cream. Cook until thickened, stirring constantly. Stir in cheeses until melted.

BREAKFAST POUFF

Makes 4 to 6 servings

2 tablespoons shortening

6 eggs, beaten

1 teaspoon salt

2 tablespoons sugar

2/3 cup flour

1 cup milk

♦ Preheat the oven to 450 degrees. Melt shortening in a heavy skillet in the oven.

♦ Beat the eggs and salt until light. Add mixture of sugar and flour; mix well. Pour into the hot skillet. Bake at 450 degrees for 20 minutes or until golden and puffy.

Serve immediately topped with butter and hot maple syrup, and with side dishes of Canadian bacon and fresh fruit.

SPICY CHEESE PIE

Makes 4 servings

4 eggs, beaten
1/4 cup milk
1/2 cup chopped salami
1/2 cup chopped pepperoni
2 cups shredded mozzarella
    cheese
1/2 teaspoon basil
1/2 teaspoon oregano
1/4 teaspoon pepper
2 tablespoons chopped onion
2 tablespoons chopped green
    bell pepper
1 tablespoon butter
1 (8-ounce) can tomato sauce
1/2 teaspoon salt
1/4 teaspoon pepper
1 unbaked (8-inch) pie shell

- Combine the eggs, milk, salami, pepperoni and cheese in a large bowl. Add the basil, oregano and pepper; mix well.

- Sauté the onion and green pepper in the butter in a small skillet until the onion is tender. Add the tomato sauce, salt and pepper. Set aside.

- Preheat the oven to 425 degrees.

- Pour the egg mixture into the pie shell.

- Bake at 425 degrees for 35 to 40 minutes or until set. Let stand for 5 minutes before cutting.

- Reheat the tomato sauce and spoon over slices of the pie.

  May prepare the filling and sauce the day before, refrigerate covered.

VEGETABLE AND RICOTTA PIE

Makes 6 servings

1 cup shredded carrots
1 cup sliced fresh mushrooms
1/2 cup chopped onion
2 cloves of garlic, minced
2 tablespoons vegetable oil
3/4 cup drained, thawed frozen
    spinach
3 eggs
15 ounces ricotta cheese
1/4 teaspoon nutmeg
3/4 teaspoon salt
1 unbaked (9-inch) pie or quiche
    shell

- Preheat the oven to 425 degrees.

- Sauté the carrots, mushrooms, onion and garlic in the oil in a skillet for 3 to 5 minutes or until tender. Stir in the spinach. Cook for 1 minute longer; remove from heat.

- Beat the eggs, cheese, nutmeg and salt in a small mixer bowl. Stir into the vegetable mixture.

- Pour into the pie shell.

- Bake at 425 degrees for 10 minutes. Reduce oven temperature to 375 degrees. Bake for 35 minutes longer or until the filling is set and the crust is golden brown.

CRABMEAT QUICHE

Makes 8 servings

The rice crust is what makes this quiche so deliciously unique.

3 cups cooked rice

2 tablespoons melted butter

1 egg, beaten

1½ cups (scant) half-and-half

⅓ cup mayonnaise

½ cup grated onion

½ teaspoon cayenne, or to taste

Curry powder to taste

1 teaspoon instant chicken
    bouillon

2 eggs, beaten

1 cup shredded Swiss cheese

1 (6-ounce) can crabmeat

♦ Preheat the oven to 350 degrees.

♦ Mix the rice, butter and 1 egg in a small bowl. Press over bottom and side of a 9- or 10-inch deep-dish pie plate.

♦ Combine the half-and-half, mayonnaise, onion, cayenne, curry powder, bouillon, 2 eggs, cheese and crabmeat in a large bowl; mix well.

♦ Pour over the rice mixture.

♦ Bake at 350 degrees for 45 to 55 minutes or until set.

May prepare the crust and filling the day before, refrigerate separately and assemble just before baking.

TERRACOTTA ENCHILADAS

Makes 4 servings

1 (13-ounce) can tomatoes or
    tomatillos, drained

1 (4-ounce) can green chiles

1 bunch cilantro, chopped

½ cup cream

1 egg, beaten

2 cloves of garlic

1 teaspoon cumin

1 bunch scallions, chopped

½ Spanish onion, chopped

3 cups shredded Colby cheese

8 corn tortillas

¼ cup vegetable oil

1½ cups shredded Monterey
    Jack cheese

♦ Preheat the oven to 350 degrees.

♦ Process the tomatoes, chiles, cilantro, cream, egg, garlic and cumin in a blender until smooth. Set aside.

♦ Combine the scallions, onion and Colby cheese in a small bowl.

♦ Cook the tortillas, one at a time, for about 8 seconds on each side in the oil in a skillet over high heat. Drain on paper towels.

♦ Spoon Colby cheese mixture onto each tortilla; roll to enclose the filling and place seam side down in a lightly greased baking dish.

♦ Spoon the tomato mixture over the top. Sprinkle with the Monterey Jack cheese.

♦ Bake at 350 degrees for 20 minutes.

FETTUCCINI ALFREDO

Makes 2 servings

4 ounces fettuccini

3 tablespoons light cream, at
   room temperature

1/3 cup grated Parmesan cheese

1 tablespoon butter, softened

Pepper to taste

Nutmeg to taste

• Cook the pasta using package directions; drain and return
  to the hot pan.

• Add the cream, Parmesan cheese and butter. Sprinkle with
  pepper and nutmeg. Toss and serve immediately.

If desired, add chopped ham or sautéed mushrooms.

SPAGHETTI ALLA CARBONARA

Makes 4 servings

1 (16-ounce) package spaghetti

1 (8-ounce) slice pancetta or 8
   ounces thick-slice bacon or
   Canadian bacon

4 cloves of garlic, crushed

2 tablespoons olive oil

1 tablespoon butter

1/4 cup dry white wine

3 eggs

4 to 5 tablespoons freshly grated
   pecorino Romano cheese

1/2 cup (heaping) freshly grated
   Parmesan cheese

8 to 10 twists of freshly ground
   pepper

2 tablespoons chopped parsley

• Cook the spaghetti al dente using package directions; drain
  and set aside.

• Remove the rind from the pancetta and cut into 1/4-inch strips.

• Sauté the garlic in the olive oil and butter in a small skillet
  until a deep golden brown. Remove the garlic; discard.

• Add the pancetta to the skillet. Cook over medium-high
  heat until slightly crisp at the edges. Add the wine and bring
  to a boil. Cook until wine is boiled away. Turn off heat.

• Beat the eggs lightly in a large mixer bowl. Add the
  pecorino Romano and Parmesan cheeses, pepper and
  parsley; mix well. Add the spaghetti and toss until well
  coated with the cheese mixture. Add the pancetta and toss
  again. Serve immediately.

BEEF AND BLACK PEPPER PASTA

Makes 4 to 6 servings

4 to 8 ounces beef tenderloin
8 ounces fresh mushrooms, sliced
1/4 cup butter
1/2 cup sweet red vermouth
1 cup whipping cream
Salt and pepper to taste
Parmesan cheese to taste
16 ounces black pepper pasta

♦ Cut the tenderloin into 2-inch strips. Sauté beef with the mushrooms in butter in a skillet.

♦ Add the vermouth, whipping cream, salt, pepper and Parmesan cheese. Cook over medium heat until thickened, stirring frequently.

♦ Cook the pasta using package directions; drain.

♦ Serve beef mixture over hot cooked pasta.

RIGATONI WITH TOMATO AND VODKA SAUCE

Makes 6 servings

Sauce may be prepared a day ahead and reheated while cooking the pasta.

1/2 cup finely chopped onion
1 teaspoon crushed dried red pepper
2 tablespoons olive oil
1/2 cup vodka
1 1/2 cups light cream
1 1/2 cups tomato sauce
16 ounces rigatoni
4 ounces thinly sliced prosciutto, chopped
1 cup shredded Asiago cheese
2 tablespoons chopped fresh parsley
1/4 cup chopped fresh basil or 1 tablespoon dried basil

♦ Sauté the onion and red pepper in the olive oil in a large skillet over medium heat for 5 minutes or until the onion is translucent. Add the vodka and ignite with a long match. Simmer for 2 minutes or until the flames subside, shaking the pan occasionally.

♦ Increase the heat to high, add the cream and boil for 3 minutes or until the mixture thickens. Add the tomato sauce and boil for 2 minutes or until the sauce thickens and coats the back of a spoon. Remove from heat.

♦ Cook the rigatoni using package directions; drain.

♦ Bring the sauce to a simmer. Stir in the pasta, prosciutto, 2/3 cup of the Asiago cheese, parsley and basil; toss to coat.

♦ Transfer to a large warmed serving bowl. Sprinkle with the remaining 1/3 cup Asiago cheese and serve immediately.

BACON AND MUSHROOM LINGUINI

Makes 4 to 6 servings

8 ounces bacon, chopped

2 medium onions, finely chopped

6 cloves of garlic, chopped

1/2 cup olive oil

2 cups chopped mushrooms

1 1/2 cups cream

Freshly ground pepper to taste

1 cup Asiago cheese

16 ounces linguini

1/2 cup parsley

♦ Sauté the bacon, onions and garlic in the olive oil in a skillet over low heat for 20 minutes or until tender. Add the mushrooms. Cook for 10 minutes longer. Stir in the cream, pepper and cheese; mix well.

♦ Cook the linguini al dente; drain. Place on serving plate

♦ Spoon the sauce over the linguini and sprinkle with parsley.

Serve with a simple green salad and a glass of beaujolais for an easy, yet elegant, dinner.

THE BEST THAI NOODLES IN TOWN

Makes 8 servings

A wild and exotic combination of many tastes.

2 whole boneless chicken breasts

6 ounces boiled ham

1 (4-ounce) can water chestnuts

1 red bell pepper

1 small yellow squash

1 bunch scallions, chopped

1/2 cup chopped walnuts

16 ounces thin vermicelli or Chinese noodles

1 cup vegetable oil

2 tablespoons sesame oil

3/4 cup soy sauce

1 teaspoon five-spice powder

2 tablespoons chopped parsley

2 tablespoons toasted sesame seeds

1/2 teaspoon (about) hot chili oil

♦ Poach the chicken. Cut the chicken and ham into thin strips. Drain and slice the water chestnuts. Cut the red pepper and squash into thin strips.

♦ Combine the chicken, ham, water chestnuts, red pepper, squash, scallions and walnuts in a large bowl.

♦ Cook the vermicelli using package instructions; drain.

♦ Whisk the vegetable and sesame oils with the soy sauce, five-spice powder, parsley and sesame seeds in a medium bowl. Add the hot chili oil.

♦ Combine the vermicelli and chicken mixture. Add the soy sauce mixture; toss to coat.

♦ Chill until serving time.

PASTA WITH FISH AND VEGETABLES

Makes 4 servings

4 cloves of garlic, minced

2 tablespoons olive oil

2 cups chopped fresh vegetables

1 pound swordfish or tuna, cut into cubes

12 oil-cured olives, pitted, chopped

1/2 cup chopped fresh basil

1/2 cup thinly sliced red bell pepper

1/4 teaspoon hot red pepper flakes

16 ounces linguini or spaghetti

Grated Parmesan cheese to taste

♦ Sauté the garlic in the olive oil in a skillet over low heat until tender.

♦ Add the chopped vegetables. Cook for 2 to 3 minutes, stirring frequently.

♦ Add the fish. Cook for 7 to 8 minutes or until the fish is almost cooked through.

♦ Add the olives, basil, red pepper and red pepper flakes. Cook until the fish flakes easily.

♦ Cook the pasta al dente using package directions; drain.

♦ Serve the sauce over the pasta; sprinkle with Parmesan cheese.

Use vegetables such as spinach, broccoli, asparagus, carrots or cauliflower in any combination.

PASTA PUTTANESCA

Makes 8 servings

1 large onion, chopped

6 to 8 cloves of garlic, crushed

Olive oil

2 (28-ounce) cans crushed tomatoes

2 (6-ounce) cans tomato paste

1/4 cup red or white wine

1 1/2 teaspoons sugar, or to taste

3 tablespoons fresh basil

2 tablespoons fresh oregano

Salt and pepper to taste

Pinch of allspice

16 ounces spaghetti

♦ Sauté the onion and garlic in a small amount of olive oil in a skillet until tender. Add the tomatoes and tomato paste. Rinse the cans with the wine and add to the tomato mixture. Add the sugar, basil, oregano, salt, pepper and allspice; mix well.

♦ Simmer for 1 hour to blend the flavors. Add a small amount of water if the sauce is too thick.

♦ Cook the spaghetti al dente using the package directions. Place on a large serving platter.

♦ Ladle the sauce over the cooked spaghetti.

For added taste, try adding soaked, sun-dried chopped tomatoes, chopped capers or mashed anchovy fillets to the sauce.

ENCHANTED SCALLOPS EUROPEAN

Makes 6 servings

The secret to this recipe is using continuous low heat and taking time between each step when adding ingredients.

3 cloves of garlic, chopped

3 tablespoons olive oil

2 tablespoons chopped fresh basil

2 tablespoons chopped fresh parsley

1 medium onion, thinly sliced

1 (14-ounce) can artichoke hearts, quartered

1 pound fresh sea scallops

1 pound fresh mushrooms, sliced

1 fresh tomato, chopped

24 pitted black olives, thinly sliced

Juice of 1 lemon

Salt and pepper to taste

1 cup (or less) half-and-half

♦ Sauté the garlic in the olive oil in a large skillet over low heat. Add the basil, parsley and onion and sauté until the onion is translucent, stirring frequently.

♦ Add the artichokes. Cook for 5 minutes. Add the undrained scallops. Simmer, covered, for 10 minutes.

♦ Add the mushrooms, tomato, olives and lemon juice. Simmer for 5 minutes. Add the salt and pepper. Add enough half-and-half to make the sauce of the desired consistency. Simmer for 10 minutes longer.

Serve over angel hair pasta with a tossed green salad and white wine.

Add shrimp or clams to the scallops for variety.

LOVERS' LINGUINI WITH GALLIANO

Makes 2 servings

8 ounces linguini

12 ounces large shrimp, peeled, deveined

1/4 cup olive oil

2 cloves of garlic, minced

2 scallions, chopped

6 artichoke hearts, drained, quartered

2 tablespoons chopped fresh parsley

2 tablespoons chopped pimentos

2 tablespoons butter

1/4 cup Galliano

♦ Cook the linguini according to package directions; drain and keep warm.

♦ Sauté the shrimp in the olive oil in a skillet for 3 minutes or just until firm. Add the garlic, scallions, artichokes and parsley. Cook for 1 minute. Stir in the pimentos, butter and Galliano.

♦ Add the cooked linguini and toss until coated.

Serve with a green salad and crusty bread.

ORZO WITH SHRIMP AND FETA

Makes 4 servings

6 ounces orzo

2 teaspoons olive oil

1 tablespoon minced parsley

1/2 tablespoon grated lemon rind

Salt and pepper to taste

1 clove of garlic, minced

2 medium tomatoes, seeded, chopped

1 tablespoon olive oil

1 tablespoon tomato paste

1/2 cup dry white wine

1/4 teaspoon crushed oregano

2 bay leaves

1/8 teaspoon crushed red pepper flakes

1 pound medium shrimp, peeled

1/2 cup crumbled feta cheese

• Cook the pasta using package directions; drain. Stir in 2 teaspoons olive oil, parsley, lemon rind, salt and pepper. Set aside.

• Sauté the garlic and tomatoes in a skillet in 1 tablespoon olive oil for 5 minutes or until tender. Add the tomato paste, wine, oregano, bay leaves and red pepper flakes. Cook for 2 minutes or until thickened.

• Add the shrimp. Cook for 5 minutes or until the shrimp turn pink.

• Sprinkle the cheese over the shrimp. Remove and discard the bay leaves. Serve over the pasta. Garnish with additional crumbled feta cheese.

FETTUCCINI WITH ASPARAGUS AND PEAS

Makes 6 servings

3/4 cup half-and-half

6 tablespoons butter

1 pound fresh asparagus, trimmed, cut into 1 1/2-inch pieces

1 cup fresh green peas

16 ounces fettuccini

1/2 cup lemon juice

1/2 teaspoon grated lemon rind

1/3 cup freshly grated Parmesan cheese

1/4 cup toasted pine nuts

Salt and pepper to taste

• Heat the half-and-half and butter in a small saucepan over low heat until the butter melts. Set aside; keep warm.

• Cook the asparagus and peas in a small amount of water until tender-crisp; drain.

• Cook the fettuccini using package directions; drain.

• Place the cooked fettuccini in a large bowl. Add the lemon juice and toss to coat. Let stand for 1 minute.

• Add the lemon rind, Parmesan cheese, pine nuts, asparagus and peas. Add the butter mixture, salt and pepper. Toss gently and serve.

Serve with butterflied grilled lamb.

PASTA PRIMAVERA

Makes 4 to 6 servings

1 medium onion, chopped
1 clove of garlic, minced
1/2 cup pine nuts
1/2 cup unsalted butter
1 pound asparagus
1 1/2 cups snow peas
1/4 cup chopped parsley
8 ounces mushrooms, sliced
1 1/2 cups sliced broccoli florets
1 medium zucchini, thinly sliced
1 cup whipping cream
1/2 cup chicken broth
2 tablespoons chopped fresh basil
1 cup frozen tiny peas, thawed
5 green onions, chopped
1 1/2 cups grated Parmesan cheese
Salt and pepper to taste
16 ounces linguini or fettuccini

♦ Sauté the onion, garlic and pine nuts in the butter in a large skillet or wok over medium heat for 2 minutes or until the pine nuts are lightly browned.

♦ Cut the asparagus into 1-inch pieces. Add the asparagus, snow peas, parsley, mushrooms, broccoli and zucchini. Stir-fry for 2 minutes or until vegetables are tender-crisp.

♦ Increase heat to high. Add the whipping cream, broth and basil. Boil for 3 minutes or until slightly reduced, stirring constantly. Stir in the peas, green onions and 1 cup of the Parmesan cheese. Cook for 1 minute. Season with salt and pepper.

♦ Cook the pasta al dente using package directions. Add the cooked pasta to the vegetable mixture and toss gently. Sprinkle with the remaining 1/2 cup Parmesan cheese. Serve immediately.

May add 5 slices ham that have been chopped or slivered or 1 pound cooked shelled shrimp with the peas and green onions for a heartier meal.

PASTA WITH SUMMER GARDEN TOMATO SAUCE

Makes 6 servings

A cold sauce for hot pasta; delicious and refreshing on a hot day.

6 medium ripe tomatoes
1 bunch green onions, minced
3 tablespoons minced parsley
2 tablespoons minced fresh basil
1 teaspoon each salt and sugar
Pepper to taste
2 teaspoons red wine vinegar
2 cloves of garlic, minced
1/4 cup olive oil
16 ounces spaghetti
1/2 cup grated Parmesan cheese

♦ Chop the tomatoes; combine with the green onions, parsley, basil, salt, sugar, pepper and vinegar in a large bowl.

♦ Sauté the garlic in olive oil in a small saucepan until golden brown. Remove and discard the garlic. Pour the olive oil over the tomato mixture; toss to mix.

♦ Chill the vegetable mixture for 3 hours or longer.

♦ Cook the pasta using package instructions; drain. Place in a warmed serving bowl. Add the tomato sauce and toss to mix. Serve with cheese.

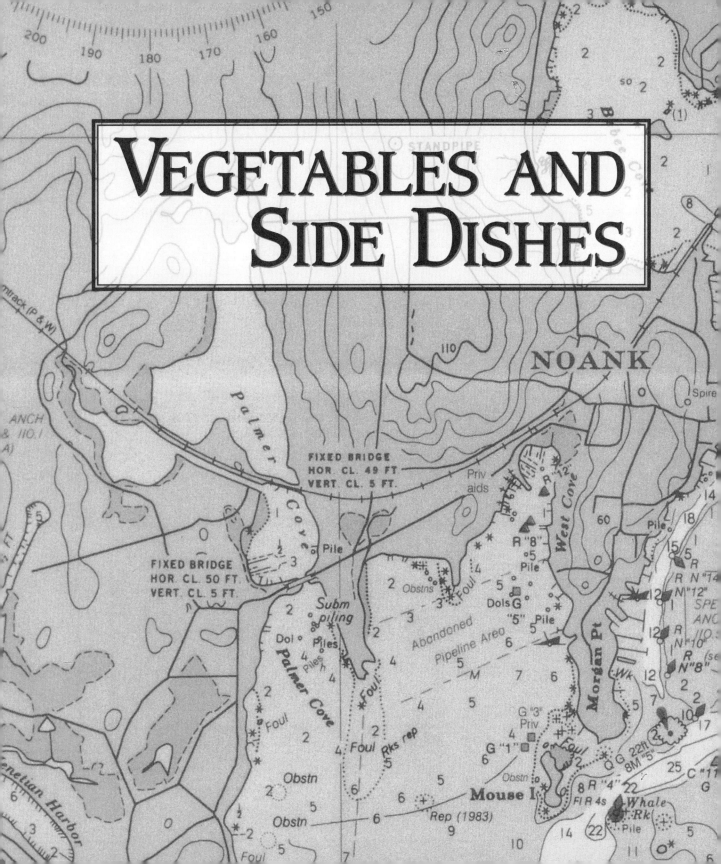

VEGETABLES AND SIDE DISHES

VEGETABLES AND SIDE DISHES

♦ ♦ ♦ ♦ ♦ ♦ ♦ ♦ ♦ ♦ ♦ ♦ ♦

ASPARAGUS BUNDLES WITH LEMON MAYONNAISE Makes 4 servings

1½ pounds fresh asparagus

¼ cup water

¾ cup mayonnaise

Juice of ½ lemon, or to taste

1 tablespoon capers, rinsed, drained

- ◆ Rinse the asparagus, break off the tough ends, remove scales if sandy or tough, but leave asparagus spears whole.

- ◆ Arrange the asparagus spears lengthwise with tips toward center in a 6x10-inch baking dish; add water.

- ◆ Microwave, tightly covered, on High for 5 to 6 minutes or until tender-crisp, rotating the dish ½ turn after 3 minutes.

- ◆ Place asparagus in cold water in a bowl to cool; drain. Chill.

- ◆ Combine the mayonnaise, lemon juice and capers in a small bowl. Spoon a small dollop of the sauce on top of each serving of asparagus.

Serve with chicken or seafood salad.

SLOW-COOKED BEAN COMBO Makes 10 servings

8 slices bacon

4 large onions, sliced into rings

1 cup packed brown sugar

1 teaspoon dry mustard

½ teaspoon garlic powder

1 teaspoon salt

½ cup cider vinegar

2 (15-ounce) cans Great Northern beans, drained

1 (10-ounce) package frozen green lima beans, thawed, drained

1 (16-ounce) can red kidney beans, drained

1 (28-ounce) can pork and beans

- ◆ Fry the bacon in a small skillet; drain, reserving 1 tablespoon of the drippings. Crumble the bacon and set aside.

- ◆ Pour the reserved drippings into a slow cooker. Add the onions, brown sugar, mustard, garlic powder, salt and vinegar. Cook, covered, on High for 20 minutes.

- ◆ Add the Great Northern beans, lima beans, kidney beans and pork and beans; stir to mix well. Add the bacon.

- ◆ Cook, covered, on Medium for 2 to 4 hours.

If a slow cooker is not available, combine the ingredients as above in a Dutch oven, bring to a simmer and bake at 250 degrees for 2 to 4 hours.

BROCCOLI CASSEROLE

Makes 8 servings

2 (10-ounce) packages frozen chopped broccoli

2 cups frozen whole small onions

2 tablespoons butter

2 tablespoons flour

¼ teaspoon nutmeg

¼ teaspoon salt

Dash of pepper

1 cup milk

3 ounces cream cheese, cut into small pieces

2 tablespoons butter

1 cup soft bread crumbs

¼ cup grated Parmesan cheese

♦ Cook the broccoli and onions using package instructions; drain.

♦ Preheat the oven to 350 degrees.

♦ Melt 2 tablespoons butter in a medium saucepan over low heat. Blend in the flour, nutmeg, salt and pepper. Remove from heat; stir in the milk gradually.

♦ Cook over low heat until thickened, stirring constantly. Add cream cheese; whisk until smooth.

♦ Combine the sauce with the vegetables and spoon into a 2-quart casserole.

♦ Bake at 350 degrees for 20 minutes.

♦ Melt the remaining 2 tablespoons butter in a small saucepan; toss with the bread crumbs and Parmesan cheese. Sprinkle over the top of the casserole.

♦ Bake for 15 to 20 minutes longer.

CABBAGE BOHEMIAN

Makes 4 to 6 servings

½ head cabbage

3 slices bacon

1 tablespoon vegetable oil

1 large onion, thinly sliced

½ cup chicken stock

1 teaspoon cider vinegar

Salt and pepper to taste

½ teaspoon caraway seeds

♦ Shred the cabbage with a knife; do not use a grater.

♦ Fry the bacon in a large skillet until crisp; drain and crumble. Discard the bacon drippings. Pour the oil into the skillet and heat over high heat.

♦ Add the cabbage and onion. Stir-fry until golden brown at the edges. Stir in the chicken stock and vinegar.

♦ Cook, covered, for several minutes or until tender-crisp.

♦ Season with salt, pepper and caraway seeds. Stir in the crumbled bacon.

♦ Serve immediately.

Spiced Red Cabbage

Makes 4 to 6 servings

6 peppercorns
2 whole allspice
2 whole cloves
1 bay leaf
1½ cups water
½ cup sugar
2 medium cooking apples, sliced
1 medium head red cabbage
1 medium onion, sliced
1 tablespoon bacon drippings
3 tablespoons cornstarch
¾ cup white vinegar

♦ Enclose the peppercorns, allspice, cloves and bay leaf in a cheesecloth spice bag.

♦ Bring the water to a boil in a 5-quart Dutch oven with the spice bag. Add the sugar, apples, cabbage and onion; reduce heat. Simmer for 10 to 15 minutes or until the cabbage is tender-crisp, stirring occasionally.

♦ Discard the spice bag. Add the bacon drippings to the cabbage mixture.

♦ Combine the cornstarch and vinegar in a small bowl; blend until smooth. Add to the cabbage mixture gradually, stirring constantly. Cook over low heat until thickened, stirring constantly.

♦ Serve immediately.

For a lighter flavor, omit the bacon drippings and stir in 2 slices crumbled crisp-fried bacon just before serving.

Cauliflower Casserole

Makes 8 servings

1 large or 2 medium heads cauliflower
¼ cup butter
2 tablespoons flour
1 bouillon cube, crumbled
1 cup milk
6 to 8 ounces Gruyére cheese, shredded
¼ cup water
¼ cup butter
½ cup herb-seasoned stuffing
¼ cup slivered almonds

♦ Rinse the cauliflower and separate into florets. Cook in boiling water to cover in a saucepan for 15 minutes; drain.

♦ Preheat the oven to 400 degrees.

♦ Melt the butter in a small skillet. Add the flour and crumbled bouillon, stirring to make a paste. Cool. Add the milk and cheese. Cook until thickened and smooth, stirring constantly.

♦ Pour the bouillon mixture over the cauliflower, tossing gently to coat. Spoon into a 2-quart casserole.

♦ Topping: Heat the water and butter in a small skillet. Stir in the stuffing and almonds. Sprinkle over the cauliflower mixture.

♦ Bake at 400 degrees for 30 minutes.

GINGER CARROTS

Makes 4 servings

Even people who dislike carrots will like this recipe.

7 or 8 medium carrots
Salt to taste
1 tablespoon sugar
1 teaspoon cornstarch
1/4 teaspoon salt
1/4 teaspoon ground ginger
1/4 cup orange juice
2 tablespoons butter
Chopped parsley to taste

- Slice the carrots diagonally into 1/2-inch slices.
- Cook, covered, in salted water until tender.
- Combine the sugar, cornstarch, 1/4 teaspoon salt and ginger in a saucepan. Add the orange juice and cook over medium heat until thick and bubbly, stirring constantly. Stir in the butter.
- Pour the ginger mixture over the hot carrots; toss to coat. Top with the parsley.

SCALLOPED CORN AND TOMATOES

Makes 8 servings

1 cup thinly sliced onion
3 tablespoons butter
2 pounds tomatoes, peeled, chopped
1 tablespoon sugar
1 teaspoon salt
1 teaspoon dried marjoram leaves
1/4 teaspoon pepper
2 (10-ounce) packages frozen Shoe Peg corn, thawed
1 tablespoon butter
2 cups seasoned croutons or 1/2 cup Italian bread crumbs
2 teaspoons chopped parsley

- Preheat the oven to 350 degrees.
- Sauté the onion in 3 tablespoons butter in a skillet for 5 minutes or until tender and golden brown. Stir in the tomatoes, sugar, salt, marjoram, pepper and corn; mix well.
- Spoon into a greased 2-quart baking dish.
- Melt 1 tablespoon butter in a small skillet. Add the croutons and parsley; mix well. Sprinkle over the corn mixture.
- Bake at 350 degrees for 20 minutes or until browned.

Serve as an accompaniment to steaks or grilled fish.

CORN SPOON BREAD

Makes 8 to 10 servings

1 (16-ounce) can cream-style corn

1 (17-ounce) can whole kernel corn

½ cup melted margarine

2 eggs, beaten

1 (8-ounce) package corn muffin mix

1 cup sour cream

♦ Preheat the oven to 350 degrees.

♦ Combine the cream-style corn, undrained whole kernel corn, margarine, eggs, corn muffin mix and sour cream in a large bowl; mix well.

♦ Spoon into a greased 9x13-inch baking dish.

♦ Bake at 350 degrees for 45 to 50 minutes or until golden brown.

EGGPLANT DOME CASSEROLE

Makes 8 servings

1 eggplant, unpeeled, cut into ⅜-inch slices

½ cup seasoned flour

Vegetable oil for frying

1 clove of garlic, crushed

2 green bell peppers, cut into strips

2 medium onions, chopped

1 cup seasoned bread crumbs

2 tomatoes, thickly sliced

2 cups shredded mozzarella cheese

3 eggs

¾ cup milk

Salt and pepper to taste

Allspice to taste

Thyme and parsley to taste

Basil and parsley for garnish

♦ Preheat the oven to 350 degrees.

♦ Coat the eggplant slices with flour. Heat the desired amount of oil with garlic in a large skillet. Cook the eggplant in the oil, browning both sides. Drain the eggplant.

♦ Sauté the green peppers and onions, one at a time, in the skillet; set aside.

♦ Sprinkle a lightly greased 2-quart casserole with half the bread crumbs.

♦ Alternate layers of eggplant, tomatoes, sautéed green pepper, bread crumbs, sautéed onions and mozzarella cheese until all ingredients are used, ending with bread crumbs.

♦ Beat the eggs with the milk, salt, pepper, allspice, thyme and parsley in a small mixer bowl. Pour over the layers.

♦ Bake at 350 degrees for 45 minutes or until golden brown and set.

♦ Let stand for 10 minutes.

♦ Loosen from side of casserole with a knife. Invert onto a serving plate.

♦ Garnish with fresh basil or parsley.

MEDITERRANEAN SAUTE

Makes 4 servings

Add any fresh vegetables to this dish, such as broccoli or mushrooms. Chopped chicken, turkey or ham may be added as well.

1 cup red or green bell pepper strips
1 cup zucchini slices
1/2 cup Vidalia onion rings
1/2 teaspoon dried oregano leaves, crushed
1 tablespoon butter
1/2 cup cherry tomato halves
3/4 cup crumbled feta cheese

♦ Sauté the red pepper, zucchini, onions and oregano in the butter in a large skillet over medium heat. Stir in the tomatoes. Cook for 1 minute longer.

♦ Remove from heat and top with the feta cheese.

BAKED VIDALIA ONIONS

Makes 4 servings

4 large Vidalia onions
4 tablespoons butter
1 teaspoon salt
1/8 teaspoon pepper
Parmesan cheese to taste

♦ Preheat the oven to 375 degrees.

♦ Trim and peel each onion. Cut as if to quarter, but not through the bottom.

♦ Press 1 tablespoon butter into center of each onion. Sprinkle with salt and pepper. Coat with a generous amount of Parmesan cheese. Wrap each onion in foil.

♦ Bake at 375 degrees for 1 hour.

Serve with roast beef or steak.

SWEET-AND-SOUR VIDALIA ONIONS

Makes 4 to 6 servings

6 large Vidalia onions, sliced
1/4 cup cider vinegar
1/2 cup melted butter
1/2 cup boiling water
1/2 cup packed brown sugar

♦ Preheat the oven to 300 degrees.

♦ Place the sliced onions in a 2-quart baking dish. Combine the vinegar, butter, boiling water and brown sugar in a small bowl; pour over the onions.

♦ Bake, covered, at 300 degrees for 1 hour.

Serve with grilled hamburgers.

GRATED PARSNIPS AND CARROTS

Makes 8 servings

1/2 cup butter
2 tablespoons sugar
1 pound carrots, grated
1 pound parsnips, grated
1/4 cup white wine
Salt and pepper to taste

♦ Melt the butter and sugar in a large skillet. Add the carrots, parsnips and wine, stirring until well mixed.

♦ Cook, covered, over medium heat for 5 minutes or until tender-crisp, stirring several times. Sprinkle with salt and pepper.

POTATOES GRATIN

Makes 6 to 8 servings

2 tablespoons unsalted butter
2 cloves of garlic, minced, or
  1 tablespoon finely chopped
  onion
2 cups shredded Gruyère cheese
8 to 10 russet potatoes, peeled,
  thinly sliced
Salt and pepper to taste
1 egg, beaten
1 cup milk
1 cup half-and-half

♦ Preheat the oven to 375 degrees.

♦ Grease the bottom and sides of a 9x13-inch baking dish with butter; sprinkle garlic over the bottom.

♦ Reserve 2 tablespoons of the cheese. Alternate layers of potato slices, salt, pepper and the remaining cheese.

♦ Whisk the egg, milk and half-and-half in a small bowl. Pour over the potatoes. Sprinkle the reserved cheese on top.

♦ Bake at 375 degrees for 1 hour or until potatoes are tender and the top is bubbly and golden brown.

Sauté 1 large sliced onion in 1 tablespoon butter and layer with the potatoes for a tasty addition.

ROASTED NEW POTATO CASSEROLE

Makes 6 servings

6 large new potatoes, sliced
1 red bell pepper, seeded,
  chopped
1 large Vidalia or other sweet
  onion, chopped
6 to 8 slices prosciutto, cut into
  1-inch pieces
1 to 2 tablespoons olive oil
1 teaspoon herbed garlic salt or
  salt, pepper and rosemary to
  taste

♦ Preheat the oven to 400 degrees.

♦ Place the vegetables and prosciutto in a roasting pan. Drizzle with olive oil and sprinkle with the garlic salt. Toss to coat.

♦ Bake at 400 degrees for 45 minutes or until onion is browned and potatoes are tender, stirring occasionally.

Serve with grilled meats in the summer or pheasant in the winter.

TWICE-BAKED GARDEN POTATOES

Makes 8 servings

4 baking potatoes
1 tablespoon vegetable oil
1 small onion, chopped
¼ cup butter
2 cups shredded cabbage
1 cup grated carrots
½ cup water
⅓ cup chopped green bell pepper
½ teaspoon salt
⅛ teaspoon white pepper
Carrot curls for garnish

♦ Preheat the oven to 400 degrees.

♦ Coat the potatoes with the oil.

♦ Bake on a baking sheet at 400 degrees for 1 hour.

♦ Sauté the onion in the butter in a large skillet until tender. Add the cabbage, carrots and water. Simmer, covered, for 10 minutes. Add the green pepper. Simmer for 5 minutes longer or until liquid is absorbed.

♦ Cut the potatoes into halves lengthwise. Scoop out the pulp, leaving the shells intact. Reserve the shells.

♦ Mash the pulp and add the vegetable mixture; mix well. Season with the salt and white pepper.

♦ Stuff the reserved potato shells with the vegetable mixture.

♦ Bake on a baking sheet at 400 degrees for 15 minutes.

♦ Garnish with carrot curls.

WHIPPED PARTY POTATOES

Makes 10 to 12 servings

If refrigerated for 8 to 12 hours before baking, the taste of these potatoes improves. Increase the baking time to 1¼ hours. Leftovers can be shaped into patties, dipped in flour and sautéed in butter.

8 to 10 large potatoes, peeled, sliced
1 cup sour cream
8 ounces cream cheese, softened
2 tablespoons unsalted butter
1 teaspoon garlic salt
1 teaspoon onion salt
½ teaspoon cracked black pepper
Paprika to taste

♦ Boil the potatoes in water to cover until tender; drain.

♦ Preheat the oven to 350 degrees.

♦ Beat the sour cream, cream cheese, butter, garlic salt, onion salt and pepper in a mixer bowl until smooth. Add the hot potatoes gradually, beating until potatoes are fluffy after each addition.

♦ Spoon the potato mixture into a greased 2-quart baking dish. Sprinkle with paprika.

♦ Bake at 350 degrees for 45 to 50 minutes.

RATATOUILLE

Makes 6 to 8 servings

A good use of your fresh garden vegetables.

3 cloves of garlic, chopped

1 cup coarsely chopped onion

1 tablespoon olive oil

1 large eggplant, cubed

3 medium zucchini, sliced

1 large green bell pepper, chopped

1 teaspoon oregano

3 tomatoes, peeled, chopped

1 teaspoon sugar

1/2 teaspoon pepper

Parmesan cheese to taste

♦ Sauté the garlic and onion in the oil in a large saucepan for 5 minutes or until tender. Stir in the eggplant, zucchini, green pepper and oregano. Simmer for 5 minutes.

♦ Add the tomatoes, sugar and pepper. Cook over low heat for 30 minutes.

♦ Serve the ratatouille hot or chilled, garnished with grated Parmesan cheese.

Can be served in pita bread for lunch.

HARVEST RUTABAGA

Makes 4 servings

4 cups cubed peeled rutabagas

1/4 cup sugar

1 1/2 teaspoons Worcestershire sauce

1/4 teaspoon onion powder

1 teaspoon salt

4 drops of Tabasco sauce

1/4 cup melted butter

♦ Combine the rutabagas, sugar, Worcestershire sauce, onion powder, salt and Tabasco sauce in a saucepan. Add enough water to cover; bring to a boil.

♦ Cook, covered, over low heat for 30 minutes or until the rutabagas are tender; drain.

♦ Add the butter; mash to the desired consistency.

Serve with pot roast on a cool fall evening.

SPINACH AND ARTICHOKE CASSEROLE

Makes 6 to 8 servings

1/2 cup chopped onions
1/4 cup butter
8 ounces cream cheese, softened
3 tablespoons lemon juice
Salt and pepper to taste
2 (10-ounce) packages frozen chopped spinach, thawed, drained
1 (14-ounce) can artichoke hearts, drained, quartered
1 (8-ounce) can sliced water chestnuts, drained
1 cup shredded Swiss cheese
1/4 cup grated Parmesan cheese

♦ Preheat the oven to 350 degrees.

♦ Sauté the onions in the butter in a small saucepan until tender. Add the cream cheese. Cook over very low heat until smooth, whisking constantly. Add the lemon juice, salt and pepper.

♦ Combine the spinach, artichokes and water chestnuts in a large bowl.

♦ Pour the cream cheese mixture over the top and toss to coat.

♦ Spoon into a 2-quart baking dish. Top with the Swiss and Parmesan cheeses.

♦ Bake at 350 degrees for 30 minutes or until hot and bubbly.

TWICE-BAKED SWEET POTATOES

Makes 6 servings

6 medium sweet potatoes
1/2 cup peach or apricot preserves
1/4 cup butter, softened
1 teaspoon salt
Orange juice
Nutmeg to taste

♦ Preheat the oven to 350 degrees.

♦ Place the sweet potatoes in a small baking pan.

♦ Bake at 350 degrees for 1 hour or until tender.

♦ Slice off the top of each potato lengthwise. Scoop out the pulp, leaving the shells intact. Reserve the shells.

♦ Place the pulp in a large mixer bowl. Add the preserves, butter and salt; beat until smooth. Add enough orange juice to moisten; mix well.

♦ Stuff the reserved shells with the sweet potato mixture. Sprinkle with nutmeg.

♦ Bake at 350 degrees for 20 minutes or until heated through.

HOT HERBED TOMATOES

Makes 10 to 12 servings

4 cups cherry tomatoes

¾ cup soft bread crumbs

¼ cup each minced onion and fresh parsley

1 clove of garlic, minced

½ teaspoon salt

¼ teaspoon each thyme, marjoram and pepper

¼ cup olive oil

- Preheat the oven to 400 degrees.
- Place the tomatoes in a single layer in a lightly greased 9x13-inch baking dish.
- Mix crumbs, onion, parsley, garlic and seasonings in a small bowl. Sprinkle over the tomatoes. Drizzle with olive oil.
- Bake at 400 degrees for 6 to 8 minutes or until the tomatoes are puffed.

SUMMER TOMATOES STUFFED WITH BROCCOLI

Makes 4 servings

4 medium tomatoes

Salt to taste

2 tablespoons finely minced onion

4 tablespoons butter

1 (10-ounce) package frozen chopped broccoli, cooked

¼ cup shredded sharp Cheddar cheese

8 slices sharp Cheddar cheese

- Preheat the oven to 350 degrees.
- Slice the tomatoes into halves. Remove the stems. Arrange cut sides up in a baking dish. Salt generously.
- Sauté the onion in the butter in a small skillet until tender.
- Drain broccoli well. Mix with onion and ¼ cup cheese. Mound the broccoli mixture on tomato halves. Cover with 1 cheese slice.
- Bake at 350 degrees for 20 minutes.

CHEESE-TOPPED ZUCCHINI

Makes 5 to 6 servings

3 medium or 5 small zucchini

1 medium onion, thinly sliced

1 tablespoon vegetable oil

Salt and pepper to taste

½ teaspoon crushed oregano

1 (8-ounce) can tomato sauce

1½ cups shredded mozzarella cheese

Parmesan cheese to taste

- Cut the zucchini lengthwise into ½-inch slices; set aside.
- Sauté the onion in oil in a large heavy skillet until tender. Add the zucchini, seasonings and tomato sauce. Cook, covered, over medium heat for 10 minutes or until tender.
- Top with mozzarella cheese. Cook, uncovered, for 1 to 2 minutes. Sprinkle with Parmesan cheese.

For a fancier presentation, transfer zucchini to gratin dish, top with cheese, and bake at 350 degrees for 20 minutes.

ZUCCHINI BOATS

Makes 6 servings

3 medium zucchini

1 pound sweet Italian sausage meat

2 tablespoons olive oil

1 large onion, finely chopped

1 clove of garlic, minced

3 to 4 tablespoons light cream

1/2 cup grated Parmesan cheese

Dash of nutmeg

Salt and pepper to taste

1/2 cup shredded Cheddar or mozzarella cheese

♦ Preheat the oven to 350 degrees.

♦ Cut the zucchini into halves lengthwise. Scoop out the seeds, leaving the shells intact. Reserve the shells. Sauté the sausage in 1 tablespoon of the olive oil in a skillet, stirring until crumbly and brown; drain the sausage and set aside.

♦ Add the remaining olive oil to the drippings in the skillet. Sauté the onion and garlic in the skillet over low heat until tender.

♦ Return the sausage to the skillet with the onion and garlic. Add the cream, 1/4 cup of the Parmesan cheese and nutmeg. Season with salt and pepper. Cook over low heat until thickened, stirring constantly.

♦ Fill reserved zucchini shells with the sausage mixture. Place the shells in a baking dish. Pour a small amount of water around the zucchini. Bake, covered, at 350 degrees for 30 minutes or until the zucchini is tender.

♦ Preheat the broiler.

♦ Sprinkle the Cheddar cheese and the remaining 1/4 cup Parmesan cheese over the sausage mixture.

♦ Broil for 5 minutes or until bubbly.

VEGETABLE MEDLEY

Makes 4 to 6 servings

1/2 pound asparagus, cut into 1-inch pieces

1/2 pound carrots, julienned

1 yellow squash, sliced

3 tablespoons melted butter

3 tablespoons lemon juice

1/2 teaspoon basil

1/2 teaspoon thyme

1/4 teaspoon salt

♦ Steam the asparagus, carrots and squash in a steamer for 10 minutes or until tender-crisp.

♦ Combine the butter, lemon juice, basil, thyme and salt in a large bowl. Add the vegetables and toss gently.

♦ Serve immediately.

Fresh green beans are a good alternative to the asparagus.

CURRIED FRUIT

Makes 8 to 10 servings

1 (16-ounce) can pineapple slices, drained

1 (16-ounce) can pear halves, drained

1 (16-ounce) can peach halves, drained

1 (16-ounce) can apricot halves, drained

1 (11-ounce) can mandarin oranges, drained

1/3 cup butter

3/4 cup packed brown sugar

4 teaspoons curry powder

Pinch of salt

♦ Preheat the oven to 350 degrees.

♦ Combine the pineapples, pears, peaches, apricots and mandarin oranges in a large bowl; toss gently. Spoon into a large baking dish.

♦ Combine the butter, brown sugar, curry powder and salt in a small saucepan. Heat until well mixed and sugar is dissolved, stirring constantly. Pour over the fruit.

♦ Bake at 350 degrees for 1 hour. Drain some of the liquid before serving if desired.

Serve with chicken, ham or pork.

FRUITED RICE CURRY

Makes 6 servings

1 cup long grain rice

1 tablespoon instant minced onion

2 teaspoons curry powder

2 beef bouillon cubes

1/2 teaspoon salt

1/4 cup dried fruit bits

2 tablespoons golden raisins

1/4 cup blanched slivered almonds

2 1/2 cups water

2 tablespoons butter

♦ Combine the rice, onion, curry powder, bouillon cubes, salt, fruit bits, raisins and almonds in a large saucepan. Add the water and butter.

♦ Bring to a boil. Reduce heat. Simmer, covered, for 20 minutes or until all the water is absorbed.

Serve with grilled pork tenderloin.

PERFECT NO-PEEK RICE

Makes 6 servings

3/4 cup brown rice
3/4 cup long grain rice
1/4 teaspoon dried basil
1/4 teaspoon sage
2 chicken bouillon cubes
1 tablespoon butter
3 1/2 cups boiling water

♦ Preheat the oven to 350 degrees.

♦ Combine the brown rice, long grain rice, basil, sage, bouillon and butter in a greased baking pan. Add the boiling water, stirring until the bouillon dissolves and the butter melts.

♦ Bake, covered, at 350 degrees for 45 to 55 minutes or until liquid is absorbed.

For variety, sauté 8 ounces sliced mushrooms, the chopped white part of 2 green onions and 1/3 cup chopped pecans in 3 tablespoons butter. Add to the rice mixture before baking.

WILD RICE WITH MUSHROOMS

Makes 4 servings

1 cup uncooked wild rice
1/2 cup slivered almonds
2 tablespoons chopped green onions
8 ounces sliced fresh mushrooms
1/4 cup butter
3 cups chicken broth, heated

♦ Preheat the oven to 350 degrees.

♦ Rinse and drain the wild rice.

♦ Sauté the wild rice, almonds, green onions and mushrooms in butter in a skillet for 15 minutes or until the almonds are golden brown.

♦ Pour the rice mixture into a 1 1/2-quart baking dish and add the chicken broth.

♦ Bake, covered, at 350 degrees for 1 1/2 hours or until all the liquid is absorbed.

Serve as an accompaniment to seafood or poultry dishes.

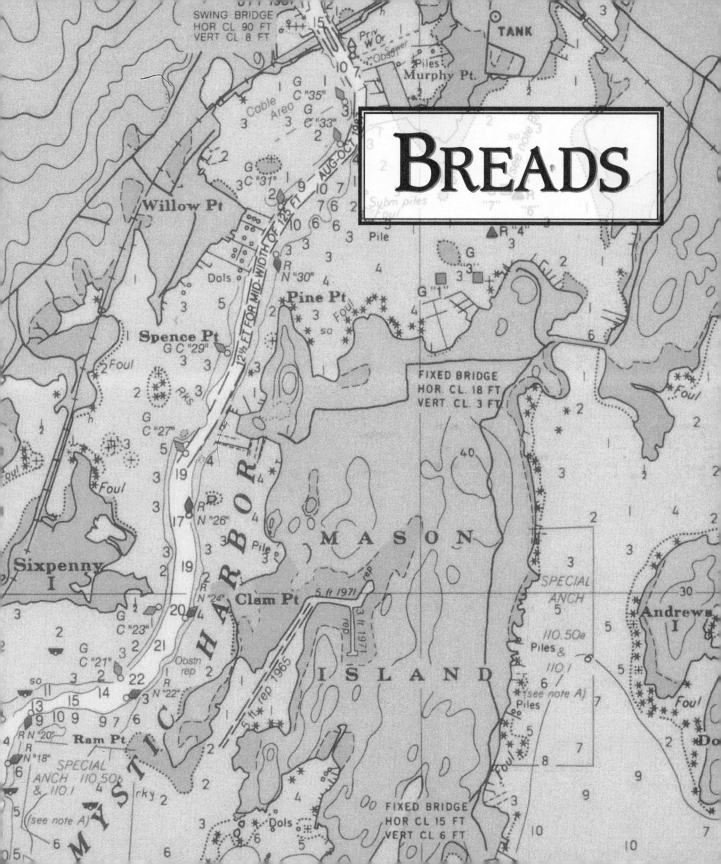

BREADS

BREADS

♦ ♦ ♦ ♦ ♦ ♦ ♦ ♦ ♦ ♦ ♦ ♦ ♦

HERBED SOUR CREAM BISCUITS

Makes 18 biscuits

4 cups flour

5 teaspoons baking powder

1/2 teaspoon baking soda

2 teaspoons dillweed

1 teaspoon dried basil

3/4 teaspoon salt

1 teaspoon pepper

1/2 teaspoon dried thyme leaves

1/2 cup butter or margarine

8 ounces sour cream

1 cup milk

♦ Preheat the oven to 450 degrees.

♦ Sift flour, baking powder, baking soda, dillweed, basil, salt, pepper and thyme into a large bowl. Cut in butter until crumbly.

♦ Make a well in the center. Add sour cream and milk; mix well with a wooden spoon. Roll to 1/2-inch thickness on lightly floured surface; cut with a 2-inch round biscuit cutter. Place on lightly greased baking sheet.

♦ Bake at 450 degrees for 15 to 18 minutes or until golden brown.

SOUR CREAM MUFFINS

Makes 12 regular or 24 small muffins

2 cups self-rising flour

1/2 cup melted margarine

1 cup sour cream

♦ Preheat the oven to 400 degrees.

♦ Combine the flour, margarine and sour cream in a medium bowl and mix until thick and creamy. Spoon into ungreased regular or miniature muffin cups.

♦ Bake at 400 degrees for 15 to 20 minutes for regular and 12 to 14 minutes for miniature muffins.

ENGLISH SCONES

Makes 12 scones

Serve with your favorite preserves at teatime.

1 1/2 cups flour

1 teaspoon cream of tartar

1/2 teaspoon baking soda

1/2 teaspoon salt

4 tablespoons butter

2/3 cup milk

♦ Preheat the oven to 425 degrees.

♦ Sift the flour, cream of tartar, baking soda and salt into a medium bowl. Cut in the butter until crumbly. Stir in the milk gradually. Roll 1/2 inch thick on a lightly floured surface; cut with a 2 to 2 1/2-inch biscuit cutter.

♦ Place close together on a greased baking sheet. Dust the tops lightly with flour.

♦ Bake at 425 degrees for 12 to 15 minutes or until golden brown.

BLUEBERRY COFFEE CAKE

Makes 9 squares

³/₄ cup sugar
¹/₄ cup butter
1 egg
¹/₂ cup milk
2 cups flour
2 teaspoons baking powder
¹/₂ teaspoon cinnamon
¹/₄ teaspoon salt
2 cups fresh blueberries
Streusel Topping

- Preheat the oven to 375 degrees.
- Cream the sugar and butter in a large bowl until light. Stir in the egg and milk.
- Sift together the flour, baking powder, cinnamon and salt. Stir into creamed mixture. Fold in the blueberries. Spoon the batter into a greased 9-inch square baking pan. Sprinkle with the Streusel Topping.
- Bake at 375 degrees for 45 to 50 minutes or until a wooden pick inserted in the center comes out clean.
- Cut into squares.

Streusel Topping

¹/₂ cup sugar
¹/₃ cup flour
¹/₂ teaspoon cinnamon
¹/₄ cup butter

- Sift the sugar, flour and cinnamon into a medium bowl. Cut in the butter until crumbly.

FRUIT AND YOGURT COFFEE CAKE

Makes 16 servings

1 (6-ounce) package dried fruit bits
¹/₂ cup butter, softened
1 cup sugar
2 eggs
1 cup vanilla yogurt
2 cups flour
1 teaspoon baking powder
1 teaspoon baking soda
¹/₂ teaspoon cinnamon
¹/₄ teaspoon salt
¹/₂ cup chopped nuts
¹/₄ cup sugar
¹/₂ teaspoon cinnamon

- Soak the fruit in hot water to cover for 10 minutes; drain.
- Cream the butter and 1 cup sugar in a large bowl until light and fluffy. Beat in eggs, one at a time. Blend in yogurt.
- Sift in the flour, baking powder, baking soda, ¹/₂ teaspoon cinnamon and salt; mix well. Mix in the fruit.
- Spoon into a greased 9x13-inch baking pan.
- Sprinkle mixture of nuts, ¹/₄ cup sugar and ¹/₂ teaspoon cinnamon over the batter.
- Chill, covered, for 8 hours or longer.
- Preheat the oven to 350 degrees.
- Bake at 350 degrees for 30 to 35 minutes or until the coffee cake tests done.

PULL-APART CINNAMON NUT BREAD

Makes 12 servings

3 (10-count) cans buttermilk
  biscuits
Cinnamon-sugar
1/2 cup butter
1 cup packed light brown sugar
1/2 to 1 cup raisins
1 cup chopped pecans

♦ Preheat the oven to 350 degrees.

♦ Cut each biscuit into quarters. Shake in cinnamon-sugar
  to coat.

♦ Melt the butter in a small saucepan over low heat. Stir in
  the brown sugar and bring to a boil. Boil for 1 minute.

♦ Alternate layers of the biscuit quarters, raisins, nuts and
  brown sugar mixture in a greased bundt or deep baking
  pan, ending with the brown sugar mixture.

♦ Bake at 350 degrees for 30 minutes.

♦ Cool in the pan for 5 minutes. Invert onto a warmed
  serving plate.

WELSH CAKES

Makes 60 small cakes

These special cakes can be made ahead of time.

4 cups flour
2 cups sugar
1 tablespoon baking powder
1 teaspoon salt
1 teaspoon nutmeg
1 cup butter
3 eggs
Milk
1 cup currants

♦ Sift the dry ingredients into a medium bowl. Cut in the
  butter until crumbly.

♦ Beat the eggs in a 1-cup measure. Add enough milk to
  measure 1 scant cup.

♦ Make a well in the center of the flour mixture and add the
  egg mixture, mixing until smooth. Stir in the currants. Chill
  for several hours or overnight.

♦ Preheat a griddle or electric skillet to 350 degrees.

♦ Roll the dough, a small amount at a time, between layers of
  waxed paper to a thickness of 1/4 inch. Cut with a 2-inch
  biscuit cutter. Keep the unrolled dough chilled.

♦ Cook on the lightly greased hot griddle or skillet until
  golden brown, turning once.

♦ Remove to a wire rack to cool.

APPLE CAKE WITH SAUSAGE

Makes 4 to 6 servings

2 tablespoons melted butter

²/₃ cup milk

1 egg, beaten

1 cup flour

2 tablespoons sugar

2 teaspoons baking powder

¼ teaspoon salt

¼ teaspoon nutmeg

¼ teaspoon cinnamon

½ cup finely chopped apple

1 (8-ounce) package frozen brown-and- serve sausage, thawed

♦ Preheat the oven to 450 degrees.

♦ Combine the butter, milk and egg in a large bowl.

♦ Sift the flour, sugar, baking powder, salt, nutmeg and cinnamon together. Add to the milk mixture; mix just until blended. Stir in the apple.

♦ Spoon the batter into a greased 7x11-inch baking dish.

♦ Arrange the sausage over the batter.

♦ Bake at 450 degrees for 15 minutes.

♦ Cut into squares and serve hot with butter and syrup.

CRANBERRY CORNBREAD

Makes 15 servings

Native grain and tart fruit make this bread a special addition to the harvest table.

½ cup butter, softened

1 cup sugar

2 eggs, beaten

1 cup buttermilk

1 cup yellow cornmeal

2 cups flour

4 teaspoons baking powder

½ teaspoon salt

2 cups cranberries, chopped

♦ Preheat the oven to 350 degrees.

♦ Cream the butter and sugar in a medium bowl until light. Stir in the eggs and buttermilk.

♦ Sift the cornmeal, flour, baking powder and salt together. Stir into the creamed mixture gradually.

♦ Fold in the cranberries.

♦ Spoon the batter into a greased 9x13-inch baking pan.

♦ Bake at 350 degrees for 30 to 35 minutes or until the center springs back when touched lightly.

MEXICAN CORNBREAD

Makes 12 servings

1 cup cornmeal

1 teaspoon baking powder

1/2 teaspoon baking soda

1/2 teaspoon salt

2 eggs

1/2 cup melted butter

1 cup buttermilk

1 cup cream-style corn

1 small onion, grated

1 (4-ounce) can chopped green
chiles, drained

1 cup shredded sharp Cheddar
cheese

♦ Preheat the oven to 350 degrees.

♦ Combine the cornmeal, baking powder, baking soda and
salt in a large bowl. Add eggs, butter and buttermilk; mix
well. Stir in the corn and onion.

♦ Pour half the batter into a greased 9x9-inch square baking
pan. Sprinkle with the chiles and cheese. Top with the
remaining batter.

♦ Bake at 350 degrees for 1 hour.

ONION CORNBREAD

Makes 9 servings

1 sweet Spanish onion, sliced

1/4 cup butter

1 cup sour cream

1/4 teaspoon salt

1/4 teaspoon dillweed

1 cup shredded sharp Cheddar
cheese

1 1/2 cups corn muffin mix

1 egg, beaten

1/3 cup milk

2 drops of Tabasco sauce

1 cup cream-style corn

♦ Preheat the oven to 425 degrees.

♦ Sauté the onion in the butter in a medium skillet over low
heat until tender. Cool slightly.

♦ Stir in the sour cream, salt, dillweed and half the cheese.

♦ Combine the muffin mix, egg, milk and Tabasco sauce in a
medium bowl and beat until well mixed. Stir in the corn.

♦ Spoon into a greased 8x8-inch square baking pan.

♦ Spoon the onion mixture over the batter and top with the
remaining cheese.

♦ Bake at 425 degrees for 25 to 30 minutes or until golden
brown.

♦ Cut into squares and serve warm.

SKIER'S FRENCH TOAST

Makes 8 servings

A make ahead breakfast that's sure to please your houseguests.

1 (10-ounce) loaf French bread

8 eggs

3 cups milk

4 teaspoons sugar

1/2 teaspoon salt

1 tablespoon vanilla extract

2 tablespoons butter, cut into small pieces

♦ Cut the bread into 1-inch thick slices and arrange in a greased 9x13-inch baking pan.

♦ Combine the eggs, milk, sugar, salt and vanilla in a large bowl and beat until smooth. Pour over the bread and dot with the butter.

♦ Chill, covered with foil, overnight.

♦ Uncover; place in cold oven.

♦ Bake at 350 degrees for 45 to 50 minutes or until the bread is puffy and lightly browned. Remove from the oven and let stand for 5 minutes before serving.

Serve with syrups of choice and sausage links browned, then simmered with apple slices, brown sugar and lemon juice.

RUM RAISIN FRENCH TOAST

Makes 3 to 4 servings

3/4 cup rum raisin ice cream, melted

3 eggs, beaten

1 tablespoon dark rum

1/4 teaspoon cinnamon

5 tablespoons finely ground pecans

6 to 8 slices cinnamon bread

Butter

Rum raisin ice cream

Maple syrup

♦ Combine the melted ice cream, eggs, rum, cinnamon and pecans in a medium bowl and mix well.

♦ Dip the bread slices in the ice cream mixture, coating both sides.

♦ Sauté in butter in a medium skillet over medium-low heat until golden brown.

♦ Top each serving with a scoop of the rum raisin ice cream and maple syrup.

ALL-SEASONS MUFFINS

Makes 1½ dozen

2 eggs
1 cup sugar
¼ cup light vegetable oil
1 cup plain yogurt
1 teaspoon vanilla extract
1¾ cups chopped fresh rhubarb
2 cups flour
2 teaspoons baking powder
½ teaspoon baking soda
½ teaspoon salt
¼ teaspoon cinnamon

♦ Preheat the oven to 375 degrees.

♦ Combine the eggs, sugar, oil, yogurt and vanilla in a large bowl; mix well. Stir in fruit.

♦ Sift the flour, baking powder, baking soda, salt and cinnamon together. Fold into the egg mixture; do not over mix.

♦ Fill greased muffin tins ⅔ full.

♦ Bake at 375 degrees for 25 minutes.

♦ Remove from the muffin tins and cool on a wire rack.

For a summer muffin use 1 cup blueberries. For an autumn muffin use 1 cup coarsely chopped cranberries.

YANKEE APPLESAUCE MUFFINS

Makes 1 dozen

Chunky homemade applesauce adds to the taste and texture of these muffins.

3 cups flour
⅓ cup sugar
1 teaspoon cinnamon
4 teaspoons baking powder
¾ teaspoon baking soda
½ teaspoon salt
1½ cups applesauce
6 tablespoons melted butter
½ cup milk
1 egg
¾ cup chopped walnuts
Cinnamon-sugar

♦ Preheat the oven to 400 degrees.

♦ Combine the flour, sugar, cinnamon, baking powder, baking soda and salt in a large bowl; mix with a fork.

♦ Blend the applesauce, butter, milk and egg in a medium bowl. Add to the flour mixture; mix until just moistened. Mixture will be lumpy. Stir in the walnuts.

♦ Spoon into greased muffin tins. Sprinkle with cinnamon-sugar.

♦ Bake at 400 degrees for 20 to 25 minutes or until a wooden pick inserted in the center comes out clean. Remove from pan immediately.

BUTTERMILK RAISIN BRAN MUFFINS

Makes 4 to 5 dozen

1 (15-ounce) package raisin bran cereal

3 cups sugar

5 cups flour

5 teaspoons baking soda

2 teaspoons salt

4 eggs

4 cups buttermilk

1 cup melted butter

- Preheat the oven to 400 degrees.
- Combine the cereal, sugar, flour, baking soda and salt in a large bowl and toss to mix.
- Beat the eggs, buttermilk and butter in a medium bowl. Fold into the cereal mixture.
- Fill greased muffin tins almost to the top for large muffins.
- Bake at 400 degrees for 15 to 20 minutes or until the muffins test done.

Batter may be stored in a covered container for up to six weeks in the refrigerator. (The editors recommend that the recipe be prepared with egg substitute instead of fresh eggs for long-term storage.)

CINNAMON MUFFINS

Makes 3 dozen miniature muffins

These are a favorite with children.

^{1}/$_3$ cup butter

1 egg

^{1}/$_2$ cup milk

1^1/$_2$ cups flour

^{1}/$_2$ cup sugar

^{1}/$_4$ teaspoon nutmeg

1^1/$_2$ teaspoons baking powder

^{1}/$_2$ teaspoon salt

6 tablespoons melted butter

^{1}/$_2$ cup sugar

1 teaspoon cinnamon

- Preheat the oven to 350 degrees.
- Beat ^{1}/$_3$ cup butter in a medium bowl. Stir in the egg and milk alternately with mixture of flour, sugar, nutmeg, baking powder and salt.
- Fill miniature muffin tins sprayed with nonstick cooking spray ^{2}/$_3$ full.
- Bake at 350 degrees for 10 to 15 minutes or until the muffins test done.
- Remove from the muffin tins, dip tops in melted butter, and coat with mixture of sugar and cinnamon.

This recipe may be prepared ahead of time, frozen and wrapped in foil to reheat.

Oat Bran Muffins

Makes 1 dozen

Mix and match the spices to your choice of fruit. Don't omit the banana or you'll be sorry.

2 cups oat bran

2 teaspoons baking powder

1/4 teaspoon cinnamon or a dash of allspice, ginger, cloves, nutmeg or orange rind

1 banana, mashed

1/4 cup raisins or chopped dates or dried apricots or apples

1/4 cup chopped pecans

1 cup skim milk

2 egg whites, beaten

1/4 cup molasses

2 tablespoons vegetable oil

Cinnamon-sugar

Minced pecans

- Preheat the oven to 425 degrees.
- Combine the oat bran, baking powder and cinnamon in a large bowl.
- Add the banana, raisins, pecans, milk, egg whites, molasses and oil; mix well.
- Spray bottoms of paper-lined muffin tins with nonstick cooking spray. Fill 1/2 to 3/4 full. Sprinkle with mixture of cinnamon-sugar and minced pecans.
- Bake at 425 degrees for 17 minutes. Invert onto a wire rack to cool.

  May substitute 1/2 cup blueberries, chopped fresh peaches or apples for raisins or almonds or walnuts for the pecans.

Piña Colada Muffins

Makes 1 dozen

Serve as a festive accompaniment to a springtime breakfast or luncheon.

1/2 cup sugar

1 egg

1/4 cup butter, softened

1 cup sour cream

1 teaspoon rum extract

1 1/2 cups flour

1 teaspoon baking powder

1/2 teaspoon baking soda

1/2 teaspoon salt

1 (8-ounce) can crushed pineapple, drained

1/2 cup flaked coconut

- Preheat the oven to 375 degrees.
- Cream the sugar, egg and butter in a medium bowl until light. Add the sour cream and rum extract; beat until smooth. Sift in the flour, baking powder, baking soda and salt; mix just until moistened. Mix in the pineapple and coconut.
- Spoon into greased muffin tins.
- Bake at 375 degrees for 15 to 20 minutes or until the muffins test done.

APRICOT BREAD

Makes 1 loaf

This teatime bread can be made ahead and frozen.

1 cup dried apricots
1 cup sugar
2 tablespoons margarine, softened
1 egg, beaten
1/4 cup water
1/2 cup orange juice or apricot
 nectar
2 cups flour
1 tablespoon baking powder
1/4 teaspoon baking soda
1/4 teaspoon salt
1/2 cup chopped walnuts

♦ Preheat the oven to 350 degrees.

♦ Soak the apricots in hot water to cover in a bowl for 30 minutes; drain and chop.

♦ Cream the sugar and margarine in a medium bowl until light. Add the egg, beating until smooth. Stir in the water and orange juice. Add mixture of flour, baking powder, baking soda and salt; mix well. Stir in the walnuts and apricots.

♦ Spoon into a greased 5x9-inch loaf pan.

♦ Bake at 350 degrees for 1 hour or until a wooden pick inserted in the center comes out clean.

♦ Cool in the pan for 10 minutes. Invert onto a wire rack to cool completely.

BANANA BREAD

Makes 1 loaf

2 medium ripe bananas, mashed
2 eggs
1/2 cup vegetable oil
5 tablespoons buttermilk
1 1/2 cups sugar
1 teaspoon vanilla extract
1 3/4 cups flour
1 teaspoon baking soda
1/2 teaspoon salt
1 cup chopped walnuts

♦ Preheat the oven to 325 degrees.

♦ Combine the bananas, eggs, oil, buttermilk, sugar and vanilla in a large bowl; mix until well blended. Add a mixture of flour, baking soda and salt; mix well. Stir in walnuts.

♦ Pour into a greased and floured 5x9-inch loaf pan or 2 miniature loaf pans.

♦ Bake at 325 degrees for 1 hour and 20 minutes for large loaf or 40 minutes for smaller loaves or until the top is golden brown with a slight split.

♦ Invert onto a wire rack to cool.

May substitute 1/2 cup chocolate chips for half the walnuts.

BEER BREAD

Makes 1 loaf

3 cups self-rising flour

3 tablespoons sugar

1 (12-ounce) can beer, at room
temperature

1 egg (optional)

• Preheat the oven to 350 degrees.

• Combine the flour, sugar, beer and egg in a medium bowl;
mix well. Spoon the batter into a greased 5x9-inch loaf pan.

• Bake at 350 degrees for 45 to 50 minutes or until the bread
tests done.

• May substitute all-purpose flour with 1 teaspoon salt and 3
tablespoons baking powder for self-rising flour or substitute
1 cup oat or whole wheat flour for 1 cup of the self-rising
and add 2 teaspoons baking powder.

*May add desired amounts of caraway seeds, sunflower seeds
or bran or, for sweeter bread, add raisins or grated apple
and cinnamon and nutmeg to taste.*

LEMON BLUEBERRY TEA BREAD

Makes 1 loaf

2/3 cup butter, softened

1 cup sugar

2 eggs

1/2 cup milk

2 2/3 cups flour

2 teaspoons baking powder

1/4 teaspoon salt

3/4 cup chopped walnuts

2 teaspoons grated lemon rind

1 1/3 cups blueberries or coarsely
chopped cranberries

1/4 cup lemon juice

1/3 cup sugar

• Preheat the oven to 350 degrees.

• Cream the butter and 1 cup sugar in a medium bowl. Add
the eggs and milk, stirring until smooth.

• Combine flour, baking powder, salt, walnuts and lemon rind
in a bowl. Add to the creamed mixture; mix well. Fold in
the blueberries.

• Spoon into a greased 5x9-inch loaf pan.

• Bake at 350 degrees for 1 hour or until a wooden pick
inserted in the center comes out clean.

• Glaze: Bring lemon juice and 1/3 cup sugar to a boil in small
saucepan. Boil for 1 minute or until syrupy. Pour over
hot loaf.

• Cool in the pan for 10 minutes. Remove to a wire rack to
cool completely.

IRISH SODA BREAD

Makes 1 loaf

Makes St. Patrick's Day special.

2 cups raisins
4 cups flour
¼ cup sugar
1 teaspoon salt
1½ teaspoons baking powder
¼ cup butter
1⅓ cups buttermilk
1 egg, beaten
½ teaspoon baking soda

- Preheat the oven to 350 degrees.
- Cover the raisins with warm water to plump; drain well.
- Sift the flour, sugar, salt and baking powder into a medium bowl. Cut in the butter until crumbly.
- Stir in the raisins and buttermilk.
- Beat the egg with the baking soda. Add to the flour mixture; mix well.
- Shape the dough into a semicircle and place on a greased baking sheet.
- Bake at 350 degrees for 45 minutes or until a wooden pick inserted in the center comes out clean.

SPICY PUMPKIN BREAD

Makes 2 or 3 loaves

For a lovely gift from your kitchen, wrap this spicy bread in a tea towel and tie with a ribbon.

1 teaspoon nutmeg
1 teaspoon cinnamon
3 cups sugar
1½ teaspoons salt
1 cup vegetable oil
4 eggs
2 cups canned pumpkin
3 cups flour
2 teaspoons baking soda
⅔ cup water
1 cup chopped nuts

- Combine the nutmeg, cinnamon, sugar, salt, oil and eggs in a large bowl and mix until smooth. Add the pumpkin, flour, baking soda and water, mixing well. Fold in the nuts.
- Fill 3 greased and floured 1-pound coffee cans or 2 greased and floured 5x9-inch loaf pans ⅔ full.
- Bake at 350 degrees on the lowest oven rack for 1 hour or until a wooden pick inserted in the center comes out clean.
- Cool in the pans for 10 minutes after baking, then invert carefully onto wire racks to cool completely.

ANADAMA BREAD

Makes 2 loaves

This is a do-ahead bread that disappears quickly.

2 tablespoons dry yeast
1/2 cup warm water
1 cup scalded milk
1 cup boiling water
1 cup yellow cornmeal
1/4 cup butter, melted
1/2 cup molasses
2 teaspoons salt
6 cups flour

- Dissolve the yeast in warm water.
- Combine the milk and boiling water in a large bowl and stir in the cornmeal. Add the butter, molasses and salt. Let stand until cooled to lukewarm. Stir in yeast.
- Stir in the flour with a wooden spoon. Knead on floured surface for 8 minutes or until smooth and elastic. Place the dough in a greased bowl, turning to grease surface. Let rise, covered, for 1 1/2 hours or until doubled in bulk.
- Shape into 2 loaves; place in buttered 5x9-inch loaf pans. Let rise, covered, for 45 minutes or until doubled in bulk.
- Preheat the oven to 375 degrees.
- Bake at 375 degrees for 40 to 45 minutes or until the loaves test done. Turn onto wire racks to cool.

BUTTERMILK YEAST BREAD

Makes 2 loaves

1 tablespoon active dry yeast
1/2 cup lukewarm water
1 cup boiling water
1 tablespoon margarine
1 cup buttermilk
1/4 teaspoon salt
1/2 cup honey
5 to 6 cups flour
Melted butter

- Dissolve the yeast in the lukewarm water. Let stand for 5 minutes.
- Mix boiling water with the margarine in large mixer bowl. Cool to lukewarm. Add buttermilk, salt and honey. Add flour, mixing with dough hook until mixture forms a ball.
- Place dough in bowl sprayed with nonstick cooking spray. Let rise, covered, for 1 1/2 hours or until doubled in bulk.
- Knead on a floured surface for 10 minutes, adding flour as necessary. Shape into 2 loaves; place in 5x9-inch loaf pans sprayed with nonstick cooking spray.
- Let rise, loosely covered, for 1 hour or until doubled in bulk.
- Preheat the oven to 350 degrees.
- Bake at 350 degrees for 45 to 50 minutes or until brown.
- Remove from pans to wire rack; butter tops.
- Cool covered with waxed paper and a dish towel for a softer crust.

ENGLISH MUFFIN BREAD

Makes 2 loaves

Make this tasty bread ahead of time, slice and toast for a breakfast treat. The bread freezes well.

2 envelopes dry yeast

3 cups flour

1 tablespoon sugar

2 teaspoons salt

1/4 teaspoon baking soda

2 cups milk

1/2 cup water

3 cups flour

Cornmeal

- ♦ Combine the yeast, 3 cups flour, sugar, salt and baking soda in a large bowl.

- ♦ Heat the milk and water to 120 to 130 degrees in a medium saucepan. Stir the milk mixture into the flour mixture; beat until smooth. Stir in the remaining 3 cups flour to make a stiff batter.

- ♦ Sprinkle cornmeal into 2 greased 5x9-inch loaf pans. Spoon the batter into the pans and sprinkle tops with cornmeal. Let rise, covered, in a warm place for 45 minutes.

- ♦ Preheat the oven to 400 degrees.

- ♦ Bake at 400 degrees for 25 minutes. Remove from the pans and invert onto wire racks to cool.

HERBED CASSEROLE BREAD

Makes 1 loaf

1 3/4 cups flour

3 tablespoons instant nonfat dry milk

2 tablespoons sugar

2 tablespoons vegetable oil

1 envelope dry yeast

1 teaspoon salt

1 1/2 teaspoons caraway seeds

3 tablespoons fresh sage or 1 tablespoon dry sage

1/2 teaspoon fresh rosemary or pinch of dried rosemary

Pinch of basil or thyme

Pinch of ginger

1 teaspoon nutmeg

1 cup 120- to 130-degree water

1 cup flour

- ♦ Combine 1 3/4 cups flour, dry milk, sugar, oil, yeast, salt, caraway seeds and seasonings in food processor fitted with steel blade. Process for 5 seconds. Add the water. Process for 30 seconds or until blended.

- ♦ Add the remaining 1 cup flour 1/4 cup at a time, processing for 5 to 10 seconds after each addition or until well blended. Pour the batter into a greased 1 1/2-quart baking dish.

- ♦ Let rise, covered, in a warm place for 40 to 45 minutes or until almost doubled in bulk.

- ♦ Preheat the oven to 375 degrees.

- ♦ Bake at 375 degrees for 25 to 30 minutes or until the bread tests done.

- ♦ Cool in the pan for 10 minutes. Remove to wire rack to cool completely.

FRENCH BREAD

Makes 2 loaves

This make-ahead recipe may be mixed in a food processor to lessen the mixing time, or by hand, if desired.

5¹/₂ to 6¹/₂ cups flour
2 envelopes dry yeast
1 tablespoon sugar
1 tablespoon salt
2 tablespoons shortening
2¹/₄ cups hot water
Vegetable oil

♦ Combine 2 cups flour, yeast, sugar and salt in a large mixer bowl or food processor. Add the shortening and hot water. Beat for 2 minutes. Add 1 cup flour. Beat at high speed for 1 minute. Add enough remaining flour to make medium dough.

♦ Shape into ball on floured surface. Let rest, covered with plastic wrap and towel, for 20 minutes.

♦ Punch dough down. Divide into 2 portions. Roll each into 8x15-inch rectangle; roll as for jelly roll. Place on greased baking sheet. Brush with oil. Refrigerate, covered, for 2 to 24 hours.

♦ Preheat the oven to 350 degrees.

♦ Let loaves stand at room temperature for 10 minutes. Brush with cold water. Bake at 350 degrees for 30 to 40 minutes or until golden brown.

NAUTICAL KNOTS

Makes 16 rolls

2 (11-ounce) cans refrigerated breadsticks
French Herb Spread
Grated Parmesan cheese to taste

♦ Preheat the oven to 350 degrees.

♦ Separate the dough strips and tie each loosely into a knot. Place 1 inch apart on a greased baking sheet. Brush with the French Herb Spread. Sprinkle with the cheese.

♦ Bake at 350 degrees for 15 minutes or until golden brown.

French Herb Spread

¹/₂ cup butter, softened
1 teaspoon parsley flakes
¹/₂ teaspoon each oregano, sweet basil and celery seeds
Pinch of sage
¹/₈ teaspoon salt
¹/₄ teaspoon pepper
1 teaspoon grated Parmesan cheese

♦ Combine all ingredients in a medium bowl; mix well.

♦ May spread on sliced French bread, wrap in foil and bake at 350 degrees for 15 minutes, open foil and bake for 5 minutes longer.

THE RECTORY'S SALLY LUNN BREAD

Makes 1 loaf

This version of Sally Lunn is a Virginia treasure. This "better than pound cake" treat was baked for "after services faithful" who came by the rectory for luncheon. "The sermon was inspiring, but the Sally Lunn was divine!" the parishioners always said. If there was any left, it was wonderful toasted the next day for breakfast.

1 envelope dry yeast
1/2 cup warm water
1/2 cup butter, softened
3 egg yolks
1/2 cup sugar
4 cups flour
1 teaspoon salt
1 cup milk, scalded, slightly cooled

♦ Dissolve the yeast in the warm water. Cream the butter, egg yolks and sugar in a large bowl. Mix in the flour and salt gradually.

♦ Mix in the milk and yeast; batter will be consistency of thick honey. Spoon into a lightly greased and floured bundt pan.

♦ Let rise, covered, in a warm place for 1 hour or until doubled in bulk.

♦ Preheat the oven to 350 degrees.

♦ Bake at 350 degrees for 30 minutes or until a cake tester inserted in the center comes out clean.

♦ Cool in the pan for 10 minutes. Invert onto a serving plate. Turn over crust up. Serve warm with honey butter.

SAUSAGE BREAD

Makes 1 loaf

1 1/2 pounds hot or sweet Italian sausage
1 pound frozen bread dough, thawed
1 egg, beaten
1 (10-ounce) jar roasted red peppers, drained, chopped
Garlic powder to taste
1 medium onion, chopped (optional)
1 tablespoon olive oil (optional)

♦ Remove sausage casings. Brown sausage in a medium skillet, stirring until crumbly; drain.

♦ Roll the bread dough into a 7x17-inch rectangle. Brush lightly with the beaten egg; reserve remaining egg. Cover with sausage and peppers to within 1 inch of edges. Sprinkle with the garlic powder, onion and olive oil.

♦ Roll as for jelly roll from the long side, sealing edge. Place seam side down on a greased baking sheet.

♦ Let rise, covered, in a warm place for 30 minutes.

♦ Preheat the oven to 350 degrees.

♦ Brush with remaining egg. Bake at 350 degrees for 20 to 30 minutes or until golden brown on top.

♦ Cut into 1/2-inch slices and serve warm.

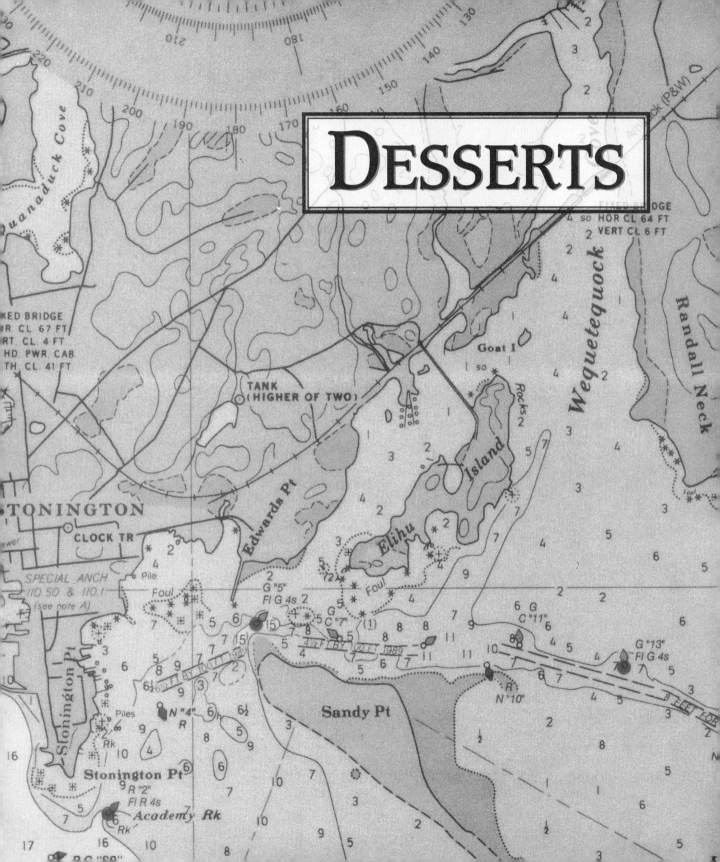

DESSERTS

DESSERTS

♦ ♦ ♦ ♦ ♦ ♦ ♦ ♦ ♦ ♦ ♦ ♦ ♦

APPLE CAKE

Makes 16 servings

This tasty cake can be sliced and frozen, then eaten one slice at a time.

1 cup vegetable oil
3 eggs
2 cups sugar
2 cups flour
1 teaspoon cinnamon
1 teaspoon nutmeg
1 teaspoon salt
1 teaspoon vanilla extract
1 teaspoon baking soda
1 (21-ounce) can apple pie filling

♦ Preheat the oven to 350 degrees.

♦ Beat the oil and eggs in a large bowl. Add the sugar, flour, cinnamon, nutmeg, salt, vanilla, baking soda and apple pie filling; mix well.

♦ Spoon the mixture into a greased 10-inch tube pan.

♦ Bake at 350 degrees for 1¼ hours or until cake tests done.

BLITZEN TORTE

Makes 8 servings

½ cup butter, softened
½ cup sugar
Dash of salt
4 egg yolks, beaten
1½ teaspoons vanilla extract
6 tablespoons milk
1 cup (scant) flour
1 tablespoon baking powder
4 egg whites
1 cup sugar
1 cup walnuts
1 cup whipping cream, whipped
¼ to ½ cup confectioners' sugar
½ teaspoon vanilla extract

♦ Preheat the oven to 350 degrees.

♦ Cream the butter and ½ cup sugar in a small bowl until light and fluffy. Add the salt, egg yolks, 1½ teaspoons vanilla and milk; mix well. Add mixture of flour and baking powder; mix well.

♦ Spoon the batter into 2 greased 8-inch round cake pans lined with waxed paper on the bottoms.

♦ Beat the egg whites in a mixer bowl until soft peaks form. Add 1 cup sugar gradually, beating until stiff peaks form. Spread half the meringue over each layer. Sprinkle half the walnuts on each layer.

♦ Bake at 350 degrees for 30 minutes. Cool.

♦ Remove from pans carefully.

♦ Sweeten the whipped cream with the confectioners' sugar and ½ teaspoon vanilla. Place 1 layer, walnut side up, on cake plate. Spread with whipped cream. Place remaining layer, walnut side up, on top.

Sliced strawberries between layers and as garnish are a springtime treat.

TWO-WAY CARROT CAKE

Makes 16 servings

1 (8-ounce) can crushed pineapple in syrup
3 cups flour
2 cups sugar
1 1/2 teaspoons baking soda
1 teaspoon baking powder
1/2 teaspoon salt
2 teaspoons ground cinnamon
1 1/2 cups vegetable oil
3 eggs
2 teaspoons vanilla extract
2 cups coarsely shredded carrots
1 1/2 cups broken pecans

♦ Preheat the oven to 325 degrees.

♦ Drain the pineapple and reserve the syrup.

♦ Combine the flour, sugar, baking soda, baking powder, salt and cinnamon in a large mixer bowl. Make a well in the center. Add the oil, eggs, the reserved pineapple syrup and vanilla; beat until smooth. Stir in the pineapple, carrots and pecans. Pour into a greased 10-inch tube pan.

♦ Bake at 325 degrees for 1 1/2 hours or until the cake tests done.

♦ Cool in pan on a wire rack for 10 minutes. Remove to the wire rack to cool completely.

♦ Serve with warm Rum Sauce.

For a change of pace, frost with Maple Frosting.

Rum Sauce

1 cup packed dark brown sugar
1/2 cup dark corn syrup
1/2 cup light cream
1/4 cup butter
1/4 cup light rum
1 teaspoon vanilla extract

♦ Combine the brown sugar, corn syrup, cream and butter in a 2-quart saucepan. Bring to the boiling point over low heat, stirring constantly.

♦ Let stand until just warm, stirring occasionally. Stir in the rum and the vanilla.

Maple Frosting

1/2 cup butter, softened
8 ounces cream cheese, softened
4 cups confectioners' sugar
1 teaspoon vanilla extract
2 tablespoons maple syrup

♦ Cream the butter and cream cheese in a small mixer bowl until light.

♦ Add the confectioners' sugar gradually, beating until smooth and creamy. Stir in the vanilla and the maple syrup.

DEEP DARK CHOCOLATE FUDGE CAKE

Makes 12 to 14 servings

2 cups sugar
¾ cup margarine
1½ cups boiling water
2 cups flour
½ cup baking cocoa
½ teaspoon salt
2 teaspoons baking soda
2 eggs, beaten
1 teaspoon vanilla extract
Chocolate Frosting

• Preheat the oven to 350 degrees.

• Combine the sugar and margarine in a medium bowl. Add the boiling water. Sift in the dry ingredients; beat until smooth. Beat in the eggs and vanilla.

• Pour into greased and floured 9x13-inch cake pan.

• Bake at 350 degrees for 40 minutes.

• Spread warm Chocolate Frosting over top.

Chocolate Frosting

1 cup sugar
3 tablespoons cornstarch
6 tablespoons baking cocoa
Dash of salt
1 cup boiling water
3 tablespoons butter
1 teaspoon vanilla extract

• Combine the sugar, cornstarch, baking cocoa and salt in a medium saucepan. Add the boiling water. Cook over low heat until thickened, stirring constantly. Stir in the butter and vanilla.

• Frosting will be thin but quite rich. Double the recipe if desired.

CHOCOLATE DECADENCE

Makes 12 servings

1⅓ cups sugar
½ cup water
8 ounces baking chocolate
4 ounces semisweet chocolate
1 cup unsalted butter, softened
5 extra-large eggs, at room temperature, beaten
Whipped cream for garnish
Chocolate curls for garnish

• Preheat the oven to 350 degrees.

• Bring sugar and water in a medium saucepan to a boil over low heat, stirring frequently.

• Melt the chocolates in a double boiler over boiling water. Pour into a large bowl. Blend in sugar mixture. Cool slightly. Stir in the butter gradually. Beat in the eggs; do not overbeat. The mixture will be lumpy. Spoon the batter into a greased 8-inch springform pan. Set the pan in a shallow pan of water.

• Bake at 350 degrees for 25 to 30 minutes or until the cake tests done. Cool completely. Remove sides of pan.

• Garnish with whipped cream and chocolate curls.

CHOCOLATE SOUFFLE CAKE

Makes 8 to 10 servings

This not-too-sweet cake sinks in the center after baking, making room for the filling.

4 ounces German's sweet chocolate

½ cup unsalted butter

4 egg yolks

½ cup sugar

½ teaspoon vanilla extract

4 egg whites

Whipped cream

Chocolate curls for garnish

- Preheat the oven to 300 degrees.
- Coat the bottom of a greased 8-inch springform pan with sugar. Shake out excess.
- Melt the chocolate and the butter in a medium saucepan over low heat, stirring constantly. Remove from heat and whisk in the egg yolks, one at a time. Whisk in the sugar and vanilla gradually.
- Beat the egg whites in a medium bowl until stiff peaks form. Fold in the chocolate mixture. Spoon into the prepared pan.
- Bake at 300 degrees for 1 hour and 20 minutes or until the cake tests done.
- Cool on a wire rack for 5 minutes. Loosen cake from sides of pan; remove sides of pan.
- Fill the indented center with whipped cream and garnish with chocolate curls.

CHOCOLATE NUT ZUCCHINI CAKE

Makes 16 to 20 servings

3 cups flour

1½ teaspoons baking powder

1 teaspoon baking soda

1 teaspoon salt

4 eggs

3 cups sugar

1½ cups vegetable oil

4 packets liquid unsweetened chocolate

3 cups finely grated zucchini

1 cup finely chopped nuts

1 cup semisweet chocolate chips

- Preheat the oven to 350 degrees.
- Sift the flour, baking powder, baking soda and salt together.
- Beat the eggs in a large mixer bowl until fluffy. Add the sugar gradually, beating constantly. Add the oil and chocolate; blend well. Add the sifted dry ingredients; beat at low speed until smooth. Stir in zucchini, nuts and chocolate chips.
- Pour the batter into a greased and floured 10-inch tube pan.
- Bake at 350 degrees for 1¼ hours or until the cake tests done.
- Cool in the pan on a wire rack for 15 minutes. Turn onto the rack to cool completely.

Frost with favorite frosting if desired. Garnish with whipped cream.

LEMON GLAZE CAKE

Makes 16 servings

Decorate center of cake with a bouquet of seasonal flowers.

1/2 cup fine bread crumbs
3 cups flour
1 tablespoon baking powder
1 tablespoon salt
1 cup butter, softened
2 cups sugar
4 eggs
1 cup milk
2 tablespoons grated lemon rind
1/2 cup lemon juice
3/4 cup sugar

- Preheat the oven to 325 degrees.
- Grease 9-inch tube pan; sprinkle with bread crumbs.
- Sift the flour, baking powder and salt together.
- Cream the butter and 2 cups sugar in a mixer bowl until light and fluffy. Beat in the eggs, one at a time. Add the sifted dry ingredients alternately with the milk, mixing well after each addition. Stir in the lemon rind.
- Pour into the prepared pan.
- Bake at 325 degrees for 1 1/4 hours or until the cake tests done. Invert the cake onto a wire rack immediately. Poke holes in the cake.
- Glaze: Heat lemon juice and 3/4 cup sugar in saucepan until sugar dissolves, stirring constantly. Spoon hot glaze over the hot cake gradually until absorbed.

MAPLE SYRUP CAKE

Makes 8 to 10 servings

1 cup maple syrup
1 cup cold water
1 cup dried blueberries or raisins
1/2 cup butter
1 teaspoon each ground cloves, nutmeg and cinnamon
1 teaspoon salt
2 cups sifted flour
1 teaspoon baking soda
1/2 cup chopped walnuts

- Preheat the oven to 350 degrees.
- Combine the maple syrup, cold water, blueberries, butter and seasonings in a medium saucepan over medium-high heat. Bring to a boil. Boil for 4 minutes, stirring constantly. Cool to lukewarm.
- Add the flour, baking soda and walnuts; mix well.
- Pour into a greased and floured 5x9-inch loaf pan or 7-inch tube pan.
- Bake at 350 degrees for 1 hour or until the cake tests done. Turn onto wire rack to cool.

RAISIN SPICE CAKE

Makes 8 to 10 servings

3 cups flour

2 cups sugar

2 teaspoons baking soda

1/2 teaspoon each nutmeg and salt

1/4 teaspoon ground cloves

1 1/2 teaspoons cinnamon

1 cup mayonnaise

1/3 cup milk

2 eggs

3 cups chopped peeled apple

1 cup raisins

1/2 cup chopped nuts

2 cups whipped cream

- Preheat the oven to 350 degrees.

- Combine the flour, sugar, baking soda, nutmeg, salt, cloves and cinnamon in a large mixer bowl. Add mayonnaise, milk and eggs; beat until well mixed, scraping bowl frequently. Batter will be thick. Stir in apple, raisins and nuts.

- Spoon the batter into 2 greased and floured 9-inch round cake pans.

- Bake at 350 degrees for 45 minutes.

- Cool in the pans for 10 minutes. Invert onto a wire rack to cool completely.

- Spread whipped cream between layers and over top and side of cake.

Omit whipped cream and frost with favorite cream cheese frosting.

TROPICAL DREAM CAKE

Makes 12 to 16 servings

2 cups sugar

1 cup vegetable oil

3 eggs

1 (8-ounce) can crushed pineapple

1 1/2 teaspoons vanilla extract

1 cup whole wheat flour

2 cups all-purpose flour

1 teaspoon each salt, baking soda, baking powder and ground cinnamon

2 cups mashed bananas

1 cup chopped nuts

1 cup raisins (optional)

1 3/4 cups sifted confectioners' sugar

2 tablespoons (or more) orange juice

- Preheat the oven to 350 degrees.

- Beat sugar and oil in a medium bowl until smooth. Beat in eggs, one at a time. Stir in undrained pineapple and vanilla. Add mixture of flours, salt, baking soda, baking powder and cinnamon; mix well. Add the bananas, nuts and raisins; mix well.

- Spoon into a greased and floured 10-inch fluted tube pan.

- Bake at 350 degrees for 60 to 70 minutes or until the cake tests done.

- Cool in the pan for 10 minutes. Invert onto a wire rack to cool completely.

- Blend confectioners' sugar and enough orange juice to make glaze. Drizzle over cool cake.

Substitute 3 cups all-purpose flour for the 1 cup whole wheat and 2 cups all-purpose flour.

APRICOT BISCOTTI

Makes 2 dozen

2 1/2 cups flour
3/4 cup sugar
1 teaspoon baking powder
1/2 teaspoon baking soda
1/2 teaspoon nutmeg
1/2 cup chopped apricots
1/2 cup chopped almonds
2 teaspoons finely grated lemon rind
3 eggs
1 teaspoon vanilla extract
1/4 teaspoon lemon extract

- Preheat the oven to 350 degrees.
- Sift the flour, sugar, baking powder, baking soda and nutmeg in a large bowl. Stir in the apricots, almonds and lemon rind. Make a well in the center.
- Place the eggs and the flavorings in the well and beat with a fork until frothy. Stir the flour mixture into the egg mixture gradually, mixing well by hand when the dough begins to take shape.
- Knead on a lightly floured surface until smooth. Shape into two 12-inch logs. Place on a baking sheet sprayed with nonstick cooking spray. Flatten to 3x12-inch rectangles, leaving 6 inches between.
- Bake at 350 degrees for 20 to 30 minutes or until golden brown on top and firm to the touch.
- Remove from the oven and reduce the heat to 300 degrees. Transfer the logs to a cutting board. Cool for several minutes.
- Cut into 3/4-inch slices. Arrange the slices cut side up 1/2 inch apart on a cookie sheet.
- Bake at 300 degrees for 15 minutes or until dry and crisp.
- Store in an airtight container.

CHERRY MERINGUES

Makes 2 dozen

1 cup dried tart cherries
2 egg whites, at room temperature
1/2 teaspoon vanilla extract
Dash of salt
1/2 cup sugar
1 cup coarsely chopped pecans

- Preheat the oven to 350 degrees.
- Cut the cherries into quarters with scissors or a sharp knife.
- Beat egg whites, vanilla and salt in a medium mixer bowl until stiff peaks form. Add the sugar gradually, beating until stiff peaks form. Fold in the cherries and the pecans.
- Drop by teaspoonfuls onto a parchment-lined cookie sheet.
- Place in the oven and turn off the heat.
- Let stand in closed oven for 5 hours or overnight.
- Store the meringues in an airtight container.

Lantern Hill Cookies

Makes 3 dozen

2 egg whites
Dash of salt
½ cup sugar
½ teaspoon vinegar
½ teaspoon vanilla extract
1 cup semisweet chocolate chips, melted
¾ cup walnuts, chopped

- Preheat the oven to 350 degrees.
- Beat the egg whites and salt in mixer bowl until foamy. Add the sugar gradually, beating until stiff peaks form. Beat in the vinegar and vanilla. Fold in the melted chocolate and walnuts gently.
- Drop by teaspoonfuls onto a greased cookie sheet.
- Bake at 350 degrees for 10 minutes. Remove to wire rack immediately.

Fudge Brownies

Makes 16 servings

2 ounces unsweetened chocolate
4 ounces semisweet chocolate
½ cup unsalted butter
¼ teaspoon salt
½ teaspoon vanilla extract
1 cup sugar
2 eggs
¼ cup flour
1 cup chopped walnuts

- Preheat the oven to 325 degrees.
- Line 8-inch square baking pan with foil shiny side up; butter foil.
- Melt the chocolate and butter in a large heavy saucepan over low heat, stirring until smooth. Remove from the heat. Stir in salt, vanilla and sugar. Beat in the eggs, one at a time.
- Add the flour; stir for 1 minute or until the mixture is shiny. Stir in the walnuts.
- Pour into the prepared pan.
- Bake at 325 degrees in the bottom third of the oven for 40 minutes. Cool completely. Chill in the freezer for 30 minutes or until firm.
- Invert onto cutting board, peel off foil and cut into squares.

For a fudge pie, pour the batter into a greased 9-inch pie pan. Bake at 350 degrees for 25 to 30 minutes. Cut into wedges and serve with whipped cream or ice cream.

CHOCOLATE WALNUT BARS

Makes 6 dozen

1 cup butter, softened
½ cup sugar
½ cup packed dark brown sugar
2 egg yolks
1 cup flour
1 cup old-fashioned oats
1 teaspoon vanilla extract
8 ounces semisweet chocolate
2 tablespoons butter
1 cup chopped walnuts

♦ Preheat the oven to 350 degrees.

♦ Cream the butter, sugar and brown sugar in a medium bowl. Stir in the egg yolks, flour, oats and vanilla.

♦ Spread the batter in a greased 10x15-inch baking pan.

♦ Bake at 350 degrees for 30 minutes.

♦ Cool slightly. Turn onto a wire rack to cool completely.

♦ Topping: Melt the chocolate and the butter in a double boiler over hot water over low heat, stirring until smooth.

♦ Spread over baked layer. Top with walnuts. Let stand until set. Cut into 1x2-inch bars.

CHOCOLATE MACAROONS

Makes 2 dozen

1 cup semisweet chocolate chips
2 egg whites
½ cup sugar
1 cup flaked coconut

♦ Preheat the oven to 325 degrees.

♦ Melt the chocolate chips in a small saucepan over low heat and set the pan in a large pan of hot water to keep warm.

♦ Beat the egg whites in a mixer bowl until soft peaks form. Add sugar gradually, beating until stiff peaks form. Fold in chocolate and coconut gently.

♦ Drop by scant teaspoonfuls onto a parchment-lined cookie sheet.

♦ Bake at 325 degrees for 15 minutes.

These cookies will keep for three to four days stored in an airtight container but become hard if exposed to air.

CHOCOLATE TURTLE BARS

Makes 2 dozen

1 (14-ounce) package caramel candies
1 (5-ounce) can evaporated milk
1 (2-layer) package Swiss chocolate cake mix
1/2 cup melted margarine
1 1/2 cups chopped pecans
1 cup semisweet chocolate chips

- Preheat the oven to 350 degrees.
- Melt the caramels with 1/3 cup of the evaporated milk in a heavy saucepan over low heat until smooth, stirring frequently and set aside.
- Combine the remaining evaporated milk, cake mix and margarine in a large bowl; mix well. Press half the mixture into the bottom of a 9x13-inch baking pan.
- Bake at 350 degrees for 8 minutes.
- Sprinkle half the pecans and half the chocolate chips over the baked layer and top with the caramel mixture.
- Top with remaining cake mix mixture; press gently into the caramel mixture. Sprinkle with the remaining pecans and chocolate chips.
- Bake for 18 minutes longer. Cool and cut into bars.

CHOCOLATE RAISIN COOKIES

Makes 3 dozen

32 ounces semisweet chocolate
8 cups cornflakes
1/2 cup raisins
1/2 cup nuts

- Melt the chocolate in a double boiler over low heat, stirring until smooth.
- Combine the cornflakes, raisins and nuts in a large bowl. Stir in the chocolate; mix until chocolate coats everything. Do not allow any water to drip into the chocolate.
- Drop by spoonfuls onto cookie sheets lined with waxed paper.
- Refrigerate for 15 to 20 minutes or until the cookies are firm to the touch.

  Use half white chocolate and half dark chocolate and/or add coconut.

JOE FROGGERS

Makes 7 dozen

These spicy, dense cookies went to sea with colonial fishermen and still go out today with cruising families from Maine to Connecticut.

3/4 cup water
1/4 cup dark rum
8 cups flour
1 tablespoon salt
1 tablespoon ginger
1 teaspoon cloves
1 teaspoon nutmeg
1/2 teaspoon allspice
2 cups dark molasses
2 teaspoons baking soda
1 cup shortening
2 cups sugar

- Combine the water and rum. Sift the flour together with the salt and spices. Blend the molasses and baking soda.
- Cream the shortening and sugar in a large mixer bowl until light. Add the rum, flour and molasses mixture half at a time, mixing well after each addition. Chill in the refrigerator.
- Preheat the oven to 375 degrees.
- Roll the dough on a well floured surface to a 1/4 to 1/3-inch thickness. Cut with 4-inch round cookie cutter and place on greased cookie sheets.
- Bake at 375 degrees for 10 to 12 minutes or until golden brown. Let stand on the sheets for 5 minutes before removing to wire rack to cool completely.
- Store in an airtight container.

GINGER SPICE COOKIES

Makes 6 dozen

3/4 cup butter, softened
1 cup packed brown sugar
1 egg, beaten
1/4 cup molasses
2 1/4 cups flour
2 teaspoons baking soda
1 teaspoon ginger
1 teaspoon cinnamon
1/2 teaspoon ground cloves
1/4 teaspoon salt
Sugar

- Cream the butter and brown sugar in a medium mixer bowl until light. Add the egg and molasses and blend well.
- Sift the flour, baking soda, ginger, cinnamon, ground cloves and salt together 2 or 3 times. Add to the creamed mixture; mix well.
- Chill in the refrigerator.
- Preheat the oven to 350 degrees.
- Shape the dough into walnut-size balls. Roll in sugar and place 2 to 3 inches apart on an ungreased cookie sheet.
- Bake at 350 degrees for 10 minutes.

LEMON CREAM CHEESE COOKIES

Makes 6 to 8 dozen

1 cup margarine, softened
3 ounces cream cheese, softened
1 cup sugar
1 egg
1 teaspoon grated lemon rind
1 tablespoon lemon juice
2½ cups flour
1 teaspoon baking powder
1 cup confectioners' sugar
2 tablespoons lemon juice
Chocolate sprinkles, colored
    sprinkles, coconut, chopped
    nuts

+ Cream the margarine, cream cheese and sugar in a medium bowl until light and fluffy. Add the egg, lemon rind and lemon juice; mix well. Sift in the flour and baking powder; mix well.

+ Chill for 30 minutes.

+ Preheat the oven to 375 degrees.

+ Force the dough through the ribbon disk of a cookie press onto an ungreased cold cookie sheet.

+ Bake at 375 degrees for 8 to 10 minutes or until light golden brown. Cool.

+ Blend the confectioners' sugar and lemon juice in a small bowl.

+ Dip one end of each cookie into the glaze and then into the sprinkles.

For chocolate lovers—dip cookie into melted semisweet chocolate.

HAZELNUT COOKIES

Makes 2 dozen

2 cups ground hazelnuts
1 cup (scant) sugar
2 eggs, lightly beaten
Pecans or chocolate chips

+ Preheat the oven to 400 degrees.

+ Combine the hazelnuts, sugar and eggs in a medium bowl; mix well. Shape by teaspoonfuls into small balls. Place on well greased cookie sheet. Top with pecans or chocolate chips.

+ Bake at 400 degrees for 8 to 10 minutes or until golden brown.

+ Cool on a wire rack.

Nice cookie to serve with ice cream or fruit.

GINGERBREAD COOKIES

Makes 2 dozen

This recipe is great to use for making gingerbread houses. To celebrate different holidays, use different cookie cutters.

1 cup shortening
1 cup sugar
1 cup molasses
1 egg
2 tablespoons vinegar
5 cups flour
1 1/2 teaspoons baking soda
1/2 teaspoon salt
2 to 3 teaspoons ground ginger
1 teaspoon cinnamon
1 teaspoon cloves

♦ Cream the shortening and sugar in a large mixer bowl. Add the molasses, egg and vinegar; mix well. Add mixture of flour, baking soda, salt and spices; mix well. Knead until smooth.

♦ Place the dough in a sealable plastic bag; chill overnight.

♦ Preheat the oven to 375 degrees.

♦ Roll half the dough at a time 1/4-inch thick and cut with cookie cutter. Place on ungreased cookie sheets.

♦ Bake at 375 degrees for 6 to 7 minutes. Cool on the cookie sheets for 2 minutes before removing to wire racks.

Make gingerbread heart necklaces for Valentine's Day by using a straw to make holes in the cookies before baking and then threading red licorice strings through the holes.

Note: Use 1/4-inch wooden dowels to make uniformly thick cookies. The rolling pin should roll on the dowels, pushing the dough to 1/4-inch thickness. Rolling the dough between waxed paper and using a small amount of dough at a time makes an easier task of transferring the cookies to the cookie sheets.

NEW ENGLAND HERMITS

Makes 4 dozen

1 cup sugar
1/2 cup vegetable oil
3 cups sifted flour
1 teaspoon cinnamon
1/2 teaspoon nutmeg
1/4 teaspoon salt
1 teaspoon baking soda
1/2 cup milk
1/2 cup molasses
3/4 cup raisins

♦ Preheat the oven to 350 degrees.

♦ Blend the sugar and oil in a large bowl.

♦ Sift the flour, cinnamon, nutmeg, salt and baking soda together. Add to the sugar mixture alternately with the milk and molasses, mixing well after each addition.

♦ Stir in the raisins.

♦ Spread in a greased 10x15-inch baking pan.

♦ Bake at 350 degrees for 25 minutes.

♦ Let cool and cut into squares.

CRUNCHY OATMEAL COOKIES

Makes 4 dozen

1 cup margarine or butter, softened
¾ cup packed brown sugar
¾ cup sugar
2 eggs, beaten
¾ cup flour
1 teaspoon salt
1 teaspoon baking soda
5 cups old-fashioned oats
½ cup raisins
½ cup chocolate chips

+ Preheat the oven to 350 degrees.
+ Cream the margarine, brown sugar and sugar in a medium bowl until light. Beat in the eggs. Sift in the flour, salt and baking soda; mix well. Mix in the oats. Stir in the raisins and chocolate chips.
+ Drop by teaspoonfuls onto a greased cookie sheet.
+ Bake at 350 degrees for 10 minutes or until brown.
+ Cool on a wire rack.

OATMEAL SPICE COOKIES

Makes 3½ to 5 dozen

1½ cups sifted flour
2 teaspoons cinnamon
2 teaspoons allspice
1½ teaspoons ground cloves
1½ teaspoons ginger
⅛ teaspoon salt
½ teaspoon pepper
½ teaspoon baking soda
1 cup butter, softened
1 cup sugar
1 cup packed light brown sugar
1 teaspoon vanilla extract
2 eggs
3 cups quick-cooking oats

+ Preheat the oven to 375 degrees.
+ Line cookie sheets with foil shiny side down. Grease the foil.
+ Sift the flour, cinnamon, allspice, cloves, ginger, salt, pepper and baking soda together; set aside.
+ Combine the butter, sugar, brown sugar, vanilla and eggs in a medium mixer bowl; beat until blended. Stir in the flour mixture. Add the oats; mix well.
+ Let stand for 2 hours.
+ Drop by spoonfuls onto greased cookie sheets.
+ Bake at 375 degrees for 10 to 12 minutes or until brown.

SHORTBREAD COOKIES

Makes 2½ dozen

1 cup butter, softened
½ cup confectioners' sugar
2 cups flour
¼ teaspoon baking powder
⅛ teaspoon salt

- Cream the butter and confectioners' sugar in a medium bowl. Sift in the flour, baking powder and salt; mix well.
- Shape into a 1½x10-inch log.
- Chill, covered, for 2 hours or longer.
- Preheat the oven to 325 degrees.
- Cut chilled dough into ⅓-inch slices and place on an ungreased cookie sheet.
- Bake at 325 degrees for 12 minutes or until golden brown.

  Dough can be rolled ⅓-inch thick and cut with cookie cutters. Bake as above.

SNOWBALL SURPRISES

Makes 3 dozen

1 cup butter, softened
½ cup sugar
1 teaspoon vanilla extract
2 cups flour
1 cup finely chopped walnuts
5 ounces milk chocolate kisses
Confectioners' sugar

- Preheat the oven to 375 degrees.
- Cream the butter, sugar and vanilla in a medium bowl until light.
- Stir in the flour and walnuts. Shape the dough around the chocolate kisses and gently roll into balls. Place on an ungreased cookie sheet.
- Bake at 375 degrees for 12 minutes.
- Remove to a wire rack to cool. Sprinkle with confectioners' sugar.

CHRISTMAS SNOWDROPS

Makes 4 dozen

1 cup butter, softened
3 tablespoons confectioners' sugar
1 teaspoon vanilla
2 cups flour
1 cup chopped walnuts
Confectioners' sugar

- Cream the butter, 3 tablespoons confectioners' sugar and vanilla in a small bowl until light. Add the flour; mix well. Stir in the walnuts. Knead lightly.
- Chill in the refrigerator.
- Preheat the oven to 350 degrees.
- Shape dough into 1-inch balls and place 2 inches apart on greased cookie sheets.
- Bake at 350 degrees for 25 to 30 minutes or until golden. Roll warm cookies in confectioners' sugar; cool on wire rack. Roll again in confectioners' sugar when cool.

ST. NICK'S WHISKERS

Makes 4½ dozen

1 cup butter, softened
1 cup sugar
2 tablespoons milk
1 teaspoon vanilla extract
2½ cups flour
½ cup each chopped red and green candied cherries
½ cup chopped pecans
1 cup flaked coconut

- Cream the butter and sugar in a mixer bowl until light and fluffy. Add the milk and vanilla, beating until smooth. Stir in the flour, candied cherries and pecans.
- Shape the dough into two 2x8-inch logs. Roll in coconut. Wrap in plastic wrap.
- Chill overnight.
- Preheat the oven to 375 degrees.
- Cut the dough into ¼-inch slices. Place on ungreased cookie sheets.
- Bake at 375 degrees for 12 to 14 minutes or until the edges begin to brown.

Substitute miniature chocolate chips for the candied cherries.

SOUR CREAM SUGAR COOKIES

Makes 5 to 6 dozen

Both children and adults find these soft, cake-like cookies irresistible.

1 cup butter, softened
2 cups sugar
4 eggs
1 teaspoon baking soda
1 cup sour cream
1 teaspoon vanilla or orange
  extract
3½ cups flour
½ teaspoon salt

♦ Preheat the oven to 375 degrees.

♦ Cream the butter and sugar in a large bowl until light and fluffy. Beat in the eggs, one at a time.

♦ Dissolve the baking soda in the sour cream. Blend in the vanilla. Add to the creamed mixture alternately with a mixture of flour and salt, mixing well after each addition.

♦ Drop by spoonfuls onto greased cookie sheets.

♦ Bake at 375 degrees for 10 to 12 minutes or until light brown.

  Frost cookies with a favorite butter frosting in colors to suit the season.

SUGAR AND SPICE ROLL-UPS

Makes 4 dozen

¾ cup finely chopped blanched
  almonds
⅓ cup sugar
1 teaspoon cinnamon
½ teaspoon nutmeg
1 tablespoon butter, softened
Sugar
1 puff pastry sheet
1 egg white, slightly beaten

♦ Combine the almonds, ⅓ cup sugar, cinnamon, nutmeg and butter in a small bowl; mix well.

♦ Sprinkle a flat surface generously with sugar. Roll the puff pastry to 12x15 inches with a rolling pin and sprinkle with the almond mixture; roll as for jelly roll. Brush edge with beaten egg white; press to seal.

♦ Chill in the refrigerator.

♦ Preheat the oven to 400 degrees.

♦ Cut the roll into ¼-inch slices and place 2 inches apart on a cookie sheet lined with foil that is lightly greased.

♦ Bake at 400 degrees for 8 to 10 minutes or until golden brown. Cool on a wire rack.

♦ Store in an airtight container.

TRADITIONAL APPLE PIE

Makes 8 servings

Apple pie recipes come and go, but this one has stood the test of time. Both the pie filling and the crust may be made ahead of time. During the peak apple season, you may make several batches of apple pie filling, adding 1 tablespoon of fruit preservative to each pie to prevent the apples from darkening. Then freeze the filling in foil pie plates. When ready to bake, place the apple mixture over the crust in a 9-inch pie plate and proceed as directed below. The baking time is approximately the same as for the fresh pie filling.

3/4 to 1 cup sugar

2 tablespoons flour

1 teaspoon cinnamon

1/8 teaspoon nutmeg

1/8 teaspoon salt

6 to 8 cooking apples, peeled, cored, sliced

Pie Pastry for 2-crust pie

2 tablespoons butter, sliced

- Preheat the oven to 400 degrees.
- Sift the sugar, flour, cinnamon, nutmeg and salt into a small bowl. Mix in the apples until coated. Spoon into a pastry-lined 9-inch pie plate.
- Dot with pats of the butter. Top with the remaining pastry, sealing the edge and cutting vents.
- Bake at 400 degrees for 50 minutes or until the apples are tender and the crust is browned.

Pie Pastry

Makes 5 pie crusts

4 cups flour

1 tablespoon sugar

2 teaspoons salt

1 3/4 cups vegetable shortening

1 egg, beaten

1 tablespoon vinegar

1/2 cup water

- Combine the flour, sugar and salt in a medium bowl and cut in the shortening until crumbly.
- Beat the egg with vinegar and water. Add to the flour mixture; stir just until mixed. Chill for 15 minutes.
- Divide into 5 portions. Roll on lightly floured surface or between waxed paper.
- May freeze unused pastry for future use.

BLUE AND RED BERRY PIE

Makes 6 to 8 servings

1/2 small orange, cut into pieces

4 cups frozen blueberries, thawed, drained

12 ounces cranberries

1 1/2 cups sugar

3 tablespoons cornstarch

Sour Cream Pastry

2 tablespoons (about) butter

1 to 2 tablespoons milk

Sugar to taste

♦ Grind the orange in a food processor; set aside.

♦ Combine the blueberries, cranberries, 1 1/2 cups sugar and cornstarch in a heavy saucepan. Bring to a boil over medium heat and cook until thickened, stirring constantly. Mix in the orange.

♦ Let stand until cool.

♦ Preheat the oven to 350 degrees.

♦ Spoon the berry mixture into pastry-lined 9-inch glass pie plate. Dot with butter. Top with the remaining pastry, sealing the edge and cutting vents.

♦ Brush lightly with milk; sprinkle with sugar

♦ Bake at 350 degrees for 1 hour or until golden brown.

Sour Cream Pastry

Makes 2 pie crusts

6 tablespoons sour cream

2 tablespoons ice water

1 teaspoon sugar

3/4 teaspoon salt

2 1/4 cups all-purpose flour

1/4 cup cake flour

1/2 cup butter

1/2 cup vegetable shortening

♦ Blend the sour cream, ice water, sugar and salt in a small bowl.

♦ Sift the flours into a large bowl. Cut in the butter and the shortening until crumbly.

♦ Add the sour cream mixture. Stir until dough forms. Divide into 2 portions; shape into balls.

♦ Chill, tightly wrapped in plastic wrap, for 1 hour.

♦ Roll on lightly floured surface or between waxed paper.

PEACHES AND CREAM PIE

Makes 6 to 8 servings

1 cup sour cream
2 tablespoons flour
¾ cup sugar
1 egg, beaten
1 teaspoon vanilla extract
2 cups diced peeled fresh
    peaches
1 unbaked (9-inch) pie shell
Crumbly Topping

• Preheat the oven to 400 degrees.
• Combine the sour cream, flour, sugar, egg and vanilla in a medium bowl and mix until smooth.
• Stir in the peaches. Spoon into the pie shell.
• Bake at 400 degrees for 25 minutes.
• Sprinkle the Crumbly Topping over the pie filling. Bake for 10 minutes longer or until golden brown.
• Chill before serving.

Crumbly Topping

¼ cup flour
2 tablespoons butter
¼ teaspoon nutmeg
¼ cup finely chopped pecans

• Combine the flour, butter, nutmeg and pecans in a small bowl and mix until crumbly.

FROZEN PEANUT BUTTER PIE

Makes 8 to 10 servings

4 ounces cream cheese, softened
½ cup peanut butter
½ cup milk
1 cup confectioners' sugar
1 cup whipping cream, whipped
1 (9-inch) graham cracker pie shell

• Combine the cream cheese and the peanut butter in a medium bowl and beat until smooth.
• Add the milk and confectioners' sugar and blend well.
• Fold in the whipped cream gently.
• Pour into the pie shell. Freeze until firm.
• Let the pie stand at room temperature for several minutes to soften slightly before serving.

Garnish with chopped peanuts and semisweet chocolate shavings.

PECAN PIE

Makes 6 to 8 servings

The slow baking called for in this recipe makes a chewy pecan pie.

3 eggs
1 cup packed brown sugar
1 cup dark corn syrup
Dash of salt
2 tablespoons bourbon
2 cups broken pecans
1 unbaked (9-inch) pie shell
1 egg white, beaten

◆ Preheat the oven to 450 degrees.

◆ Combine the eggs, brown sugar, corn syrup, salt, bourbon and pecans in a food processor. Pulse for 10 to 15 seconds or until smooth.

◆ Brush the pie shell with beaten egg white to prevent sogginess.

◆ Pour the pecan mixture into the prepared pie shell.

◆ Bake at 450 degrees for 7 minutes.

◆ Reduce the oven temperature to 275 degrees. Bake for 2 hours longer.

PUMPKIN ICE CREAM PIE

Makes 6 to 8 servings

Pumpkin Ice Cream Pie is a great alternative to traditional pumpkin pie at Thanksgiving.

1/4 cup packed light brown sugar
1 cup canned pumpkin
1/2 teaspoon cinnamon
1/4 teaspoon ginger
Dash of nutmeg
Dash of ground cloves
1/4 teaspoon salt
1 quart vanilla ice cream, softened
1 (9-inch) gingersnap or graham cracker pie shell, chilled
1/3 cup pecans

◆ Combine the brown sugar, pumpkin, cinnamon, ginger, nutmeg, cloves and salt in a medium bowl, mixing well.

◆ Stir in the ice cream; mix until smooth.

◆ Spoon into the pie shell. Top with the pecans.

◆ Freeze until firm.

◆ Let the pie stand at room temperature for several minutes to soften slightly before serving.

PUMPKIN MAPLE PIE

Makes 6 to 8 servings

A blending of New England flavors.

1 unbaked (9-inch) pie shell
2 cups dried beans
2 cups canned solid-pack
    pumpkin
1¼ cups whipping cream
¾ cup maple syrup
3 eggs
1 teaspoon vanilla extract
½ teaspoon ground allspice
½ teaspoon fresh grated nutmeg
½ teaspoon ground ginger

- Chill the pie shell for 30 minutes.
- Preheat the oven to 400 degrees.
- Line the pie shell with foil and fill with the dried beans.
- Bake at 400 degrees for 10 minutes. Remove the foil and beans from the pie shell. Return the pie shell to the oven. Bake at 400 degrees for 10 minutes longer. Let stand until cool.
- Reduce the oven temperature to 350 degrees.
- Combine the pumpkin, whipping cream, maple syrup, eggs, vanilla, allspice, nutmeg and ginger in a large bowl; mix well. Spoon into the prepared pie crust.
- Bake at 350 degrees for 50 to 60 minutes or until set.

RHUBARB CUSTARD PIE

Makes 6 to 8 servings

1½ cups sugar
¼ cup flour
½ teaspoon nutmeg
½ teaspoon salt
2 eggs, beaten
3 cups rhubarb, cut in ½-inch
    slices
2 tablespoons butter
Pie pastry for 2-crust pie

- Preheat the oven to 450 degrees.
- Sift the sugar, flour, nutmeg and salt into a medium bowl. Add the eggs and beat until smooth. Stir in the rhubarb.
- Pour the rhubarb mixture into a pastry-lined pie plate. Dot with butter. Top with the remaining pastry, sealing the edge and cutting vents.
- Bake at 450 degrees for 10 minutes. Reduce the oven temperature to 350 degrees. Bake for 40 minutes longer.

BAVARIAN APPLE TART

Makes 8 servings

1/2 cup butter, softened
1/3 cup sugar
1/4 teaspoon vanilla extract
1 cup flour
8 ounces cream cheese, softened
1 egg
1/4 cup sugar
1/2 teaspoon vanilla extract
1/2 cup sliced almonds (optional)
1/3 cup sugar
1/2 teaspoon cinnamon
4 cups thinly sliced apples

- Preheat the oven to 450 degrees.

- Cream the butter, 1/3 cup sugar and 1/4 teaspoon vanilla in a mixer bowl until light and fluffy. Cut in the flour until crumbly. Press over the bottom and partially up sides of a 9-inch springform pan.

- Cream together the cream cheese, egg, 1/4 cup sugar and 1/2 teaspoon vanilla in a small mixer bowl until light and fluffy. Spread in the prepared pan.

- Toss the almonds, 1/3 cup sugar, cinnamon and apples in a large bowl until the apples are coated; fan the apple slices over the cream cheese layer.

- Bake at 450 degrees for 10 minutes. Reduce the temperature to 400 degrees. Bake for 25 minutes longer.

- Cool in pan. Loosen sides of pan; remove.

SWISS APPLE TART

Makes 8 servings

1 sheet prepared puff pastry
1 egg yolk, beaten
Ground nuts or coarse dry bread crumbs
3 or 4 apples, thinly sliced
2 eggs
1/4 to 1/3 cup sugar
Nutmeg to taste
1 cup whipping cream

- Preheat the oven to 425 degrees.

- Line a 9-inch quiche pan with the puff pastry. Brush the edges with beaten egg yolk. Sprinkle bottom with ground nuts.

- Arrange the apple slices over the nuts in a circular pattern, starting from the center.

- Beat the eggs and sugar lightly in a small bowl. Add the nutmeg and the cream, mixing well. Pour over the apples.

- Bake at 425 degrees for 35 to 45 minutes or until golden brown. (Reduce oven temperature to 400 degrees if the tart appears to brown too quickly.)

Substitute other fruit in season for apples such as quartered Italian prune plums, apricot halves or other fresh or canned fruit.

BERRIES AND CREAM TART

Makes 10 to 12 servings

1 cup graham cracker crumbs
½ cup finely chopped pecans
2½ tablespoons sugar
¼ cup unsalted butter
8 ounces cream cheese, softened
⅓ cup confectioners' sugar
1 teaspoon vanilla extract
2 tablespoons Grand Marnier
1 cup whipping cream, whipped
4 cups fresh blueberries, rinsed, drained
½ cup (or more) melted raspberry jam

♦ Preheat the oven to 350 degrees.

♦ Combine the graham cracker crumbs, pecans, sugar and butter in a food processor. Process for 10 seconds. Press over bottom and sides of a buttered fluted 11-inch tart pan with a removable bottom.

♦ Bake at 350 degrees for 10 minutes. Cool completely.

♦ Beat the cream cheese and confectioners' sugar in a small bowl until light and fluffy. Blend in the vanilla and the liqueur. Whisk the cream cheese mixture into the whipped cream gently.

♦ Spoon into the cooled crust.

♦ Heat the blueberries with the melted jam in a small saucepan over low heat to release flavor. Spread the blueberry and jam mixture over the cream cheese filling.

♦ Chill, covered, for up to 6 hours before serving.

Substitute strawberry slices, raspberries or sliced peaches or nectarines. Toss peach or nectarine slices with a small amount of lemon juice and brown sugar to prevent browning. Arrange the fruit on the filling and brush with melted jam. It is not necessary to heat any fruit with the jam except the blueberries.

BLUEBERRY TART

Makes 8 servings

1 cup flour
Dash of salt
2 tablespoons sugar
½ cup butter
1 tablespoon white vinegar
3 cups blueberries
1 cup sugar
2 tablespoons flour
Dash of cinnamon
Confectioners' sugar to taste

♦ Preheat the oven to 400 degrees.

♦ Combine 1 cup flour, salt, 2 tablespoons sugar, butter and vinegar in a food processor. Process until smooth; spread in the bottom of a 9-inch tart pan.

♦ Combine 2 cups of the blueberries, 1 cup sugar, 2 tablespoons flour and cinnamon in a medium bowl; mix well. Spoon into the prepared pan.

♦ Bake at 400 degrees for 1 hour.

♦ Spread the remaining 1 cup blueberries on top.

♦ Cool completely. Dust with confectioners' sugar.

NUTTY CURRANT TARTLETS

Makes 12 servings

1 cup flour
1/4 teaspoon salt
3/4 cup margarine, softened
1/4 cup ice water
1/3 cup butter
1/2 cup light corn syrup
1/2 cup packed dark brown sugar
1 cup currants
1/3 cup chopped pecans or
    walnuts
1/4 teaspoon nutmeg
1/4 teaspoon salt
2 eggs

♦ Sift the flour and 1/4 teaspoon salt into a medium bowl. Cut in the margarine until crumbly. Add the ice water gradually, mixing with a fork until blended. Shape into a ball; wrap in waxed paper. Chill for 15 minutes.

♦ Melt the butter in a large saucepan over low heat. Add the corn syrup, brown sugar, currants, pecans, nutmeg and 1/4 teaspoon salt; mix well. Let stand until cool.

♦ Beat eggs just enough to mix whites with yolks. Add to currant mixture; mix well.

♦ Preheat the oven to 425 degrees.

♦ Roll the dough on a lightly floured surface and cut in circles to fit 2 1/2-inch tartlet pans. Line pans with the pastry.

♦ Spoon the filling into the pastry-lined tartlet pans.

♦ Bake at 425 degrees on the lowest rack of the oven for 15 to 20 minutes or until the tops are toasty-crisp and the insides are soft.

FRUIT KABOBS WITH LEMON-MINT SAUCE

Makes many servings

1 large cantaloupe
1 medium honeydew melon
1 large pineapple
4 cups strawberries
1 large bunch white grapes
4 bananas, sliced
Lemon-Mint Sauce

♦ Cut melons and pineapple into bite-size pieces. Stem strawberries and grapes. Slice the bananas.

♦ Thread the fruit onto wooden skewers. If preparing early, add the bananas just before serving.

♦ Serve the Lemon-Mint Sauce in a shallow dish for easy dipping.

Lemon-Mint Sauce

24 ounces lemon yogurt
1 cup minced fresh mint

♦ Combine the lemon yogurt and the mint; mix until smooth. Chill until serving time.

ALMOND CREAM PUFF RING

Makes 10 servings

Prepare this buttery dessert about three hours before serving.

1 cup water
½ cup butter
¼ teaspoon salt
1 cup flour
4 eggs
Almond Cream Filling
Chocolate Glaze

♦ Combine the water, butter and salt in a 2-quart saucepan. Bring to a boil. Remove from heat. Add the flour all at once and stir vigorously with a wooden spoon until the mixture forms a ball and pulls away from the sides of the pan. Add the eggs, one at a time, beating after each addition until smooth and satiny in appearance. Cool slightly.

♦ Preheat the oven to 400 degrees.

♦ Trace a 7-inch circle using a plate as a guide on a lightly greased and floured baking sheet. Drop the batter by heaping teaspoonfuls into 10 mounds inside the circle to form a ring.

♦ Bake at 400 degrees for 40 minutes, or until golden brown. Turn off the oven. Let stand in closed oven for 15 minutes. Remove to a wire rack to cool.

♦ Slice top from the cooled puff ring with a serrated knife. Reserve the top portion; scoop out doughy center. Spoon in the Almond Cream Filling; replace the top.

♦ Drizzle the Chocolate Glaze over the top of the ring. Chill for 1 hour before serving.

Almond Cream Filling

1 (4-ounce) package vanilla
  instant pudding mix
1¼ cups milk
1 cup whipping cream, whipped
1 teaspoon almond extract

♦ Prepare the pudding mix with milk using package directions. Blend in the whipped cream and almond extract.

Chocolate Glaze

½ cup semisweet chocolate chips
1½ teaspoons milk
1 tablespoon butter
1½ teaspoons light corn syrup

♦ Combine the chocolate chips and milk in a medium saucepan. Heat over low heat until the chocolate melts, stirring constantly. Add the butter and corn syrup and stir until the mixture is thick and smooth.

APPLE CRUMB CAKE

Makes 6 to 9 servings

2 cups flour

1 cup sugar

1 cup butter, softened

1/2 cup chopped pecans or walnuts

1 egg

5 or 6 apples, peeled, sliced

1 teaspoon cinnamon

♦ Preheat the oven to 350 degrees.

♦ Combine the flour and sugar in a medium bowl. Cut in the butter until crumbly.

♦ Stir in the pecans. Add the egg and mix well with a fork.

♦ Pat 2/3 of the mixture into the bottom of a greased 9-inch square baking pan. Spread the apple slices over the crumb mixture and sprinkle cinnamon on top.

♦ Spread the remaining crumb mixture over the apples.

♦ Bake at 350 degrees for 50 minutes.

Serve warm, plain or with whipped cream.

SOUR CREAM APPLE DELIGHT

Makes 8 servings

1 egg

1 1/2 cups sour cream

3/4 cup sugar

1/2 teaspoon salt

2 teaspoons vanilla extract

1/4 cup flour

6 to 8 large Granny Smith apples, peeled, cored, thinly sliced

1/3 cup sugar

1/3 cup packed brown sugar

1/2 cup flour

1 cup chopped nuts

6 tablespoons melted butter

Cinnamon to taste

♦ Preheat the oven to 375 degrees.

♦ Combine the egg, sour cream, 3/4 cup sugar, salt, vanilla and 1/4 cup flour in a large bowl and stir until smooth. Add the apples and toss to coat.

♦ Combine the remaining 1/3 cup sugar, brown sugar, 1/2 cup flour, nuts, butter and cinnamon in a large bowl and mix until crumbly.

♦ Alternate layers of the apple mixture and the brown sugar mixture in a greased 9x9-inch baking dish, ending with the brown sugar mixture. Sprinkle with additional cinnamon.

♦ Bake at 375 degrees for 40 to 50 minutes or until apples are tender and topping is golden brown.

APPLE-CRANBERRY CRISP

Makes 6 servings

¾ cup packed brown sugar

¾ cup old-fashioned oats

½ cup flour

¾ teaspoon cinnamon

¾ teaspoon nutmeg

½ cup butter, cut into pieces

4 to 6 Granny Smith apples, peeled, cored, cut into ¼-inch slices

1 cup cranberries

♦ Preheat the oven to 350 degrees.

♦ Combine the brown sugar, oats, flour, cinnamon and nutmeg in a small bowl. Cut in the butter until crumbly.

♦ Place the apple slices and cranberries in a greased 9-inch baking dish. Top with the oats mixture.

♦ Bake at 350 degrees for 35 to 40 minutes or until the top is golden brown and the apples are tender.

♦ Cool slightly. Spoon into bowls to serve.

Serve with ice cream or whipped cream flavored with maple syrup.

PASTRY CREME WITH BLUEBERRIES

Makes 4 servings

3 egg yolks

⅓ cup sugar

1 tablespoon flour

1 tablespoon cornstarch

2 cups hot milk

½ teaspoon vanilla extract

1 cup blueberries

♦ Combine the egg yolks, sugar, flour and cornstarch in a medium bowl and beat until smooth. Whisk in the milk.

♦ Pour the mixture into a medium saucepan. Cook over low heat just to the boiling point; do not boil. Remove from heat and stir in the vanilla.

♦ Spoon into wineglasses and chill. Top with blueberries at serving time.

CHERRY-NUT CRUNCH

Makes 6 to 8 servings

This sweet cobbler can be served warm or cold and keeps well.

1 cup flour
1½ cups sugar
1 teaspoon baking soda
1 teaspoon cinnamon
1 egg
1 tablespoon vegetable oil
2 (16-ounce) cans water-pack tart red pitted cherries
½ cup chopped walnuts
1 cup whipping cream, whipped
Tart Sweet Topping

♦ Preheat the oven to 350 degrees.

♦ Combine the flour, sugar, baking soda, cinnamon, egg and oil in a large bowl and mix well; the mixture will seem dry. Drain the cherries and reserve the juice for the topping. Stir in the cherries and walnuts.

♦ Spoon into a greased 8 or 9-inch square baking dish.

♦ Bake at 350 degrees for 35 to 40 minutes or until golden brown.

♦ Cool and cut into squares. Top with whipped cream or ice cream and drizzle warm Tart Sweet Topping over the top.

Tart Sweet Topping

½ cup sugar
1 tablespoon cornstarch
Dash of salt
Reserved cherry juice

♦ Combine the sugar, cornstarch, salt and reserved cherry juice in a medium saucepan. Bring to a boil, stirring constantly.

CRANBERRY SLUMP

Makes 8 servings

2½ cups cranberries
½ cup chopped walnuts
½ cup sugar
¾ cup melted butter, cooled
1 cup sugar
2 eggs, beaten
1 cup flour
½ teaspoon almond extract

♦ Preheat the oven to 375 degrees.

♦ Combine the cranberries, walnuts and sugar in a medium bowl; mix well. Pour into an ungreased 9-inch springform pan.

♦ Combine the butter, sugar, eggs, flour and almond flavoring in a medium bowl; mix well.

♦ Pour the batter over the cranberry mixture.

♦ Bake at 375 degrees for 35 to 40 minutes or until golden brown.

AMARETTO CHEESECAKE

Makes 12 to 16 servings

2 cups graham cracker crumbs
¼ cup sugar
½ cup melted margarine
Cream Cheese Filling
Sugared Almonds

- Preheat the oven to 350 degrees.
- Combine the graham cracker crumbs, sugar and margarine in a small bowl, stirring until moist. Press into an ungreased 10-inch springform pan.
- Pour the Cream Cheese Filling into the prepared pan.
- Bake at 350 degrees for 45 to 60 minutes or until the center is almost firm.
- Arrange the Sugared Almonds in a circle around the outer edge of the cheesecake. Bake for 15 minutes longer.
- Cool for 15 minutes. Loosen cheesecake from sides of pan. Remove the pan sides carefully. Cool completely.
- Chill for several hours to overnight.

Cream Cheese Filling

16 ounces cream cheese, softened
1 cup sugar
3 eggs
1 cup sour cream
½ cup whipping cream
¼ cup Amaretto
½ teaspoon almond extract

- Beat the cream cheese and sugar in a large bowl until light and fluffy. Add the eggs, sour cream, whipping cream, Amaretto and almond flavoring; whisk or beat until smooth and creamy.

Sugared Almonds

½ cup sugar
¼ cup boiling water
½ cup sliced almonds
1 teaspoon Amaretto

- Dissolve the sugar in the boiling water in a small saucepan over medium heat. Boil for 2 minutes and remove from heat. Stir in the almonds and Amaretto. Remove the almonds; spread on waxed paper to cool.

CHOCOLATE CHEESECAKE

Makes 12 servings

1 cup chocolate wafer crumbs

1/4 cup melted butter

3 eggs

24 ounces cream cheese, softened

2 cups chocolate chips, melted

1 teaspoon vanilla extract

1/8 teaspoon salt

1 cup sour cream

1 cup whipping cream, whipped

2 tablespoons confectioners' sugar

♦ Preheat the oven to 350 degrees.

♦ Combine the chocolate crumbs and the butter. Pat over bottom and sides of a buttered 9-inch springform pan.

♦ Combine the eggs, cream cheese, chocolate, vanilla, salt and sour cream in a large mixer bowl and beat until smooth.

♦ Pour into the prepared pan.

♦ Bake at 350 degrees for 1 hour. Let stand until cool.

♦ Chill, covered, overnight. Remove sides of pan. Serve with mixture of whipped cream and confectioners' sugar.

EASY-AS-PIE LIME CHEESECAKE

Makes 8 servings

1 3/4 cups graham cracker crumbs

1/3 cup melted butter

8 ounces cream cheese, softened

1/2 cup sugar

1 tablespoon lime juice

1/4 teaspoon vanilla extract

Dash of salt

1 teaspoon finely grated lime rind

2 eggs

1 cup sour cream

2 tablespoons sugar

1/2 teaspoon vanilla extract

♦ Preheat the oven to 325 degrees.

♦ Mix the crumbs and butter in a small bowl. Press over bottom and up the sides of a greased 9-inch pie plate.

♦ Beat the cream cheese in a medium bowl until fluffy. Stir in 1/2 cup sugar, lime juice, 1/4 teaspoon vanilla, salt and lime rind. Beat in the eggs, one at a time.

♦ Spoon into the prepared pie plate.

♦ Bake at 325 degrees for 25 to 30 minutes or until set.

♦ Blend the sour cream, 2 tablespoons sugar and 1/2 teaspoon vanilla in a medium bowl. Spread over the hot cheesecake. Bake for 10 minutes longer. Cool.

♦ Chill for several hours.

ORANGE SUPREME CHEESECAKE

Makes 10 servings

¾ cup flour

3 tablespoons sugar

1 teaspoon finely shredded
    orange rind

6 tablespoons butter

1 egg yolk, slightly beaten

Orange Filling

Orange Sauce

2 oranges, peeled, sectioned

Orange rind for garnish

Mint leaves for garnish

♦ Preheat the oven to 400 degrees.

♦ Combine the flour, sugar and orange rind in a medium
  bowl. Cut in the butter until crumbly. Stir in the egg yolk.

♦ Pat ⅓ of the dough over the bottom of a 9-inch springform
  pan with the sides removed.

♦ Bake at 400 degrees for 7 minutes. Cool. Butter the sides of
  the pan; attach to the bottom. Pat the remaining dough
  from bottom 1¾ inches up sides of pan. Reduce oven
  temperature to 375 degrees. Spoon the Orange Filling into
  the prepared pan.

♦ Bake at 375 degrees for 35 to 45 minutes or until the
  center is set. Cool for 15 minutes. Loosen cheesecake from
  sides of pan with a spatula. Cool for 30 minutes. Remove
  the sides of the pan. Cool for 2 hours. Spoon Orange Sauce
  over the top. Chill.

♦ Arrange the orange sections on top. Garnish with twists of
  orange rind or mint leaves.

Orange Filling

24 ounces cream cheese, softened

1 teaspoon finely shredded
    orange rind

¼ teaspoon vanilla extract

1 cup sugar

3 eggs

¼ cup orange juice

♦ Beat the cream cheese in a large mixer bowl until fluffy.
  Add the orange rind, vanilla and sugar, stirring until smooth.
  Add the eggs all at once, beating until just blended; do not
  overbeat. Stir in the orange juice.

Orange Sauce

2 tablespoons sugar

1 tablespoon cornstarch

1 cup orange juice

2 tablespoons orange marmalade

1 tablespoon orange liqueur

♦ Combine the sugar and cornstarch in a medium saucepan.
  Stir in the orange juice. Cook over low heat until thickened,
  stirring constantly. Cool slightly. Stir in the orange
  marmalade and orange liqueur.

BANANA CREPES

Makes 6 servings

3 tablespoons butter

2 tablespoons packed brown sugar

1/8 teaspoon nutmeg

3 bananas, sliced

1 cup apricot preserves

1 teaspoon grated lemon rind

2 teaspoons (or more) lemon juice

2 tablespoons dark rum

Crêpes

1 cup whipped cream

1/4 cup sliced toasted almonds

- Melt the butter in a medium saucepan over low heat. Add the brown sugar and the nutmeg. Cook for 2 to 3 minutes or until the brown sugar is dissolved.

- Stir in the bananas, preserves, lemon rind, lemon juice and rum. Heat through but do not cook.

- Spoon some of the hot banana mixture onto each crêpe; roll up or fold into quarters; place on dessert plates.

- Top with whipped cream and sprinkle with toasted almonds.

Crêpes

1 1/2 cups milk

4 eggs

1 cup flour

2 tablespoons dark rum

1 tablespoon sugar

1/4 cup melted butter

- Combine the milk, eggs, flour, rum, sugar and butter in a large mixer bowl and beat until smooth. Let rest for 1 hour.

- Ladle a small amount of batter into a preheated crêpe pan or small skillet, tilting to coat pan. Bake for several seconds or until firm but not too brown. Stack between plastic wrap.

Crêpes can be frozen, stacked between plastic wrap.

PEACH MELBA SAUCE FOR CREPES

Makes 8 servings

1 (10-ounce) package frozen raspberries, thawed

1/3 cup currant jelly

3 tablespoons butter

1/4 teaspoon almond extract

1 (16-ounce) can peach slices, drained

- Force the thawed raspberries through a sieve.

- Combine the raspberry purée, jelly, butter and almond flavoring in a medium saucepan and bring to a boil over medium heat, stirring constantly.

- Add the peach slices and toss to coat. Cool for 15 minutes.

- Serve over filled crêpes.

Sauce can be served over vanilla ice cream or frozen yogurt. Top with slivered almonds.

FRESH FRUIT TRIFLE

Makes 10 servings

24 ladyfingers, split

1/3 cup strawberry or raspberry jam

Grated rind of 1 lemon

2/3 cup dry sherry

3 tablespoons brandy (optional)

12 coconut macaroons, crushed

2 cups mixed fresh fruit pieces (kiwifruit, banana, orange, peaches, berries, etc.)

Custard

2 cups whipping cream, whipped

1/2 cup toasted slivered almonds

- Spread all the ladyfingers with jam.

- Layer half the ladyfingers in a glass trifle bowl. Sprinkle with about 1/4 of the lemon rind, 2 1/2 tablespoons sherry and 2 teaspoons brandy.

- Add a layer of half the macaroons and sprinkle with 1/3 of the remaining lemon rind, 2 1/2 tablespoons sherry and 2 teaspoons brandy.

- Layer half the fruit over the macaroons. Let stand for 1 hour.

- Spread half the Custard over the layers.

- Repeat the layers with half the remaining ladyfingers, half the remaining lemon rind, 2 1/2 tablespoons sherry, 2 teaspoons remaining brandy, macaroons, remaining lemon rind, sherry, brandy and remaining fruit. Let stand for 30 minutes.

- Cover with the remaining Custard. Chill for 2 to 3 hours.

- Top with whipped cream and almonds just before serving. Garnish with additional fresh fruit.

May substitute thinly sliced sponge cake for ladyfingers.

Custard

3 egg yolks or 1 whole egg and 1 egg yolk, beaten

1/4 to 1/2 cup sugar

1/8 teaspoon salt

2 cups milk, scalded

1/2 to 1 teaspoon vanilla extract

- Beat the egg yolks in the top of a double boiler. Add the sugar and salt; mix well. Add the hot milk very gradually, whisking constantly.

- Place the double boiler over hot, not boiling, water. Cook until mixture coats a spoon or to 175 degrees on a candy thermometer, stirring constantly.

- Let stand until cool. Blend in the vanilla.

CHARLOTTE RUSSE WITH APRICOT SAUCE

Makes 9 to 12 servings

Heaven isn't always chocolate.

6 egg yolks, beaten

1 cup sugar

2 cups milk

2 envelopes unflavored gelatin

1/4 cup cold water

1 teaspoon vanilla extract

2 tablespoons cream sherry

2 cups whipping cream, whipped

12 ladyfingers, split

Canned peeled apricot halves, drained

Maraschino cherries for garnish

Whipped cream for garnish

Apricot Sauce

♦ Blend the egg yolks, sugar and milk in a double boiler over hot water with a wooden spoon. Cook until thickened, stirring constantly.

♦ Soften the gelatin in the cold water for 5 minutes. Stir into the hot custard until completely dissolved. Let stand until cool. Stir in the vanilla and cream sherry.

♦ Fold in whipped cream. Cool until partially set.

♦ Line the bottom and sides of a 9-inch springform pan with the split ladyfingers. Pour in the cooled custard mixture. Chill for 1 hour or until set.

♦ Loosen from sides of pan if necessary; remove sides of pan.

♦ Top with apricot halves and maraschino cherries. Top with additional whipped cream.

♦ Serve the warm Apricot Sauce over the cold Charlotte.

Apricot Sauce

2 (16-ounce) cans peeled apricot halves, drained

1 tablespoon cornstarch

1/2 cup sugar

Juice of 1 lemon

Cointreau to taste

♦ Purée the apricot halves in a food processor or blender. Add the cornstarch, sugar and lemon juice; mix well.

♦ Pour into double boiler over hot water. Cook until thickened, stirring constantly. Blend in the liqueur.

If sauce is prepared ahead, add the liqueur to the sauce after reheating.

BRANDIED BREAD PUDDING

Makes 8 servings

1 (1-pound) loaf dry home-style white bread

2¼ to 2½ cups milk

⅓ cup each raisins and brandy

1 teaspoon grated orange rind

1¼ cups half-and-half

2 eggs

2 egg yolks

¾ cup sugar

¼ teaspoon vanilla extract

¼ teaspoon each cinnamon, freshly grated nutmeg and ground mace

• Preheat the oven to 350 degrees.

• Cut enough bread into ½-inch cubes to fill a buttered 9x13-inch baking pan. Stir in enough milk to soften the bread.

• Simmer the raisins in brandy in a small saucepan until the brandy is absorbed. Stir raisins and orange rind into bread mixture.

• Combine the half-and-half, eggs, egg yolks, sugar, vanilla, cinnamon, nutmeg and mace in a large bowl; whisk until blended.

• Pour over the bread mixture. Cover with a buttered sheet of baking parchment or foil. Place the baking pan in a larger pan of hot water in the oven.

• Bake at 350 degrees for 1¼ hours or until a knife inserted in the center comes out clean.

INDIAN PUDDING

Makes 8 servings

Few puddings are as old and treasured as this one.

½ cup cornmeal

3 cups milk

½ teaspoon salt

1 tablespoon butter

2 eggs, beaten

½ cup brown sugar

¾ cup molasses

1 tablespoon butter

1 teaspoon cinnamon

½ teaspoon ginger

2 cups milk

• Preheat the oven to 300 degrees.

• Combine cornmeal, 3 cups milk, salt and 1 tablespoon butter in a 2-quart saucepan. Bring to a boil over medium heat, stirring constantly. Remove from heat.

• Beat the eggs with brown sugar, molasses, 1 tablespoon butter and spices. Add to the cornmeal mixture with 1 cup of the milk; mix well. Pour into greased 2-quart baking dish.

• Bake at 300 degrees for 1 hour, stirring every 20 minutes. Stir in the remaining cup of milk. Bake for 1 hour longer, stirring every 20 minutes.

• Turn off the oven. Let stand in closed oven for 30 minutes.

• Serve warm with ice cream or whipped cream.

CHOCOLATE POTS DE CREME

Makes 4 to 6 servings

Elegant taste belies the simple ingredients.

1 cup chocolate chips
2 tablespoons sugar
Dash of salt
2 eggs
1 teaspoon vanilla extract
3/4 cup milk, scalded

- Process the chocolate chips, sugar, salt, eggs and vanilla in a blender until smooth.
- Pour the hot milk over the chocolate mixture. Blend at high speed for 1 minute. Pour into dessert dishes.
- Chill for 2 hours or until firm. Garnish with whipped cream.

FROZEN LEMON MOUSSE WITH STRAWBERRIES

Makes 8 servings

2 cups lemon yogurt
1 cup sugar
1/4 cup fresh lemon juice
Zest of 1 lemon
1 cup whipping cream, whipped
3 to 4 cups strawberries, sliced
Sugar to taste
Cointreau or Grand Marnier

- Blend the yogurt, sugar, lemon juice and lemon zest in a large bowl. Fold in the whipped cream gently. Freeze for several hours.
- Sprinkle the strawberries generously with sugar and liqueur. Let stand for several hours.
- Serve strawberries over slightly softened mousse.

  Substitute French vanilla yogurt for half the lemon yogurt.

FROZEN PEACH MOUSSE

Makes 6 servings

1 teaspoon unflavored gelatin
2 tablespoons cold water
3 tablespoons boiling water
1 cup fresh peach purée
1/2 cup sugar
Several drops of almond extract
Dash of salt
1 cup whipping cream, whipped
Sliced fresh peaches

- Soften the gelatin in cold water in a medium bowl. Add boiling water; stir until gelatin dissolves.
- Add the peach purée, sugar, almond flavoring and salt and stir until smooth. Chill for 1 hour or until thickened.
- Fold in the whipped cream gently.
- Spoon into a 4-cup mold. Freeze for 1 hour or until firm.
- Unmold onto a serving plate. Surround the mousse with fresh peach slices.

CHOCOLATE RASPBERRY MERINGUE

Makes 8 servings

Meringues like this one can be made ahead and kept in an airtight container. This recipe should be made at least three hours before serving so that the meringue can be cut without splintering.

4 egg whites

Dash of salt

1½ cups sugar

¼ cup baking cocoa

1 teaspoon vanilla extract

½ cup finely ground hazelnuts or almonds

1 cup whipping cream, whipped

2 cups fresh raspberries

♦ Preheat the oven to 350 degrees.

♦ Grease two 8-inch cake pans; line with baking parchment.

♦ Beat the egg whites with the salt in a medium bowl until stiff peaks form. Add the sugar gradually, beating until very stiff.

♦ Sift the baking cocoa over the mixture and fold in gently. Fold in the vanilla and hazelnuts. Spoon into prepared pans.

♦ Bake at 350 degrees for 45 minutes.

♦ Cool in the pans for 10 minutes; turn onto a wire rack to cool completely.

♦ Sandwich the meringues with half the whipped cream and half the raspberries, ending with the raspberries. Top with the remaining whipped cream and raspberries.

RASPBERRY BAVARIAN CREAM

Makes 8 to 10 servings

¼ cup sugar

½ cup margarine

1 cup flour

¼ cup almonds, finely chopped

1 (10-ounce) package frozen raspberries, thawed, drained

2 egg whites

1 cup sugar

1 tablespoon lemon juice

¼ teaspoon vanilla extract

¼ teaspoon almond extract

Dash of salt

1 cup whipping cream, whipped

♦ Preheat the oven to 350 degrees.

♦ Combine ¼ cup sugar, margarine, flour and almonds in a small bowl; mix until crumbly. Pat into a 9x13- inch baking pan; do not pack.

♦ Bake at 350 degrees for 20 minutes. Cool and crumble. Reserve some of the crumbs for the top.

♦ Press the remaining crumbs over the bottom of a lightly greased 9-inch springform pan.

♦ Combine the raspberries, egg whites, 1 cup sugar, lemon juice, vanilla and almond flavorings and salt in a large mixer bowl. Beat for 15 minutes or until the mixture increases in volume and becomes very thick. Fold in the whipped cream.

♦ Spoon into the prepared pan. Sprinkle with the reserved crumbs. Freeze for 8 hours or longer.

♦ Loosen from sides of pan; remove sides of pan.

STRAWBERRY-PECAN SHORTCAKE

Makes 8 servings

This is a real winning recipe. The cake is good alone or with the berries and filling.

4 cups sliced strawberries

1/4 cup sugar

2 cups flour

2 tablespoons (or more) sugar

1 tablespoon baking powder

1/4 teaspoon baking soda

1 teaspoon salt

1/3 cup vegetable shortening

1/2 cup chopped pecans

1 cup sour cream

1/3 cup milk

6 ounces cream cheese, softened

1/3 cup sugar

1 teaspoon vanilla extract

1 cup whipping cream

♦ Preheat the oven to 450 degrees.

♦ Combine the strawberries and 1/4 cup sugar and set aside in the refrigerator.

♦ Combine the flour, 2 tablespoons sugar, baking powder, baking soda and salt in a medium bowl. Cut in the shortening until crumbly. Mix in the pecans. Add sour cream and milk; stir until just mixed. Pat into a buttered 9-inch round cake pan.

♦ Bake at 450 degrees for 15 to 20 minutes or until golden brown. Cool slightly.

♦ Beat the cream cheese in a mixer bowl until light and fluffy. Beat in 1/3 cup sugar and vanilla gradually. Beat whipping cream in a chilled bowl until stiff. Fold the cream cheese mixture into the whipped cream gently.

♦ Split the warm shortcake into 2 layers.

♦ Spread half the cream cheese mixture on the bottom layer and top with half the strawberries. Replace the top layer. Top with the remaining cream cheese mixture and strawberries.

♦ Cut into wedges to serve.

Elegant Strawberries

Makes 10 servings

20 to 25 fresh strawberries, hulled
8 ounces cream cheese, softened
1/3 cup confectioners' sugar
1 1/2 teaspoons grated lemon rind
1 tablespoon lemon juice

♦ Rinse the strawberries. Place stem end down on paper towels to drain. Cut an X on top of each berry, taking care not to slice all the way through .

♦ Beat the cream cheese and confectioners' sugar in a mixer bowl until light. Stir in the lemon rind and lemon juice. Place the mixture in a pastry bag with a star tip. Pipe the filling into the center of each berry. Place each filled berry in a petite paper cup.

♦ Serve within 4 hours.

Strawberries Arnaud

Makes 6 servings

The wine sauce may be stored, covered, in the refrigerator for up to two weeks.

2 cups burgundy or other dry red wine
1/2 cup sugar
1 lime, sliced
1/2 orange, sliced
1 whole clove
1 (3-inch) cinnamon stick
1 pint vanilla ice cream
3 cups sliced fresh strawberries
Whipped cream (optional)
Fresh mint (optional)

♦ Bring the wine to a boil in a medium saucepan. Add the sugar, lime, orange, clove and cinnamon, stirring until the sugar dissolves. Boil for 1 minute longer. Remove from the heat. Let stand for 30 minutes.

♦ Strain the liquid and discard the lime, orange, clove and cinnamon.

♦ Spoon the ice cream into serving dishes and top with the strawberries. Drizzle about 1/4 cup of the sauce over each serving. Top with whipped cream and mint.

CONTRIBUTORS

♦ ♦ ♦ ♦ ♦ ♦ ♦ ♦ ♦ ♦ ♦ ♦ ♦ ♦

We would like to express our sincere appreciation to the members and friends of the Child and Family auxiliaries who graciously contributed and tested recipes as well as offered artistic talent to this project. Content similarity and space limitation prevented us from including all recipes.

Jean Abbot
Dolores Albrecht
Mary M. Allingham
Jette Altshul
Dianne Anderson
Lynette Anderson
Liz Ardolino
Dot Arthur
Dorothy A. Askelson
Carol C. Barnes
Victoria W. Barri
Adarienne Battey
Pat Belcher
Helen Benoit
Stephanie Bentz
Charlie Berry
Pat Berry
Cam Bertsche
Hetsy Bisbee
Eleanor H. Bishop
Diana Blair
Sandra Blazensky
Ginny Bliss
Doris W. Boas
Mary H. Boatwright
Lil Bohannan
Peggy Boos
Pat Brand
Joyce Brennan
Debbie Brooke

Jo An Brouwer
Hetsy Brown
Jane Bucklin
Ann M. Buonocore
Marty Burd
Ann T. Burdick
Nancy Burdick
Linda M. Burrows
Joan Butler
Vera A. Cafaro
Peggy Callahan
Tina Campbell
Sarah Canning
Suzie Canning
Linda Cantner
Pat Carlson
Dawn Hellier Carnese
Ben Carpenter
Evelyn Casey
Sheila M. Cash
Sharyne Cerullo
Joyce Christianson
Donna Clary-David
Janith Clay
Charlotte Colby-Danly
Ellen Cole
Pat Cole
Gretchen Comstock
Carol Connor
Marjorie Conway

Christine F. Crawford
Sue Curtiss
Diane Davis
Janice Davis
Joan Davis
Kim DeBoer
Ruth Demarest
Anne Marie Deren
Nancy W. DeVoe
Mary Dirks
Connie Dixon
Marilyn Doane
Dale Dodd
Jane Donnell
Sylvia Dorsey
Jamie Doubleday
"Jim" Douglass
Lynne Drahan
Connie Dreyman
Patty Dunn
Cindy Earle
Joyce Eddy
Pam Ehrlich
Debbie English
Lillian Erb
Lynn Fairfield-Sonn
Deb Fallen
Candy Feinberg
Vera Ficken
Barbara Fiore

Kappy Fisher
Janice Fitton
Kathleen Flaherty
Jim Fleishell
Tina Forster
Virginia Fowler
Nancy Carr Fox
Joyce French
Patsy Fritzsche
Deb Fuller
R. Lee Funsten
Phyllis Gada
Alva Gahagan
Joan W. Gates
Lois Geary
Edie Geer
Barbara Ginsberg
Charlie Gordan
Dorothy Gorra
Christiane Gottman
Patti Green
Nedine Grim
Connie Haberman
Barbara Hallwood
Barbara Harreys
Eileen Haskell
Liz Hartmann
Eleanor A. Harvey
Eileen A. Haskell
Elaine Haughton
Claire Helmboldt
Mary Lou Henkin
Marjorie Hess
Emily Higgins
Mary Highmore
Sally Hill
Caroline F. Hobart
Grissel Hodge
Linda Ann Hollis
Patricia D. Holmes

Anne G. Holmstedt
Judi Honiss
Barbara Hoops
Betsy Horn
Daryl L. Hornby
Ann-Marie Howell
June M. Hoye
Janet S. Hughes
Astrea S. Hupfel
Ethel M. Ives
Betty Jacobsen
Dottie Jalbert
Eleanor T. Jamieson
Sarah Janssens
Nancy Jensen
Alby Johnson
Charlotte Johnson
Elizabeth Johnstone
Carol June
Alicia Kent
Pat King
Carol Klimek
Shirley Koke
Hedy Korst
Joanne Kraska
Pat Krause
Ellie Krusewski
Amy Kubuchka
Dana Kubuchka
Jane Larson
Sally LaRue
Jennifer Latici
Joan Lauler
Judy Leeney
Dorothy Leib
Jeanne Lena
Lucy Leo
Sally Lepore
Beverly Letz
Rachel H. Levine

Jane Lionelli
Elaine Livingston
Shirley Londregan
Rose C. Longo
Jerry Lord
Judy Lovelace
Adrianne Loweth
Kathi Lynch
Linda Lyon
Diane MacFadyen
Pamela A. Maletz
Linda Mariani
Jeanne Martin
Mabel Matschulat
Dottie Matteson
Joyce Mayfield
Gail S. Mayhew
Debbie Mazer
Carol H. McBee
Betty McCarthy
Susan McConnell
Natalie McCormick
Dorothy McGill
Isabel McGowan
Wendy McGuire
Nancy McLoughlin
Kate Mercer
Libbe Miceli
Peggy Miller
Robin E. Miller
Judy Miner
Judi Mitchell
Tom Mitchell
Christina Moore
Patricia Moukawsher
Mac Mummert
Ginnie Murphy
Loretta Murphy
Nancy Murray
Trish Murray

Sally Myers
Claudia Nielsen
Barbara Noyes
Joyce Nunez
Judy Oat
Lucille Olson
Sandy Olson
Carolyn Y. Orkney
Marion Orkney
Hope Orkney
Carole A. Otto
Betty R. O'Donnell
Susan O'Donnell
Mary O'Loughlin
Marilyn O'Malley
Deborah Palmer
Patty Pape
Penny Parr
Barbara Parfitt
Kay Patrell
Lillias M. Paul
Sally Perkins
Joy Peterle
Alma H. Peterson
Susan Peterson
Pam Pethick
Terry Pfeil
Alice Phillips
Linda Pinn
Janet Pitchford
Jo Plant
Chris Platt
Rita Ponzo
Margaret Porter
Jane Potter
Patricia Proctor
Bev Pryor
Mary Pullan
Mary Read
Tal Renault

Mary Ann Renehan
Diane Reynolds
Jeanne Rhodes
Nancy Richartz
Carol Ridgway
Wendy Rieder
Meredith G. Robbins
Charlotte Robe
Muriel Roberts
Colleen Robertson
Karen Roccon
Pat Rogerson
Nancy Rosser
Lynn Ruenzel
Denise Russo
Amanda Rutledge
Pamela Ryan
Cemmy Ryland
Kay Sachs
Ellie Sandgren
Dede Savage
Eleanore Schweppe
Cele Seeley
Susan Senning
Anne Sergeant
Judy Shapiro
Nancy Sheets
Kelly Sherwood
Katie Shuck
Britt Sinay
Carol Sinnamon
Liz S. Sistare
Toni Slifer
Florence Small
Zita Smith
Martha Snyder
Martha Sproul
Ann Stark
Sally Starzec
Betty F. Steadman

Brooke Steinle
Helen H. Stockwell
Lolly Stoddard
Jackie Stoltz
Regina A. Strand
Fay Taylor
Helen Thompson
Bette Thomson
Laurel Tiesinga
Wendy Traub
Irene Trimble
Barbara B. Tuneski
Ainslie Turner
Roberta Turner
Joyce Vlaun
Rita P. Volkmann
Alice Vross
Ida Wadsworth
Cindy Wagner
Toni Wagner
Carol Warner
Conway W. Warnom
Linda V. W. Watkins
Nancy T. Weinstein
Marion Weisert
Michele Welch
Carter Welling
Sue Westner
Mary Wheeler
Elaine White
Nancy White
Emily Wildes
Rosemary Willis
Judith E. Woodman
Cicely Worrall
Margaret V. Wyper
Pat Ziegler
Karen Zoller

INDEX

◆ ◆ ◆ ◆ ◆ ◆ ◆ ◆ ◆ ◆ ◆ ◆ ◆

BIBLIOGRAPHY

♦ ♦ ♦ ♦ ♦ ♦ ♦ ♦ ♦ ♦ ♦ ♦ ♦

For those who may be interested in additional reading about our area, please consider the following:

♦ ♦ ♦ ♦

Coastal Connecticut. Barry and Susan Hildebrandt. Peregrine Press. Old Saybrook, CT, 1979.

Historic Coastal New England. Barbara Clayton and Kathleen Whitley. The Globe Pequot Press. Old Saybrook, CT, 1992.

"Mystic Built" Ships and Shipyards of the Mystic River, Connecticut 1784–1919. William N. Peterson. Mystic Seaport Museum, Inc. Mystic, CT, 1989.

ORDER FORM

♦ ♦ ♦ ♦ ♦ ♦ ♦ ♦ ♦ ♦ ♦ ♦ ♦

Charted Courses
Child and Family Agency of Southeastern Connecticut, Inc.
255 Hempstead Street
New London, Connecticut 06320   Phone: (203) 443-2172

Please send me _____ copies of *Charted Courses* @ $16.95 each $_____
add postage and handling @ $ 3.50 each $_____
Connecticut residents add 6% sales tax @ $ 1.02 each $_____
Total $_____

☐ Check   ☐ MasterCard   ☐ Visa   Card Number _____

Expiration Date _____ Signature _____

Name _____ Phone (____) _____
(please print)

Address _____

City _____ State _____ Zip _____

Please make checks payable to Child & Family Agency of S.E. CT, Inc.

Charted Courses
Child and Family Agency of Southeastern Connecticut, Inc.
255 Hempstead Street
New London, Connecticut 06320   Phone: (203) 443-2172

Please send me _____ copies of *Charted Courses* @ $16.95 each $_____
add postage and handling @ $ 3.50 each $_____
Connecticut residents add 6% sales tax @ $ 1.02 each $_____
Total $_____

☐ Check   ☐ MasterCard   ☐ Visa   Card Number _____

Expiration Date _____ Signature _____

Name _____ Phone (____) _____
(please print)

Address _____

City _____ State _____ Zip _____

Please make checks payable to Child & Family Agency of S.E. CT, Inc.

GIFT CARD FORM

◆ ◆ ◆ ◆ ◆ ◆ ◆ ◆ ◆ ◆ ◆ ◆ ◆ ◆

(   ) Please enclose a gift card to read:

_____

_____

_____

_____

_____

All copies of *Charted Courses* will be sent to same address unless otherwise specified. If you wish one or more books sent as gifts, furnish a list of names and addresses of recipients. If you wish to enclose your own gift card with each book, please write name of recipient on outside of the envelope, enclose with order, and we will include it with your gift.

(   ) Please enclose a gift card to read:

_____

_____

_____

_____

_____

All copies of *Charted Courses* will be sent to same address unless otherwise specified. If you wish one or more books sent as gifts, furnish a list of names and addresses of recipients. If you wish to enclose your own gift card with each book, please write name of recipient on outside of the envelope, enclose with order, and we will include it with your gift.